D1179711

3 0450 01205 0580

William Crookes and "Katie King"

The Medium and the Scientist

The
Medium
and the
Scientist

The Story of
Florence Cook
and
William Crookes

Trevor H. Hall

Prometheus Books

700 East Amherst St. Buffalo, New York 14215

Library of Congress Card Catalog No. 84-43102
ISBN: 0-87975-276-9

CONTENTS

LIST OF ILLUSTRATIONS

PREFACE

During the course of the investigation upon which this book is based, I have tried to make myself acquainted with the very extensive literature relating to the mediumship of Florence Cook, and I hope that nothing of importance has been omitted. This survey has included an examination of the newspapers and other periodicals of the times, and in particular those devoted to spiritualism.

In the case of Kate Cook, who was virtually an unknown medium compared with her famous sister, it was found that little reliable information was available from published sources, and in an endeavour to trace the events of her life I have had recourse to other fields of inquiry, and in particular to a mass of unpublished correspondence found in the Britten Memorial Library at Manchester. The existence of these letters, between several of the principal characters in this story of a series of remarkable events in the late nineteenth century, does not seem to be generally known among either spiritualists or psychical researchers. Many significant facts concerning both Florence and Kate, their family and certain of the other more important actors in this drama of the "golden age" of spiritualism, have been assembled from official records of the period, whilst some information has been obtained from visits to the districts in which the events occurred.

It remains my pleasant duty to acknowledge the assistance I have received whilst making the inquiry. My warm thanks are due to Mr. J. H. P. Pafford and Mr. A. H. Wesencraft of the University of London Library, who allowed me to retain in my own home on extended loan many volumes of nineteenth-century spiritualist journals which are now almost unobtainable. I am grateful to Dr. A. R. G. Owen who spent much time finding and copying references for me in Cambridge University Library, and to Mr. F. Beckwith of the Leeds Library and Mr. R. Ellidge of the Britten Memorial Library at Manchester who helped me in many ways.

I am especially indebted to Mr. G. H. Brook of Huddersfield, who gave me unlimited access to his large collection of books on spiritualism, assisted me in the work in Manchester and as a chartered electrical engineer advised me authoritatively in regard to the Varley experiments. I am under a considerable obligation to Miss K. M. Haigh, my secretary, who not only kept my notes in order and put the manuscript into decipherable form but interested herself generally in the inquiry and made many valuable suggestions. The Byron stanza would not have been easily found without the help of my daughter, Miss K. E. Hall of St. Andrews University, and I appreciate the assistance of Mr. C. E. Morris and Mr. A. G. Matthew of the Huddersfield Building Society who provided the photographs of the houses occupied by Charles Blackburn and the Cook family in London and Monmouthshire. The draft manuscript was read by Sir James Croysdale and Mr. Ralph Cleworth, Q.C., whose advice on the evidential aspects of the case was most helpful, and I have valued the kind and constructive criticisms of Mr. Bertrand Mather in regard to the presentation of the material. I am indebted to Mr. H. E. Pratt who drew my attention to the modern literature on the mysterious death of Charles Bravo.

Most importantly of all, my gratitude is due to Mrs. Eileen J. Garrett, the President of the Parapsychology Foundation in New York, who invited me to undertake the research, made funds available for the investigation and gave me constant encouragement, and to my colleague of many years, Dr. Eric J. Dingwall. Dr. Dingwall described his formidable assistance as merely "looking up a few dates and references for an old friend". In fact, he placed at my disposal his unique knowledge of the literature of psychical research and spiritualism, did most of the translations and devoted unlimited time to helping me at every stage of the inquiry, including the final preparation of the manuscript for the publisher.

INTRODUCTION

IN THE latter half of the nineteenth century superstition and credulity were as widely spread in England among all classes of the population as they are today. One reason for this was the religious ferment in the atmosphere of the times. In 1859 *The Origin of Species* was published, and in the following year the battle between Huxley and Wilberforce took place at the meeting of the British Association. Modernism in theology was beginning to become apparent, and to many it seemed that something more was required than scientific agnosticism and a Christianity which was divided against itself even under the shelter of one church. Something surer than belief was needed. Spiritualism, claiming scientific proof for its faith, had been flourishing in the United States for a decade, and the ground for its enthusiastic reception in this country was already prepared through interest in mesmerism and similar phenomena.

Inquiry into the occult became an obsession, not only among the upper classes of society but also among working people. Louis Blanc, the famous French commentator and political historian, made good use of his enforced sojourn in England to survey the social scene. He declared that fortune tellers could be counted by the thousand; that astrologers flourished both in town and country; and that business was excellent, so considerable was the number of their dupes. How was it possible, Blanc asked, to escape from such a popular epidemic, for, as he put it, it required courage to stand up against fashion?

In Victorian England as many heads as tables were being turned, and the various interpretations put upon the mysterious dances of the furniture reflected the state of mind of those who advanced them. Spiritualists were certain that the tables moved under the influence of spirits; the clergy thought that this was probably true, but whether these discarnate entities were good or bad, angelic or demonic, was open to question. The few scientific men who deigned to pay any attention to the matter considered the phenomena to be caused by various forms of unconscious muscular action on the part of the sitters. Various pieces of apparatus were designed which prevented action by the sitters, conscious or unconscious, but which at the same time often stopped the movements of the tables altogether.

Meanwhile in the United States the picture was changing. The craze over the new occult movements had started earlier than in Europe and development was rapid. People had become a little tired of turning tables, and more exciting phenomena were being exhibited. American mediums, moreover, were beginning to travel abroad; and when they arrived in England the dancing tables seemed of little account when compared with the startling manifestations which occurred in the presence of the visitors from across the ocean. New techniques appeared, and the alleged phenomena occurring in the presence of such famous mediums as the Davenport Brothers filled the spectators with amazement not unmixed with awe. Spirit hands emerged from holes in the wooden cabinets where the mediums sat, in spite of the fact that the said mediums were securely fastened inside: pale faces showed themselves at other openings and then rapidly withdrew.

The mediums operating in England during this period presented phenomena of a more of less stereotyped pattern. Darkness or subdued light was the general rule: there were rappings both on the table and in other parts of the room: lights hovered in the air: the sitters were touched by invisible hands, and tambourines were shaken and stringed instruments plucked. It was a period in which *physical* phenomena interested people more than did messages from the spirit world, which meant little and might have come from anywhere, although these were more exciting when they appeared written on freshly cleaned slates.

While these things were happening in England and were being observed by people like the Brownings, Dickens and John Bright, the mediums in the United States were once again the pioneers. It was all very well to get the spirit friends to raise tables, show their waxen faces now and then through peepholes in the cabinet, and write sentimental messages on the sitters' own slates. Why could they not show themselves complete and fully formed, building themselves up out of some mysterious substance extruded from the bodies of medium and sitters? With the doors of the séance room locked and with the entranced medium visible inside the cabinet, the production of a form almost indistinguishable from that of a living person, who could walk and talk and then finally disappear under the very eyes of the circle, would be a feat which would bring fame and riches to any medium in whose presence such a phenomenon occurred.

Among those who produced this manifestation in America was Mrs. Leah Underhill, one of the famous Fox sisters. Her fully formed materialization began as a semi-luminous figure clothed in veiling and carrying what looked like a luminous card which it passed up and down before it in order to afford the spectators a better view. The success of the earlier efforts was seen in the long series of similar sittings given to the American banker Charles F. Livermore by Miss Kate Fox, where the supposed materialized form of his deceased wife appeared, walked about, talked with the sitters, and often showed herself carrying large bunches of roses and violets.

As a result of her triumphs with these manifestations Kate Fox was enabled to visit England in 1871, where she not only produced phenomena which puzzled Mr. (later Sir) William Crookes, the famous chemist and physicist, but found a husband in the well-known barrister Mr. H. D. Jencken, the following year producing for him a sturdy infant who showed signs of powerful mediumship within six weeks of his arrival.[1]

It is possible that Kate Jencken gave a few sittings for full-formed materializations when in England, although I am not aware whether detailed accounts of these have been published. With Mr. Crookes her phenomena were of a much more simple type, and were of great interest from every point of view. Her fame spread rapidly and English mediums saw themselves being left behind in the race for recognition if they did not themselves show their spirits walking about the séance room, conversing with the sitters and then disappearing into thin air. However, it seemed that the ultimate miracle of the full-form materialization was of necessity approached by degrees, as if the attitude of the spectators had first of all to be tested. The mediums began by using the old method of

[1] Child mediums had been popular in the United States for some time. For example, little Miss Attwood was supposedly carried about by the spirits in her chair from place to place while she calmly sat on it munching candy; while Miss Lovejoy of Cincinnati at only four months enraptured her visitors with her rapping messages and cradle rockings.

being seated inside wooden cabinets provided with openings, such as the Davenports had formerly employed, and it was through these openings that the hands of the spirits were thrust, or their faces exhibited momentarily for the delectation of the company. Later, however, in 1872, two well-known mediums, Messrs. Herne and Williams, of whom we shall hear more later, began to give public sittings and full-formed phantoms glided about the room in a much subdued light. Among the sitters was now and then a young woman from Hackney, by name Florence Eliza Cook, who was destined to become the most famous materialization medium of her age, for she was supported and sponsored by Mr. William Crookes himself, who publicly and without qualification declared her phenomena to be genuine.

It is against the background of the conditions of the times that we have to study the story of Florence Cook and her family. To the devotee of spiritualism, the history of Florence's mediumship is convincing and entirely satisfying, since it seems to provide unassailable scientific evidence of the actuality of materialization as a repeatable experiment. To the psychical researcher the story is a remarkable one, worth the most careful scrutiny, and it is in many ways surprising that until now no effort seems to have been made to subject it to serious examination.

Such an inquiry can now be made, since fresh material is available derived not only from statements of persons who were acquainted with the family but also from the discovery, to be detailed later, of a mass of manuscript sources which throw a flood of light on aspects of the story hitherto hardly suspected.

The importance of the mediumship of Florence Cook in the history of spiritualism can hardly be exaggerated. It is indeed one of the cornerstones of the faith. Not only was it one of the most famous cases of the nineteenth century, but even today it is still regarded as outstanding, ranking with events of historical importance. Broadly speaking, the story is as follows. After a series of minor events to be described in detail later, Florence's mediumship developed from its initial conventional phenomena to the materialization in 1873 of an alleged full spirit form, calling itself "Katie King". This figure, which seems to have been as solid as a human being, could emerge from the cabinet in which Florence lay entranced, and walk freely amongst those present at the séance. It

I*a*. Florence Cook
(*circa* 1874)

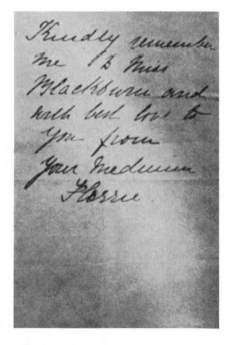

I*b*. Part of a letter from Florence Cook to Charles Blackburn (*circa* June 1872), showing the maturity of her handwriting at a time when she said she was sixteen years old

IIa. Charles Blackburn

IIb. William Crookes
(*circa* 1872)

was photographed successfully on a number of occasions, and could converse with the sitters and even be embraced.

Over a period of some months in the winter of 1873 and the spring of 1874, the scientist William Crookes conducted a long series of experiments with Florence Cook, the results of which he communicated to Mr. W. H. Harrison's paper *The Spiritualist* in a number of letters which were afterwards republished as part of his book *Researches in the Phenomena of Spiritualism* (London, 1874). Crookes declared that his investigation had satisfied him of the complete honesty and integrity of Florence Cook and of the actuality, paranormal nature and separate existence of the materialization "Katie King". Crookes in later years became, *inter alia*, the President of the Royal Society, and received a number of honorary university degrees and many other distinctions in recognition of his outstanding scientific work, including a knighthood in 1897 and the coveted Order of Merit in 1910. His period as the President of the Society for Psychical Research was one of the longest in the history of that organization.

It was the active sponsorship of Florence Cook by William Crookes that raised her to that pinnacle of fame from which her many critics failed to dislodge her. Crookes's support alone was sufficient not only for English investigators but also for many on the European continent. It is true that in his general psychical inquiries Crookes failed to convince or even, in many cases, to interest, his scientific colleagues. This in itself roused the indignation of many psychical researchers. Thus the well-known French parapsychologist P. T. Bret, writing in 1939, stated that:

> "The Katie King episode, made glorious through the courage of William Crookes, will remain in the annals of science an even sadder and more shameful chapter than the condemnation of Galileo by the Inquisition (1633) because there one can see all the orthodox scientists yielding to their hatred of the new instead of accepting the offer to come and examine the facts presented and proved by the most illustrious among them in a spirit of cold and impartial scrutiny."[1]

Similarly Charles Richet, the French physiologist and Nobel prizeman, speaking of the results of the experiments with Florence

[1] P. T. Bret, *Les Métapsychoses*. I. *La Métapsychorragie*. (Paris, 1939), p. 299.

Cook, said that "certainly the most celebrated and certainly the most decisive are those of Sir William Crookes which it seems it is impossible to doubt".[1]

The same point of view has been emphasized by many other foreign writers, and even as late as 1960 the French writer on parapsychology, Mr. René Sudre, speaking of Sir William Crookes, pointed out that "in any case he always reasoned in a scientific manner: the Crookes of thallium [an element discovered by Crookes] and the cathode rays is inseparable from the Crookes of Katie King".[2]

During the past few years spiritualists and others in England and abroad have become even more emphatic as to the overwhelming importance of the mediumship of Florence Cook. Current interest in the nature of the appearances of Jesus Christ after the Resurrection led them to connect these appearances with those of Katie King, who, as it were, "rose from the dead" and then finally disappeared for ever.

Thus, on 8 May, 1948, a noted English spiritualist and writer on psychical research, Mr. B. Abdy Collins, contributed a long article on the Katie King case to the spiritualist journal *Psychic News*. It was one of a series of essays entitled "The Whole Case for Survival". In it he said:

> "The most important case of complete materialization of a human form, well known to all Spiritualists, is that of Katie King, who claimed to be Annie Owen de Morgan, daughter of the famous pirate Sir Henry Owen de Morgan, who became Governor of Jamaica."

After quoting and discussing the evidence of Crookes and others at length, which he said in his opinion proved the genuineness of the case beyond any doubt whatsoever, Mr. Collins added:

> "I have devoted practically all my space to this one case because I feel that the materialization of complete figures which behave like ordinary persons in every way stands or falls by this one case."

He concluded his article by saying that materialization could

[1] C. Richet, *Traité de Métapsychique*. 2 éd. (Paris, 1923), p. 642.
[2] R. Sudre, *Treatise on Parapsychology*. (London, 1960), p. 38.

"explain all the difficulties which the Modernist feels about the Resurrection, and so is of outstanding importance to the world at large and Christians in particular". The comparison of the rising from the dead by Our Lord with the materialization of Katie King through the mediumship of Florence Cook was discussed with approval by the Dutch parapsychologist, Mr. George Zorab, in the following year[1] and again in his essay "The Resurrection—A Psychical Analysis"[2] in 1954.

He himself delivered a lecture "The Enigma of 'Katie King': Living Woman or Phantom?" at the College of Psychic Science in London on 26 January, 1960, and discussed at length four possible hypotheses by which the famous materialization could have been produced by natural means, including imposture and trickery. He said:

> "It is a sound and generally accepted principle in scientific research first to stretch the possibilities of all normal hypotheses as far as they will reasonably go, and only to resort to a paranormal or supernormal explanation when all the normal possibilities have been entirely exhausted."

After his examination of the four hypotheses Mr. Zorab declared that he was of the opinion that all were untenable, with the additional comment that the phenomena of materialization which occurred in the presence of Miss Florence Cook nearly ninety years ago were investigated "in a manner and under conditions unparalleled in later days with mediums producing the same kind of phenomena". Mr. Zorab was, however, frank enough to say that it was curious "that up to the present day these same kind of phenomena have never been repeated under the same watertight conditions of observation". The unique character of the Florence Cook case was also the subject of remark by Crookes's biographer,[3] who said that all the physical phenomena of spiritualism were ultimately based upon Crookes's work and that the evidence for "authentic materializations" was confined to the Katie King affair.

[1] G. Zorab, *Het Opstandingsverhaal in het Licht der Parapsychologie* ('s-Gravenhage, 1949), pp. 158 ff.
[2] *Tomorrow* (New York, 1954), II, No. 4, pp. 13–14.
[3] E. E. Fournier d'Albe, *The Life of Sir William Crookes, O.M., F.R.S.* (London, 1923) p. 238.

The suggestion that the mediumship of Florence Cook could be of assistance to modern Christians in accepting the story of the Resurrection was developed further by the editor of *Two Worlds*, another newspaper devoted to spiritualism. In the issue of 20 April, 1957, in an article "Easter Demonstrated in the Laboratory. World-Famous Scientist Attested Materialization" he said that it was appropriate that some of the photographs of Katie King by Sir William Crookes should illustrate the pages of *Two Worlds* at Easter. The caption under one of the photographs was "Resurrection demonstrated by materialization, the greatest of all psychic phenomena", adding that this mediumship showed that the miracle of Resurrection "was not confined to Palestine 2,000 years ago".

Again, the Rev. J. D. Pearce-Higgins of Putney, London, one of the leading members of the Churches' Fellowship for Psychical Study, went so far as to say in this connexion:[1]

> "Why the Churches do not publish the story of Mrs. Guppy and of Katie King from their pulpits passes my comprehension. They give suggestive evidence and corroboration of practically everything needed for a full belief in survival and shed unique light on processes similar to those recorded of the Resurrection of Jesus Christ."

By now the reader will have gained some idea of the importance attached to the work of Florence Cook by both spiritualists and parapsychologists. As Sir Oliver Lodge once said, the years 1871 to 1874 were of great importance to the disciples of psychic science and constitute a period in connexion with which they will always hold Crookes and his pioneering work in high honour and remembrance.[2]

In the succeeding pages of this book I shall try to give a picture of this period, to follow the chequered career of Florence Cook and her family from their early years until their deaths, and to describe in detail the development of the mediumship both of Florence and of her sister Kate. In particular, I shall examine as far as is now possible the extraordinary story of the association with the Cook family of both Sir William Crookes and Mr. Charles Blackburn,

---

[1] *Resurrection: A Study of the Facts.* (Worthing, 1957), p. 38.
[2] *Proceedings* of the Society for Psychical Research, 1924, xxxiv, p. 313.

the wealthy Manchester spiritualist who was one of the most important figures in the movement at that time. As I have said, new light can now be thrown on the strange and complicated series of events which linked together these central characters in this Victorian imbroglio.

CHAPTER ONE

THE EARLY MEDIUMSHIP
OF FLORENCE COOK

FLORENCE ELIZA COOK was the eldest daughter of Mr. and Mrs. Henry Cook who lived at Cobham in Kent. They had three other children, Henry Ridsdale Macdonald, Kate Selina, who was to become like her sister a medium, and Edith Harriet. After the birth of Kate on 22 January, 1859, the family seem to have moved to London where they found a house at 6 Bruce Villas, Eleanor Road, Hackney. It was in this house that the youngest daughter, Edith, was born on 14 August, 1867, and it was here that most of the important events in Florence's mediumship took place. Mr. Cook obtained a position which is variously described in official documents, but it appears that he was connected with the printing trade and served as a compositor and possibly in other capacities also.

The date of Florence's birth is uncertain. In May 1872, the editor of *The Spiritualist*, Mr. W. H. Harrison, said that he had "asked Miss Cook to write a little history of the development of her mediumship, and she has kindly furnished us with the following narrative". Florence's story opened with the sentence "I am sixteen years of age". Her article was reprinted *verbatim* six months later, without date or any reference to its provenance, in *The Spiritual Magazine*[1] and may readily have been assumed by the reader to have been written at that time.

As her year of birth has always previously been given simply as 1856, without any comment upon the absence of the exact date, it would appear that Florence's statement has previously been accepted at its face value without investigation, and that it has generally been assumed that the statement was made and first published in November 1872.

It is important to try to establish the date of Florence's birth, since much emphasis has been placed upon her youth in accounts of

[1] November 1872, p. 516.

1

her early mediumship. Thus, Sir William Crookes wrote that it did "violence to one's reason and common sense" to imagine that "an innocent schoolgirl of fifteen should be able to conceive and then carry out for three years so gigantic an imposture as this, and in that time should submit to any test which might be imposed upon her".[1]

Sir William's statement is hard to understand and gives an unfortunate impression of special pleading. His own *experiments* with Florence Cook did not start until the latter part of 1873 at the earliest, and were virtually confined to the year 1874. He had, as far as we know, no first-hand knowledge of any tests to which she may or may not have submitted apart from the comparatively short period of his experiments with her. As for Florence being "an innocent schoolgirl of fifteen", we know she was asked to leave her teaching post in Miss Eliza Cliff's school at 200 Richmond Road, Hackney, on 5 January, 1872—at a time when she was actually practising as a medium and four months before she stated she was sixteen. And even if she *was* only sixteen in May 1872 she would have been eighteen two years later.

The trouble is that first Florence's parents and then Florence herself have succeeded in enveloping the actual date of her birth in a fog of mystery that has so far proved impenetrable. A search at Somerset House has failed to reveal anything except that her birth was not registered in England between 1849 and 1858 inclusive under the name of her father, Henry Cook, or the maiden name of her mother, Emma Till. They were married on 12 January, 1856, at the parish church in Christ Church, Surrey,[2] where they both lived. So even if Florence was only sixteen in May 1872 she was certainly conceived some months before their wedding; and if she was actually older than she claimed, as seems likely from the maturity of her handwriting in 1872, she was born before her

---

[1] *Researches*, etc., p. 112.

[2] This address is taken precisely from the Entry of Marriage at Somerset House, although "Christ Church, Surrey" is not listed in any edition of *Bartholomew's Survey Gazetteer of the British Isles* that I have seen. *The Clergy List for* 1857 (London, 1857), however, shows that Robert Hall Baynes, who officiated at the marriage of Henry Cook and Emma Till, was the curate at "Christchurch, Southwark", where the ceremony took place. In the "List of Benefices" in the same publication, the entry appears for "Christ-Church, Surrey" in the "Post Town" of Southwark, which was part of Surrey until 1888. Green Walk, where both parties lived before their marriage, was on the site of what are now Colombo Street, Burrell Street and Hopton Street, amongst the bear pits and brothels of the Southwark of those days.

mother's marriage and may not have been Henry Cook's child at all. We are left with the conclusion that her birth was either registered under another man's name or was not registered at all, despite the penalties for concealment of birth.

The fog is thickened by the fact that when Florence was married in April 1874 she did not give her age; instead she added to her parents' deception by stating merely that she was "under age". She might have been eighteen, nineteen or twenty—up to two years older than she claimed. We may never know when she was born, but we may reasonably assume that it was some time before she said.

This suggests that (a) emphasis was placed on Florence's extreme youth when her mediumship began, both by her supporters and herself, to imply that so young and inexperienced a girl would not be capable of trickery; (b) the failure to register her birth (if this was the case) made it easier to lie about her age later; and (c) when there was an opportunity to give her age in the normal way in 1874, it was in fact concealed on purpose.

According to Florence's autobiographical account[1] her first discovery of her mediumship occurred "in the spring of 1870" when she was "invited to the house of a schoolfriend, whose name I am not at liberty to mention". During some amateurish experiments in table tilting, loud rappings followed Florence around the room and "the table rose from the floor quite four feet" to the astonishment of the company. A few days later Florence and her mother, Mrs. Emma Cook, returned to the undisclosed house of the unnamed schoolfriend, and during a further séance even more wonderful phenomena occurred. Florence wrote:

"The room was not perfectly dark, a light came in from the window. Soon I felt my chair taken from me. I was lifted up until I touched the ceiling. All in the room could see me. I felt too startled at my novel position to scream, and was carried over the heads of the sitters, and put gently on to a table at the

[1] *The Spiritualist*, 15 May, 1872, p. 36. Henceforward the name of this journal will be abbreviated to "*S*". It is of some interest to notice that Florence's announcement of the beginning of her mediumship closely followed in pattern and in some details the similar published account by which Charles E. Williams had introduced himself to the world of spiritualism five years earlier. (*The Spiritual Magazine*, November 1867, p. 524.) Williams, a notorious medium who was to become one of Florence's mentors at the suggestion of the spirits, also lived in Hackney.

other end of the room. Mamma asked if we could get manifestations at our own home. The table answered, 'Yes,' and that
I was a medium.

The next evening we sat at home, a table and two chairs
were smashed, and a great deal of mischief done. We said we
could never sit again but we were not left in peace. Books and
other articles were thrown at me, chairs walked about in the
light, the table tilted violently at mealtimes, and great noises
were sometimes made at night. At last we sat again; the table
behaved better, and a communication was given to the effect
that we were to go to 74 Navarino Road, and that there was
an association of Spiritualists there. Out of curiosity mamma
and I went, and found that we had been told quite correctly.
Mr. Thomas Blyton came to a *séance* at our house; he invited
me to a *séance* at Mr. Wilkes's library in Dalston Lane.
There I met Mr. Harrison. He came to see the manifestations
at my home."

There are a number of features of this account which cast some
doubt upon its truth. The first published reference to the mediumship of Florence Cook I have been able to find anywhere had
appeared one year previously[1] in a letter dated 9 June, 1871, and
written to the editor by Thomas Blyton, who described himself as
the Secretary to the Dalston Association of Inquirers into Spiritualism, giving his address as 74 Navarino Road, Dalston. His letter,
which was entitled "A New Medium", described the manifestations he had witnessed at Hackney and is so typical of accounts of
séances at this period that I reprint it in full:

"Sir, I write to describe some recent manifestations witnessed at the residence of a gentleman of the name of Cook,
in Hackney, whose daughter has mediumistic qualities, which
have appeared within the past fortnight or three weeks. The
young lady (aged fifteen) and her mother were sitting at a
table on the afternoon of the 31st of May last, when, among
other communications, they were urgently requested 'to go at
once to 74 Navarino-road, where they hold *séances*'. They
accordingly called at my residence during my absence. I afterwards paid them a visit. A *séance* was arranged, the sitters

[1] *S.*, 15 June, 1871, p. 175.

consisting of Mr. and Mrs. Cook, their daughter, an aunt, and myself; the light was removed, when immediately Miss Cook was placed upon the table, and, upon my holding her hand, she was removed from the table on to the floor, and on to the table again several times in a manner which convinced me she was being floated in the air. The table, a heavy oak one, was then thrown with great force over into the fireplace, and Miss Cook carried very rapidly round the room. Articles were carried about the room, and Miss Cook stated that she saw several spirits and lights during the evening; also that one spirit, known to the family, shook her by the hands, and kissed her.

On the 2nd inst. I was privileged to sit with them again. The circle consisted of Mr. and Mrs. Cook, Miss Cook, and myself. Previous to the light being removed, the table gave violent tilts, and on extinguishing the light, Miss Cook and her chair were repeatedly removed from the floor on to the table. A chair was twice placed over my head, without its legs first touching me; then a portion of Miss Cook's dress was removed, and after being whisked in our faces, was thrown over my head, while a hassock was thrown into my lap, as well as a vulcanite necklace which Miss Cook had been wearing. Table movements, of a very powerful nature, ensued, whilst the raps were remarkably loud and distinct. On the gas being lit, Miss Cook was entranced, and with her head turned from some paper, and resting on the table, wrote, for the first time under spirit influence, many very interesting communications. On my asking the reason for the condition of darkness for some of the manifestations, she wrote, 'Light destroys our conditions'; and, on a request for a few words in French, 'Je suis un esprit', with the translation, 'I am a spirit'. Another was 'Get Florrie (Miss Cook) to come to your *séances*, it will be well for both parties'. In answer to other questions of mine, the spirits intimated that she would eventually become a very powerful physical, trance, writing, and speaking medium.

THOMAS BLYTON,

74 Navarino-road, Dalston, E.   Secretary to the Dalston
9 June, 1871.   Association of Inquirers into Spiritualism.''

5

The fact that Florence either carelessly or deliberately put this episode a year earlier than it seems to have occurred makes it unlikely that the phenomena she mentioned ever happened at all in the way she described them. It is not easy to understand anyone in 1872 being incapable of remembering correctly whether so wonderful an experience took place one or two years previously.

The story of the visit to Mr. Blyton inspired by the spirit message seems to have been a curious business. Miss Cook gave much later a more detailed account of the journey to Navarino Road in the spiritualist journal *Light*:[1]

> "At last we were . . . told to go to a certain address in Dalston and ask for a Spiritualist who lived there and would help us. This seemed such a queer quest that we hesitated a long time before undertaking it, and when we did go we passed and repassed the house several times before summoning up courage enough to knock at the door. But it was all right. A rather cross old lady answered our knock, and, in response to our timid inquiries, told us she was not a Spiritualist and not likely to be; but her son was, and, if we wished, would come round and see us in the evening."

The quest certainly did not involve Florence and her mother in a long and tiring journey. Navarino Road and Eleanor Road, where the Cooks lived, are immediately adjoining streets, both running into Richmond Road where the school at which Florence taught until January 1872 was situated.[2]

Another interesting point about the accounts of these first séances is the description of the violent physical phenomena which were alleged to have occurred from the beginning. Florence claimed that during her first sitting the table rose four feet into the air, and that during her second she was levitated to the ceiling in full view of the sitters. It is noteworthy that, as in the case of the schoolfriend and her house, none of these sitters was mentioned by name. According to Mr. Blyton, Florence's third sitting took place

[1] 15 December, 1894, p. 608. Henceforth abbreviated to "*L*".
[2] The difficulty of believing that the Cooks had no prior knowledge of Mr. Blyton's presence and activities in their immediate vicinity is increased by the fact that a few weeks before their call upon him he had advertised the Dalston Association in the local newspaper. (*The Hackney and Kingsland Gazette*, 11 March, 1871.)

at her home on the evening of 31 May, 1871, when in response to Florence's call upon him, he visited the medium and her parents for the first time. He said that he was convinced that Florence floated in the air, and that the heavy oak table was flung with great force into the fireplace whilst Florence was carried rapidly round the room by the spirits.

The point is that independent accounts of Florence's subsequent séances contained no hint of these wonderful levitations and violent physical phenomena being repeated. As soon as named sitters other than Mr. and Mrs. Cook and Mr. Blyton had the opportunity of attending séances, the manifestations in the subsequent months seem to have been reduced to the mere appearance of alleged spirit faces at an aperture in the upper part of the door of a corner cupboard in the house at Hackney. Florence was seated on a chair inside the closed cupboard, below the level of the aperture, her hands being tied with tape or rope. The accounts of the observers make it clear that the arrangement of the cupboard and the position of the aperture were strongly reminiscent of the once familiar Punch and Judy cabinet.

It may be asked why such an anti-climax should follow the wonderful phenomena alleged to have been experienced at the first séances when Florence was able to float to the ceiling or project the heavy table into the fireplace. One answer might be that the descriptions of the first sittings were mostly fictitious, which would account for the medium's secrecy over the identity of her school-friend and the other sitters who could have confirmed her story if it happened to be true, and the discrepancy of a year in the dating of these events by her and Thomas Blyton.

If for the moment we assume that this theory is well founded some inferences from it immediately suggest themselves. The first is that Mr. and Mrs. Cook, who were the only people named by either Florence or Mr. Blyton as being present at the first séances, were in the deception from the beginning, or at least very dubious about it.[1] Secondly, Blyton himself must have indulged in some exaggeration since he claimed to have been a witness of the astonishing events at the sittings of 31 May and 2 June, 1871. Thirdly, W. H. Harrison, who asked Florence for her autobiographical account and published it, must at least have been willing

[1] For possible doubts on the part of Mr. Cook cf. *S.*, 15 November, 1871.

7

to assist in launching Florence as a medium with a good reason for doing so.

If a unified explanation is to be sought for the behaviour of these people, one need not look further than that of personal gain. Thomas Blyton was the Secretary of the local group of spiritualists in Hackney and Dalston. The Dalston Association, formed in 1870, thrived during the next few years on the fame of the mediumship of Florence Cook.[1] As the Dalston society increased in importance after 1871 Mr. Blyton grew with it and eventually became the Secretary of the British National Association of Spiritualists, established in 1873. A possibly more significant fact is that the principal financial supporter of the Dalston Association was the wealthy Charles Blackburn of Manchester who also contributed to the cost of publication of *The Spiritualist* from which W. H. Harrison's livelihood was presumably partially derived.[2] When Florence was safely launched, Harrison was able literally to fill his columns with accounts and eulogies of her marvellous mediumship. Indeed, so much space was devoted to the activities of Florence that the editor of *The Spiritual Magazine* annoyed Mr. Harrison by suggesting that *The Spiritualist* be renamed *Miss Florence Cook's Journal*.[3] As we shall see later, it is noteworthy that when occasional contributors to the paper were sufficiently bold to describe circumstances at Florence's sittings which seemed to indicate trickery, the editor almost invariably attempted to suppress their letters.

A final example of a suspicious feature of Florence's story of her mediumship in her account of 1872,[4] when emphasis was being placed upon her youth and innocence, is her statement that she was at first horrified at the wickedness of spirit communication, and

---

[1] According to Florence Cook's account (*L.*, 15 December, 1894, p. 608) Mr. Blyton became one of her best friends, and it was under his guidance that her mediumship developed rapidly. Other members of the Dalston Association included Mrs. Amelia Corner and Miss Caroline Corner, close friends and neighbours of the Cooks. Epes Sargent in his *The Proof Palpable of Immortality* (Boston, 1875, p. 47) refers to Florence Cook as "the daughter of a member of the Dalston Association of Inquirers into Spiritualism". If this meant that Mr. or Mrs. Cook, or both, were early members of the Association, the story of the quest in Navarino Road would seem even more dubious.

[2] It is noteworthy that from 1872 to 1875 Harrison received "an annual sum of about £200", privately subscribed, to assist him in publishing *The Spiritualist*, and that when he encountered financial difficulties in 1875 Blackburn was the maximum contributor of £50. (*S.*, 17 December, 1875, p. iv.)

[3] *S.*, 15 March, 1873, p. 135.

[4] Loc. cit.

that her mother warned her that it was "all a trick to amuse the children". In her later narrative in 1894[1] she said that the mediumistic faculty had run back in her family as far as they could trace, that she and her mother had experienced psychic phenomena when Florence was "quite a little child", and that at the age of fourteen she used to fall into trances and wake up to find her homework completed.

Whether Florence's story of her mediumship was true or, as seems possible, at least a partial fabrication, it appears to have been instrumental in quickly bringing about an event of considerable financial benefit to her and to the Cook family as a whole. Florence attracted the kindly and credulous eye of Mr. Charles Blackburn. It is of course possible that this may have been coincidental, or, on the other hand, it may have been the objective which the Cooks and their supporters had in mind when the story of the wonders of Florence's mediumship was published.

According to Mr. Benjamin Coleman, Mr. Blackburn "became interested in this young lady's career, and at once made such arrangements as should render it unnecessary for her to become a professional medium",[2] Blackburn himself saying that he had "made a little arrangement of compensation with the family".[3] Mr. Traill Taylor, the editor of *The British Journal of Photography*, who was himself interested in spiritualism, is quoted as stating "that an open-handed Manchester gentleman has, if we understand him aright, paid to the said medium or her family a sum equal to the stipend received by many a hard-working curate for his ministrations".[4]

Apart from the obvious material advantage of the receipt of a regular income by the Cooks there was another and important benefit from this comfortable arrangement. It was not necessary to charge fees to individual sitters. It is quite clear from the literature that those who attended the séances were the invited guests of the

[1] *L.*, Op. cit.
[2] *S.*, 15 May, 1874, p. 234. Mr. Coleman was a noted spiritualist at that time.
[3] *S.*, 17 April, 1874, p. 192. According to Blackburn, writing a year or two after the event, the "little arrangement" began when Florence was "aged about 17", which on the basis of her declared age would be during 1873. This was, however, an understandable approximation for Blackburn was unquestionably attending séances at Hackney in 1872.
[4] Quoted in H. E. Thompson's "Grasping a Spirit" in *The Medium and Daybreak*, 19 December, 1873, pp. 598–9.

Cook family in their own home, were mainly docile and convinced spiritualists, and conformed of necessity to the restraints and conditions imposed by the medium and her parents. The accounts of the phenomena, moreover, were principally contributed by believers to the columns of *The Spiritualist*, which, as we have seen, strongly favoured the medium and her work.

Florence Cook's story[1] in 1872 suggests that in 1871 (if we accept Mr. Blyton's date) she had received practical training as a physical medium. She wrote:

"Mr. Thomas Blyton came to a *séance* at our house; he invited me to a *séance* at Mr. Wilkes's library in Dalston-lane. There I met Mr. Harrison. He came to see the manifestations at my home. By this time we were convinced of the truth of spirit communion. About this time I was first entranced; a spirit spoke through me, telling papa that if I sat with Messrs. Herne[2] and Williams,[3] I should get the direct voice. I had several sittings with them and finally succeeded in getting the direct voice, direct writing, and spirit touches. The presiding spirit of my circles is Katie, John King's daughter. She speaks very much the same as her mother, who is the celebrated Katie King of Herne and Williams' *séances*."

[1] *S.*, 15 May, 1872.

[2] Frank Herne, a well-known physical medium of the period, whose first séances were given in January 1869. In 1871 he joined Charles Williams in partnership and their séances at 61 Lambs Conduit Street, London, became both famous and successful. At the direction of the spirits Mr. Henry Cook arranged for the youthful Florence to become the pupil of Herne. It is odd that when Florence began to practise as a medium herself the alleged materialization announced that she was "Katie King", the daughter of a spirit of the same name who was associated with Herne's séances. It would perhaps be unkind to suggest that Florence appropriated some of the "goodwill" of Herne's business, but that is what in fact seems to have occurred.

[3] Charles Williams, the English materialization medium and the partner of Frank Herne. Fraud was frequently suspected at his séances, and was on one occasion at least glaringly exposed. In September 1878 a group of Dutch spiritualists detected Williams and his fellow-medium at the time, A. Rita, in flagrant trickery at Amsterdam. "Charlie", the materialized spirit, was found to be Rita. The mediums were intercepted in an attempted flight from the house and searched by the angry spiritualists. The equipment for the impersonation, consisting of muslin, false beards, wigs and other paraphernalia, was discovered on the persons of both mediums.

For the various reports on Mr. Herne's activities see *The Medium and Daybreak*, 1871, pp. 185, 238, 282, 312: 1872, pp. 179, 237, 261, 276, 287: 1876, pp. 6, 28, 39; 1878, pp. 484, 551, 552. The account of the Dutch exposure will be found in *The Spiritualist* of September 20, 27, 1878, where various statements, by accusers and accused are printed, a German version of the facts being given in *Psychische Studien* for October 1878. An earlier and favourable account of Mr. Williams's mediumship was printed by Mr. A. J. Riko in his *Het Medium Williams in Nederland* (Den Haag, 1874).

From contemporary accounts it is clear that not only was Herne giving sittings on his own account but was actively engaged in helping Florence develop her mediumship in her own home at Hackney. One such sitting was described as occurring on 10 April, 1872,[1] where the two principal mediums were Herne and Florence. Spirit hands and arms were seen, and once or twice, not very clearly, a supposed spirit form was observed in the darkened room. The cabinet appears to have been formed by curtains hanging over an open door. On 13 April, at a public séance at Herne and Williams's rooms, materialized hands and a veiled nun-like figure appeared. On 20 April, again at Herne and Williams's rooms, "Katie King's" head materialized, wrapped up in a fabric of the purest white.

On Sunday, 21 April, another séance was held at Mr. Cook's house. Florence and Herne were again the mediums, sitting in a darkened room, the spectators being outside in the passage with curtains across the doorway. Spirit hands appeared through the opening in the curtains. Shortly after the hands disappeared a full-length robed figure, its face and head also covered by drapery, rushed out of the room, through the curtains, agitatedly seizing Mr. Cook crying "Oh, Cookey! Cookey!" and after a time retired back into the cabinet. Shortly afterwards the draped figure of John King came out into the passage shaking people by the hand, and leading or pushing them to one end of the passage leaving the end which led to the stairs clear. He even lifted up little Donald Cook, aged four, and carried him bodily down the passage with the rest of the sitters. After a time the spectators observed two shadows emerge from the dark room and ascend the stairs together.

A few seconds later the passage was plunged into pitch darkness and nothing was heard for a quarter of an hour, after which time the two alleged materializations presumably returned from their mysterious expedition upstairs. Screams were again heard from Florence Cook but she finally emerged through the curtains according to Harrison "more excited than frightened". It is perhaps noteworthy that even after this curious occurrence Florence continued to give joint séances with Herne and Williams as late as August 1872.[2]

Florence's story of her association with Mr. Herne is of

---

[1] S., 15 May, 1872. The account was contributed by the editor, Mr. Harrison.
[2] The Spiritual Magazine, 1872, pp. 240 ff.

considerable interest and importance. Not only was he at that time much more famous than herself but he had already succeeded in persuading Mr. Blackburn to give him financial support to pursue his vocation, a fact which could hardly be unknown to the Cook family.[1] Whether these payments ceased when Mr. Harrison found it was his "painful duty" to report that Mr. Herne had been discovered[2] dressed up and posing as a spirit form we have no means now of knowing. What is clear, however, is the fact that, since Mr. Harrison found it necessary to print the story of Mr. Herne's deception, the facts must have amply justified it and could hardly have escaped Florence's attention or that of her parents. Moreover, the later escapades of Mr. Herne's partner, Charles Williams, in Holland lend weight to the assumption that both had been engaged in systematic fraud for some years.

As we have already seen, Florence's startling phenomena as recorded by Messrs. Blyton and Harrison do not seem to have continued very long. Even with Herne as her assistant they could hardly be compared with her earlier manifestations such as levitations and movements of heavy furniture. Moreover, now that she was established in London as a recognised sensitive and had passed out of the tutelage of her special friends, her phenomena seemed at first to have been limited to "showing the spirit faces", an exhibition which was very popular at that period and created sometimes amazement and sometimes doubt as to what was really going on. One of the best and most amusing accounts of such a sitting with Florence was included by the Rev. C. Maurice Davies, who was on the Council of the British National Association of Spiritualists, in his book published in 1875.[3]

Dr. Davies was cautious in his outlook. He regarded the mediums then operating in London with kindly tolerance and always tried to give them the benefit of the doubt. But the doubts

[1] S., 15 June, 1872 p. 47.
[2] S., loc. cit. Three years later, Harrison had to use similar words regarding another exposure of Herne. In an article "Another fiasco in Liverpool" (S., 31 December, 1875, p. 323) Harrison reported that a group of devout sitters at the Spiritual Centre in Russell Street, Liverpool, had engaged Herne for six séances, and that the alleged spirit "John King" had been discovered to be Herne, with his scarf wrapped round his head to simulate a turban. The disgusted spiritualists described the occurrence as "imposture of the grossest kind", whilst Harrison said it was his "painful duty to record another miserable fiasco".
[3] Mystic London: or, Phases of Occult Life in the Metropolis (London, 1875), pp. 309–11.

were there. To perform such feats without at least a trace of athletic prowess was impossible and so he called the subject of his remarks "Spiritual Athletes". As to the sitting he attended with Florence, "a trim little lady of sweet sixteen" as he calls her, he wrote as follows:

"Now, I do not purpose going through the details of the séance, which was considerably irksome, being protracted by endless psalm singing. What I want to do—with Miss Cook's permission—is to calculate the chances of her being sufficiently athletic to perform the tricks herself, without the aid of spirits. Does she not underrate her unaided powers in assigning a supernatural cause for the effects produced?

Well, then, this lithe little lady is arrayed in the ordinary garb of the nineteenth century with what is technically termed a 'pannier', and large open sleeves, each of which, I fear, she must have found considerably in the way, as also the sundry lockets and other nick-nacks suspended from her neck. However, there they were. We put her in a cupboard, which had a single Windsor chair in it, and laid a stoutish new cord on her lap. Then came singing, which may or may not have been intended to drown any noise in the cupboard; but, after some delay, she was found tied around the waist, neck, and two wrists, and the ends of the cord fastened to the back of the chair. These knots we sealed, and consigned her to the cupboard again. Shortly after there appeared at an aperture in the upper portion of the cupboard a face which looked utterly unspiritual and precisely like that of the medium, only with some white drapery thrown over the head. The aperture was just the height that would have allowed Miss Cook to stand on the chair and peep out. I do not say she did; I am only calculating the height. The face remained some minutes in a strong light; then descended. We opened the cupboard and found the little lady tied as before with the seals unbroken. Spiritual, or material, it was clever.

After a pause, the same process was gone through again; only this time stout tape was substituted for rope. The cord cut the girl's wrists; and tape was almost more satisfactory. Again she was bound, and we sealed the knots; and again a face appeared—this time quite black, and not like the medium at all. I noticed that the drapery ran right round the face, and cut it off at a straight line on the lower part. This gave the idea of a mask. I am not saying it was a mask. I am only throwing out a hint that, if the 'spirits' wish to convince people they should let the neck be well seen. I am bound to say it bore a strong light for several minutes; and some people say they saw eyelids. I did not. I do not say they were not there. I know how impossible it is to prove a negative, and only say I did not see them."

The fact that Florence had been a pupil of Herne and Williams removes any doubt as to the origin of the idea of the "spirit faces" in the aperture of the Punch and Judy cupboard. In an eye-witness account dated 11 December, 1872, of a séance with these mediums,[1] Mr. David H. Wilson made it clear that a cabinet was used with a window or aperture, and that whilst the gas was turned down there was sufficient light to enable those near the cabinet to see whatever might appear at the aperture whilst Mr. Williams was tied with rope inside. "Spirit faces" appeared in due course. Similarly Mr. George Fraser described the procedure at one of these séances at which he was present,[2] saying that Florence shut herself up in a corner cupboard above the doors of which a square hole had been cut large enough to exhibit, as in a frame, the head of any spirit which might appear. In these early days the sitters were not even allowed to tie Florence up. Mr. Fraser made it plain, as did other witnesses of the period, that Florence was first shut in the cupboard with a piece of tape placed on her lap. After some time had elapsed the doors were opened "by the direct command of the spirit voice" and Florence was then discovered to be tied in her chair. Mr. Fraser, who was obviously not writing in a critical vein, nevertheless conceded in his account that the spirit faces bore a strong resemblance to Florence Cook, whom he described as being of a most prepossessing appearance.

Further confirmation of the similarity of the spirit faces at Hackney to Florence was provided by another letter dated 26

---

[1] *The Medium and Daybreak*, 13 December, 1872.
[2] *The Social Review* (London, 14 December, 1872). Mr. Fraser's article was reprinted in *Where are the Dead?* pp. 65–7. Cf. his account of the tying procedure with that described above by Dr. Maurice Davies.

December, 1872, from Mr. Henry M. Dunphy[1] describing a séance held three days earlier. The company included Miss Marie Scott, Mrs. Amelia Corner, Miss Caroline Corner and other friends invited at the request of "Katie King". The usual faces appeared in the cabinet aperture and were described by Mr. Dunphy as being similar in general character to that of Florence Cook.

The question of the tying of the medium seems to have caused as much discussion among the more critical observers as the similarity of the faces to that of the medium. It was naturally suggested that, if the spirits proposed temporarily to release the medium from her bonds during the séance in order that phenomena might occur, such a task would be made appreciably easier for the spirits if they had done the original tying themselves.[2]

Occasionally comment upon the use of the corner cupboard during the séances appeared in periodicals other than *The Spiritualist*. The following article not only provided further confirmation of the similarity of the face at the aperture to that of Florence, if this be needed, but mentioned somewhat critically the result of a simple test using a length of string tied around the medium's waist. Mr. Traill Taylor, whom I have already mentioned, wrote:

"One item of alloy in this case is that, in the opinion of those who have seen the spirit thus visibly, it too often bears a decidedly unpleasant resemblance to the medium. No means can be taken to test the genuineness of the differences between the two entities, for, by a pretty fiction, the spectators at the particular séances referred to are presumed to be invited as private guests to the residence of the medium, and no person could be guilty of such rudeness as to 'test the spirit'.

[1] *S.*, 1 January, 1873. Mr. Dunphy was a barrister-at-law and a spiritualist.
[2] There is no doubt that during later stages of Florence Cook's mediumship the sitters were allowed to do the tying. It is, however, pertinent to point out that the student of elementary conjuring procedure knows that if his hands are being tied it is extremely easy to cause a member of the audience unknowingly and infallibly to tie a slip knot, from which the performer can swiftly release himself and just as rapidly show his bonds intact once more.
It is curious to learn that Florence's friend and fellow-medium, Mary Showers, who was about the same age and of whom we shall hear more later, adopted the same earlier procedure. A piece of rope was placed in the cabinet with the medium, and the curtains drawn. At a signal from within, the curtains were opened and Miss Showers was discovered bound to her chair. (F. Podmore, *Modern Spiritualism* (London, 1902), Vol. II, p. 101.)

We had the opportunity of being present on one occasion when the spirit was expected to appear; but, whether the ghostly visitant felt disinclined to gratify our desires—or whether its non-appearance was attributable to our having tied a string round the waist of the medium (a young lady) the end of which string we passed through a hole made in the side of the cabinet, tying it to a chair outside—the result was that no spirit was that evening to be seen at the aperture; in short, the séance was characterized by a very decided want of success, in consequence of which, we presume, we have not been again invited to be present."[1]

The "spirit faces", as seen with mediums such as Herne, Williams, Mrs. Guppy and Florence Cook, were by no means universally accepted as genuine phenomena, even by convinced spiritualists. Thus, Mrs. S. B. Catherine Berry, writing in *The Medium and Daybreak* of 28 March, 1873,[2] said:

"You are aware that I never have been thoroughly satisfied with the manifestations called 'spirit faces'. I have sat at many of these séances, but always had a doubt upon my mind as to their genuineness. I am now satisfied that some are not genuine; and I would advise all who go to witness these manifestations to take my experience, and put mediums through a far stricter test than they are at present subjected to. It is no use searching the cabinet or room where they are to sit: the beard, masks, and draperies are not there, they go in with the medium. My advice is, search them, and instead of using cord to tie them with, use cotton. Fastened with cotton, they cannot move without its breaking, but with cord, never mind how many knots may be made, they can and do extricate themselves. Again, I would advise that the instant a spirit face is seen at the aperture and disappears, the cabinet, or door of · room, should be thrown open."

This passage is particularly interesting, coming from Mrs. Berry who had been introduced to spiritualism by her friend Miss Roe, and who shortly afterwards was completely converted

[1] *The Medium and Daybreak*, 19 December, 1873, pp. 598–9.
[2] This letter was reprinted in her book, *Experiences in Spiritualism* (London, 1876), 2nd Edition, pp. 116 ff.

16

by the celebrated physical medium Mrs. Mary Marshall who attempted, without any success, to rival her contemporary D. D. Home, whose phenomena were of a much more striking character. Once converted, Mrs. Berry became a devout follower. Indeed, life to her would have been a dark and dreary shadow without the comfort that spiritualism brought her for that was, as she put it, "the beacon that lights me on". Mrs. Berry acted as an enthusiastic propagandist for the mediums, especially for her friends Messrs. Herne and Williams whose séances she constantly attended but who suffered severe competition through the performances of Messrs. Kingsley and Hopkins who produced very similar phenomena. Although from her letter it is clear that Mrs. Berry knew of mediums who even she thought were fraudulent, she was very careful not to name them lest, perhaps, the Cause might be tarnished.

Florence ran into early difficulties with her production of the face of Katie King. Dr. J. E. Purdon, an American physician who had a house at the seaside resort of Sandown in the Isle of Wight, had attended a séance at Hackney on 12 May, 1872, at the invitation of Mr. Cook.[1] He was evidently impressed by the appearance of a face and hands at what appears to have been on this occasion "an opening in the curtain hung up across the door as a temporary screen", for he forthwith invited Florence to stay with him in Sandown. In a letter dated 10 June, 1872[2] he said that Florence had "been staying at my house for some time past", accompanied, we may suppose, by her mother.

Dr. Purdon revealed that the séances at Sandown had proved to be a fiasco. He said that a face had "appeared at the window of the cabinet within which Miss Cook sits as medium for the manifesta-

[1] S., 15 May, 1872, p. 35.
[2] S., 15 June, 1872, p. 46. Florence was in the habit of accepting invitations of this sort from men of substance who were attracted by her mediumship. Thus, in an undated letter to Charles Blackburn which she clearly wrote soon after the Sandown visit, to which she referred, Florence mentioned another admiring spiritualist, Mr. J. Luxmoore, who seems quickly to have replaced Dr. Purdon. Florence said that she had felt much happier since Mr. Luxmoore had taken a prominent part in her séances. She explained that he "understands everything" and by his strong will was capable, presumably in contrast with Dr. Purdon, of sending away the bad spirits such as those which had proved so upsetting at Sandown. She went on to say that on the following Tuesday Mr. Luxmoore was taking her to the Exhibition to be followed by dinner, and added "he has kindly invited Mamma and me to go with him for a run in his yacht. Will it not be nice? I should like it so much and it will do Mamma so much good."

tion", that the face seemed to be of flesh and blood and that the likeness to Miss Cook was startling. He added that the experiments had been "rendered utterly worthless" by the discovery that the bonds with which Florence had been secured to her chair had been cut and the seals broken. Florence herself wrote to her friend, W. H. Harrison, saying with commendable restraint that the sittings at Sandown had been "far from satisfactory". She explained that she was being troubled for the first time by a bad spirit calling himself the devil, who was undoing all the good work of "Katie King".

So far as I have been able to ascertain this seems to have been one of the first serious criticisms of Florence Cook, and Harrison was clearly in a considerable dilemma about it. Florence's mediumship was new; and a bad mistake such as she had evidently made at Sandown was a serious matter. He had not yet reached the stage, which was to come later, of silencing all criticism when it was within his capacity to do so. In his editorial "Trickery in Spiritualism"[1] he wisely contented himself with sitting on the fence. He divided his allegiance by pointing to the "blameless life" of Florence with the suggestion that bad spirits had "no doubt, much to do with the matter", at the same time referring to Dr. Purdon as "a thoroughly honest observer, faithfully recording all he sees".

It would seem that this may not have been the first serious doubt about Florence Cook's mediumship, and it certainly was not to be the last. In the issue of *The Lancet* of 10 January, 1874, it was reported:

> "Mr. William Hipp has also recounted in the *Echo*[2] his experience of a séance, with the celebrated Miss Cook as a medium. Among other manifestations the time arrived for the spirits to sprinkle the guests with water, a tumbler having been placed on the table for that purpose. The room was darkened and expectation was on tiptoe, but the sceptical Mr. Hipp

[1] *S.*, 15 June, 1872, p. 41. Harrison's difficulty was increased by the necessity of dealing in the same article with a glaring exposure of the medium Frank Herne, Florence's mentor, who, as we have seen, had been discovered "dressed up as a ghost".
[2] 3 January, 1874, p. 2. Mr. Hipp's letter, "The 'ghost séance' " was a reply to an earlier letter "A ghost séance in London" in the same paper by Mr. J. Enmore Jones, describing one of Florence's sittings at which Katie King wore an Eastern headdress (The *Echo*, 31 December, 1873, p. 2). Mr. Enmore Jones, although a convinced spiritualist, was, as we shall see later, to become a critic of Crookes's conduct of the final dramatic séances at Hackney.

grasped the tumbler, and in a few seconds clutched the hand that was dipped into it. As he had caught a spirit a light was procured, and a striking tableau presented itself. The spirit hand had an arm of flesh, which formed part of Miss Cook's body. The censure and ignominy, he adds, that he brought on himself was only counterbalanced by the satisfaction he felt in having a last caught a spirit."

Miss Cook was angrily defended by her friend Mr. Thomas Blyton,[1] the explanation advanced being that she had instinctively stretched her hand across the table to recover a flower which had been removed by the spirits from her dress. It is not clear from either account what she was doing amongst the sitters at all, nor did Mr. Blyton explain how, if she was entranced, the medium was able to stretch out her arm to recover a flower or even realize that it had been removed from her dress. Mr. Blyton said that this incident took place during a séance at which he was present "about two years ago". If this estimate be correct, the sitting must have been about January 1872.

That Florence's tuition by more experienced mediums was not confined to Herne and Williams is made clear by the literature. Mr. James Burns, the editor of *The Medium and Daybreak*, on the occasion of a public debate described a séance held on 14 December, 1872, at 16 Old Quebec-street, London.[2] The mediums were Mr. and Mrs. Nelson Holmes[3] and Florence Cook. Amongst the company present were Mr. W. H. Harrison, Mr. Edward W. Cox, and "Mr. Cook's family". It is of great interest to read that after a dark séance another sitting was held by the light of a candle utilizing two rooms separated by a doorway over which was fixed a temporary partition of some sort with an aperture in it. Miss Cook and Mr. Holmes went inside the room on the opposite side of the

---

[1] *S.*, 16 January, 1874, p. 34.

[2] F. A. Binney. *Where are the Dead? Or, Spiritualism Explained* (3rd Edition, London, 1875), pp. 57–60. The author published the book under the pseudonym of "Fritz".

[3] Mr. and Mrs. Holmes were two American mediums who at that time were visiting London. They claimed later that John King and his daughter Katie were their controlling guides and astonishing phenomena were said to take place at their séances, Katie appearing fully formed and floating in the air some seven feet from the ground. Suspicions as to their phenomena were voiced in various quarters and after their return to America they became the centre of a violent controversy in which the landlady of the lodgings in which they lived said that she had impersonated Katie King at the American sittings. (*The Galaxy*, 1874, XVIII, pp. 754–61.)

partition from the spectators and alleged spirit faces appeared at the aperture. One was the face of the alleged spirit "Katie King", manifesting through the mediumship of Florence Cook, and the spirit actually had to apologize for the fact that its face precisely resembled that of her medium.[1]

It is clear from contemporary accounts that Florence's "spirit-faces" aroused some scepticism, even amongst devout spiritualists. But they were important as the prelude to infinitely more startling manifestations, so before turning to the alleged materialization of the full form of Katie King it may be desirable to examine with such precision as is possible a series of events early in 1873 which seem to indicate rather clearly the methods, which, if fraudulent, may have been employed. These occurrences involve the test of the string tied around the medium's waist already mentioned by Mr. Traill Taylor. On that occasion, it will be remembered, the securing of the string to a chair outside the cupboard prevented the faces appearing at the aperture at all.

On 15 January, 1873, one of the sitters at a séance at Hackney was Mr. H. Cholmondeley-Pennell. On 16 January Mr. Cholmondeley-Pennell wrote to *The Spiritualist* describing certain "suspicious appearances" noticed by him at the sitting:

"1. That the faces which appeared, whether white or black, were always, in every feature, *exact counterparts* of the face of the medium.

2. That the 'check string', if I may use the term, was drawn into the cabinet to a sufficient distance (about two feet) to allow of the face of the medium appearing at the aperture; a circumstance to which, you will remember, I called your attention at the time, when measuring off the string. The drawing in of the string took place by intermittent—though, as it appeared to me, systematic—pulls or jerks, many of

---

[1] There was another occasion when Katie King found it expedient to apologize to the spiritualists. This was during the later period when the fully materialized form was in the habit of coming out into the room. In her article "Drapery Brought into Circles by Spirits" (*S.*, 1 November, 1878, p. 205), Miss Emily Kislingbury recalled that during one sitting it was observed that the figure had arrayed itself in a garment recognized as the property of Florence Cook. Miss Kislingbury wrote: "Katie King made full confession and excused her delinquency by saying that the power had not been very strong and she had saved herself trouble by using things belonging to the medium." Miss Kislingbury was a convinced spiritualist and a firm believer in the mediumship of Florence Cook.

which occurred before the so-called entrancement of the medium.

3. No faces appeared until the full quantity of string had been drawn in.

4. *This check or test string was the only practical impediment to the medium presenting her own face at the aperture.*

To the best of my judgment the same thing precisely took place on the only other occasion when I was present at Miss Cook's séance.

You are most welcome to show this note to Mr. Blackburn, or use it in any other way you think proper."

As was his custom with any testimony critical of Miss Cook's mediumship, Mr. Harrison refrained from publishing this letter. However, on 1 February a letter from Mr. Henry M. Dunphy was published,[1] possibly inadvertently, saying that he had heard of Mr. Cholmondeley-Pennell's criticisms, and defending Florence stoutly on the grounds that the string had not been pulled during a séance attended by him on 19 January, thus revealing that a critical comment had been made.

Mr. Cholmondeley-Pennell again wrote on 2 February, 1873, asking that the editor "be good enough to publish in its entirety my letter to you of the 16th Jan. last on the subject of the séances in question". Mr. Harrison had little choice but to do so.[2] In his covering letter of 2 February, Mr. Cholmondeley-Pennell said, charitably enough:

"I *may*, of course, have been unfortunate in the conditions under which I witnessed the faces in the presence of Miss Cook, of whose courtesy and that of her family I retain only the pleasantest remembrance; and nothing would give me more pleasure than to find my experience reversed on further investigation. If otherwise, however, the most severe censor need not be very hard on the frolics of a young lady of sixteen."

Mr. Harrison tried hard to make the best of the matter on the same page by referring again to the subsequent séance at which

[1] *S.*, 1 February, 1873, p. 87.
[2] *S.*, 15 February, 1873, p. 108.

21

Mr. Dunphy had noted that the string was not pulled into the cabinet when the faces appeared. Unfortunately, however, a letter from Lord Arthur Russell[1] in the same issue[2] made it only too clear to the reader that after the séance of 15 January, and especially after the published revelation of Mr. Dunphy on 1 February, an alternative method of obtaining freedom of movement in the cupboard despite the restraint of the string may have been adopted by the medium.

Lord Arthur Russell's letter, which would clearly have been hard to suppress, was dated 6 February, 1873, and contained the following account of a séance at Hackney the previous night:

"I had been led by the accounts of witnesses to expect a startling apparition; it was therefore, naturally, very disappointing, after Miss Florence Cook had been tied down in the cupboard, and the ghost of 'Katie' looked out of the peephole, to observe that the face of the ghost was merely Miss Florence Cook's face, with a piece of white linen wrapped round it, and that the black face which subsequently appeared was again merely Miss Cook's face with a black tissue drawn over it.

I could not feel satisfied with the explanation of the believers present, that the spirit-faces are usually found to be strikingly like their mediums. I also thought that the alarm and indignation shown by Mrs. Cook, when I proposed suddenly to open the cupboard during the apparition of the spirit was calculated to confirm the suspicions of an unbeliever. Miss Florence Cook's often-repeated request that we should talk together while I was endeavouring to listen to the shuffling noise she made inside the cupboard, before the apparition of her face at the aperture, also produced an unfavourable impression upon me.

When Miss Florence Cook was liberated, and the string with which she had been bound was cut, Lady Arthur Russell, who does not believe in ghosts, naturally picked up the string and examined it carefully. She found that the portion which passed round Miss Cook's waist, had been cut and sewn together again with white thread. The explanation suggested,

[1] Lord Arthur John Edward Russell (1825–92), brother of the 9th Duke of Bedford, was a Member of the Senate of London University and M.P. for Tavistock.
[2] S., 15 February, 1873, p. 105.

that this had probably been done in the shop where the string had been bought, was, I must say, not convincing to my mind; nor was the opinion, expressed by a lady present, that the string might have been cut and mended by an evil spirit, in order to throw discredit on the phenomena of Spiritualism, at all more conclusive.

During the second séance, when Miss Florence Cook had been effectually tied with pocket handkerchiefs and twine, no ghost appeared at the peep-hole. It was quite impossible for an unbeliever in spiritual manifestations, like myself, not to draw an unfavourable conclusion from this fact when put together with the observations of the first part of the *séance*."

In an unprinted letter to Charles Blackburn, Florence wrote "On Wednesday Lord and Lady Russell were here. They are very sceptical. They say all the Spiritualism they have seen is clever conjuring. All that they saw here was rendered worthless by a flaw being found in the string round my waist. I do not know how it came there and should feel very uneasy if the string test had not been tried so many times and always knots, seals and string found perfect."

The reader who has not studied the history of spiritualism as a popular movement in the late nineteenth century may well regard it as incredible that a medium like Florence Cook could continue to attract sitters to her séances for such a long period in the face of these published suspicions. As the editor of *The Lancet* wrote[1] in the heyday of Florence's career:

> "Scientific men are invited to investigate the phenomena of spiritualism, and their refusal to do so is regarded as a result of a narrow-minded prejudice; but we agree with the editor of the *New Quarterly Magazine* when he says that the existence of delusion, and the manner of it, being once explained, the subject ceases to possess any interest for educated and intelligent people. Discussion of such a topic affords neither instruction nor entertainment."

Frank Podmore offered a general explanation[2] of the problem sixty-four years ago:

[1] Loc. cit., 10 January, 1874.
[2] *Studies in Psychical Research* (London, 1897), pp. 20–1.

THE MEDIUM AND THE SPIRITUALIST

"The activities of the convert naturally took the form of missionary enterprise rather than of scientific investigation; and the séance room became not a laboratory but a propagandist institution. From such an attitude little sympathy was to be expected for disinterested scepticism. For most Spiritualists the time for inquiry into the foundations of their belief, if it had ever been, had long since gone by. And whilst there were at all times a few men of education and intelligence who never shut their eyes to new facts or new interpretations of old ones, these men in no sense directed the movement. Spiritualism was a democratic birth of the land of democracy, and Spiritualists in general had made up their minds that these things— the movements of tables, the apparitions of the séance room, the inspirational addresses poured forth weekly in a hundred lecture halls—were the work of spirits. Nor was it only the satisfaction of the religious instinct and the inertia of faith grown habitual which benumbed the spirit of inquiry. Vanity was with most a powerful auxiliary. To persons who had built themselves a new faith and had posed as prophets, perhaps also as martyrs, in the domestic circle and beyond it, on the strength of signs and marvels specially vouchsafed to them, it would have been a painful, often an unendurable shock, to have their signs and wonders explained as the result of clumsy fraud. Hence those who detected trickery of any kind met with scant sympathy. It was obscurely felt that they were malicious or ignorant persons who had gone out of their way to assail the new Revelation, and to make innocent people uncomfortable and even, perhaps, ridiculous.

Even when those who exposed the fraud were themselves believers, their reception was scarcely more favourable."

Against this favourable background Florence enjoyed additional advantages which helped to shield her from those who doubted. First, as I have shown, the financial support of the wealthy Charles Blackburn enabled her family to invite to her séances as guests, without fees, convinced spiritualists who could be expected to do as they were told and would not seek to apply critical tests to the phenomena. It is true that occasionally some sitters could not restrain their suspicions and embarrassing situations occurred, but these difficulties were the exceptions to the rule. Until the Volck-man upheaval[1] they seem to have been overcome, more or less satisfactorily, by explanations and denials.

Secondly, Florence had in Harrison a faithful and energetic press-agent, ready at all times to play down or conceal criticisms and write enthusiastic accounts of her mediumship. Finally, as we shall see, the phenomena were to be pronounced as genuine without qualification by William Crookes in 1874. It was the combination of these circumstances which enabled the reputation of Florence Cook to be built up during her lifetime and for posterity as a genuine medium capable of producing the miracle of a fully materialized form under scientific conditions of control.

During the spring of 1873 Katie King became a full-form materialization, stepping out of a cabinet and walking and talking amongst the sitters in the séance room. The appearance of the figure continued during séances at Mr. Cook's house throughout the summer and autumn of 1873, amidst the enthusiastic com-mendations of the spiritualists and to the delight of Charles Black-burn. The figure was always clad in white with bare arms and feet, and as the séances progressed Katie King gradually became sufficiently bold to speak and shake hands with the sitters and to stay out of the cabinet for appreciable periods. Those attending the the séances continued to be the invited guests of the Cook family.

A typical account of one of these earlier full materializations was contained in a description of a séance held at Hackney on 7 May, 1873.[2] The signatories of the report were Mrs. Amelia Corner, Miss Caroline Corner, J. C. Luxmoore, G. R. Tapp and William H. Harrison. In addition to those who signed the report Mrs. Emma Cook and her two younger children were present.

Before the séance, which lasted two hours, Florence Cook was searched in her bedroom by Mrs. Amelia Corner and Miss Caroline Corner, the mother and sister of Edward Elgie Corner, the future husband of the medium. The cabinet doors were opened and shawls hung across. By the light of a candle and a small lamp Katie King emerged from the cabinet and by degrees walked away from it to stand or move about amongst the sitters with whom she conversed.

---

[1] *See* pp. 27 ff.
[2] *S.*, 15 May, 1873, pp. 200–4. The account was republished on pp. 220–33 of E. E. Fournier d'Albe's *New Light on Immortality* (London, 1908).

Photographs of the materialization were taken by W. H. Harrison using magnesium light, although for some reason these photographs were not published. Instead, the article was illustrated by an engraving, showing only one half of the full length figure, which Harrison said "had been executed as nearly as possible with scientific accuracy, by an artist of great professional skill". The engraving was "about as faithful a copy as wood-cutting can give, of one of the photographs obtained on Wednesday night". The face depicted by the engraving did not greatly resemble that of Florence Cook, but whether the photograph showed the same difference we have no means of knowing.

Another description of the arrangements of the séances at this period was contributed by "Our Special Commissioner"[1] to the *Daily Telegraph* of 12 August, 1873:

"In a short time, however, Katie—as the familiar of Miss B was termed—thought she would be able to 'materialize' herself so far as to present the whole form, if we rearranged the corner cupboard so as to admit of her doing so. Accordingly we opened the door, and from it suspended a rug or two opening in the centre, after the fashion of a Bedouin Arab's tent, formed a semicircle and sat and sang Longfellow's 'Footsteps of Angels'. Therein occurs the passage, 'Then the forms of the departed enter at the open door'. And, lo and behold though we had left Miss B tied and sealed to her chair, and clad in an ordinary black dress somewhat voluminous as to the skirts, a tall female figure draped classically in white, with bare arms and feet, did enter at the open door, or rather down the centre from between the two rugs, and stood statuelike before us, spoke a few words, and retired; after which we entered the Bedouin tent and found pretty Miss B with her dress as before, knots and seals secure, and her boots on! This was Form No. 1, the first I had ever seen. It looked as material as myself; and on a subsequent occasion—for I

[1] It is certain that the writer was the Rev. Dr. C. Maurice Davies, who has been previously quoted, since the description was reprinted by him on pp. 342 ff. of his *Mystic London*. An earlier article under a similar pseudonym was published in the *Daily Telegraph* of 10 October, 1872, and was later included *verbatim* without mention of provenance, in his book *Unorthodox London* (London, 1873), pp. 337–44. All these accounts, in the *Daily Telegraph*, *Unorthodox London* and *Mystic London*, were written in the first person and show a marked similarity of style.

have seen it several times—we took four very good photographic portraits of it by magnesium light. The difficulty I
still felt, with the form as with the faces, was that it seemed
so thoroughly material and flesh and blood like."

At one of these séances held at Hackney on 9 December, 1873,
one of the guests was Mr. William Volckman. According to his
account of the affair he had for some nine months sought an invitation to a Hackney sitting, and had only been successful in obtaining
one after complying with a hint from Mr. Cook that a present of
jewellery would not be refused by the medium.

It is important to record that Volckman was a spiritualist, and
was indeed one of the committee appointed by the London Dialectical Society in 1869 to investigate spiritual phenomena. After
inquiring into the subject for two years the committee published
its report which was a favourable one.[1] Mr. W. H. Harrison, in an
article entitled "Evidence that Spiritualism Deserves Investigation",[2] was enthusiastic in his praise, and reported that the
members of the committee were "persons of social position, of
unimpeachable integrity, with no pecuniary object, having nothing to gain by deception, *and everything to lose by detection of
imposture*". (The italics are mine.)

It seems that Volckman may also have been a member of the
Dalston Association of Inquirers into Spiritualism, for at "the
ordinary weekly meeting"[3] little more than a week before the
dramatic séance of 9 December, 1873, he was the second speaker
in a discussion following the delivery by Harrison of a paper on
"Certain Problems connected with Mediumship". The meeting
was attended by most of Florence Cook's supporters, including
J. C. Luxmoore and Thomas Blyton, with whom Volckman was
apparently very friendly. Thus, on the face of it, Volckman seems
to have been ideally qualified to be admitted to the Hackney
séances.

During the séance of 9 December Katie King took Volckman by
the hand, a gesture to all the sitters which had become habitual
with her. His suspicions having been aroused by what he had

[1] *Report on Spiritualism of the Committee of the London Dialectical Society.*[(London,
1871.)
[2] *S.*, 1 September, 1873, p. 319.
[3] *S.*, 5 December, 1873, p. 441.

observed during the sitting, he retained in his grasp first the hand and then the waist of the apparition, with the stated conviction that he was holding Florence Cook. The gas light was hastily extinguished and Edward Elgie Corner, who was to marry Florence four months later, came to the rescue of "Katie King" assisted by Mr. G. R. Tapp. After an undignified struggle the spirit was rescued from Volckman's grasp and retired hastily to the cabinet, the scuffle being sufficiently unrestrained for Volckman to suffer the loss of part of his beard and to receive other superficial injuries. After an interval of five minutes the cabinet was opened and Florence was found in a distressed condition, but with the tape tied around her waist as it had been at the beginning of the séance. Volckman was escorted from the house, and the dishevelled medium was taken under the care of the lady sitters.

An unsigned article[1] "Gross Outrage at a Spirit Circle" was loud in its condemnation of Volckman's conduct although the anonymous author confirmed the somewhat suspicious interval of five minutes which elapsed between Katie King re-entering the cabinet and it being opened by the sitters. It seems clear that the cabinet was not opened until the permission of the spirit had been given, for the writer added that during the waiting period of five minutes "Katie gave earnest instructions to the sitters".

Not all spiritualists shared the unrestrained annoyance of the author of "Gross Outrage at a Spirit Circle". Mr. H. E. Thompson in a published letter "Grasping a Spirit"[2] showed indeed some sympathy with Volckman:

> " 'A gross outrage' is recorded by one of your contemporaries as having been perpetrated by a gentleman who is an investigator into the phenomena of spiritualism, at Miss Cook's séances.
>
> While the medium is enclosed in a cupboard, a spirit opens the door, comes out and shakes hands with those present. The 'outrage' consisted in the gentleman referred to clasping the spirit in his arms, in order to assure himself that it really was a spirit, and not the medium herself, as a number of people have attested it to be.
>
> Now, the Cook séances are said to be 'test' ones; but where,

[1] *S.*, 12 December, 1873, p. 461. The author was probably W. H. Harrison.
[2] *The Medium and Daybreak*, 19 December, 1873, p. 598.

I ask, is the test if investigators are compelled to apply only such tests as are dictated by those interested?"

Volckman himself wrote a letter on 16 December, 1873, to *The Spiritualist* replying to the accusations contained in the article "Gross Outrage at a Spirit Circle", but the editor withheld its publication. Thereupon Volckman wrote to the editor of *The Medium and Daybreak* on 22 December, 1873, explaining what had occurred and his letter, together with his earlier communication of 16 December intended for the columns of *The Spiritualist*, was published on 26 December, 1873.[1] It read as follows:

"Sir: Under the heading 'Gross Outrage at a Spirit Circle', a charge was recently brought against me in a spiritual journal. My letter in reply having been withheld by the journal in question, I begged permission to give it publicity through your widely-read columns. It was as follows:

Sir: In the report which appears in your journal of a séance lately held at Mr. Cook's, I am accused of seizing the ghost, thereby breaking the conditions by which the members of the circle were bound.

In reply I have to state that having for forty minutes carefully observed and scrutinized the face, features, gestures, size, style and peculiarities of utterance of the so-called spirit, the conviction irresistibly forced itself upon me that *no ghost*, but the medium, Miss Florence Cook herself, was before the circle. I perceived also an occasional tip-toeing by the young lady as if to alter her stature, and was much struck by the utter puerility of her remarks throughout the séance. I am confirmed in my conviction, as above stated, by the facts that the *struggling* ghost had to be *forcibly* extracted from my grasp, and afterwards to be 'aided' into her cabinet by a Justice of the Peace.

I may add that no third parties had any knowledge of my invitation to, or presence at, the séance in question.

Yours truly,
William Volckman.
16 December, 1873.

[1] *The Medium and Daybreak,* 26 December, 1873, p. 618.

While the suppression even for a single week of the above short letter does not advantage the ghost theory, it certainly prejudices that character for fairness usually aspired to by editors.

> I am, Sir,
> Yours truly,
> William Volckman.
> 22 December, 1873."

Volckman added some further details of the incident in a subsequent article "The Struggling Ghost".[1]

> "Here then was a further test, if the opportunity for applying it should occur—as fortunately it did. Would 'Katie', I mentally asked, 'make me an offer of her hand?' Would that hand dissolve in mine according to orthodox ghostly fashion? Let the sequel tell.
> 'Katie' assured (as she told us) of the harmonious character of the circle, deigned to take some of us by the hand. My turn came; and by no means to my surprise I found that her Ghost-ship could not release her fingers from my hand. Apprehending the situation she quickly made a step backwards towards her cabinet, endeavouring to tug away her hand. But, not to be thus evaded, I with equal promptness rose up and grasped her with both hands round the waist, when commenced that 'wrestling with the angel' which is now immortalized in the columns of The Spiritualist, and which completed my test."

There can be little doubt that this widely publicized and dramatic episode precipitated a crisis in the affairs of Florence Cook. The suspicions of Dr. Purdon, Mr. Cholmondeley-Pennell and Lord Arthur Russell had created difficulties which had been overcome, but which were now likely to be remembered. The actual seizure of the figure by a well-known spiritualist such as Volckman, and his repeated and published declarations that he had no doubt whatever that the alleged materialization was an imposture by Florence Cook cannot have been regarded as anything less than a catastrophe by the spiritualists. The fact that Volck-

[1] *The Medium and Daybreak*, 16 January, 1874, p. 39.

man's fairness and ability as an investigator, with everything to lose by the detection of imposture, had been praised in the columns of *The Spiritualist* only three months previously, was scarcely helpful. It is noteworthy that although Volckman's articles were openly libellous, it was evidently decided by the Cooks that it would not be prudent to commence proceedings against him for damages.

Charles Blackburn himself was at the disastrous sitting of 9 December. If any correspondence between Florence and him existed which was relevant to the Volckman affair, it has probably been lost or destroyed. We can only speculate as to what attitude he was likely to adopt, with particular regard to the fact that he was paying to Florence and her family what seems to have been a regular allowance.

In this connexion it is interesting to consider Blackburn's reaction to a somewhat similar situation which later arose with Florence's sister Kate when he discovered that, at one of her séances, the medium's chair was empty during a dark sitting.[1] Fortunately some of the correspondence covering that event is still in existence, although unpublished, and we know that Blackburn's attitude was expressed in four words which could scarcely have caused more consternation to the Cooks. He wrote:

"I shall stop payment."

Blackburn was a credulous man, but there is good evidence to show that occasionally he became extremely angry when he imagined that he was being deceived, so it is reasonable to assume that Florence's allowance was suddenly placed in serious jeopardy in December 1873, and that she and her supporters reached the conclusion that only drastic measures would rehabilitate her in the eyes of her patron and so restore the situation.

We do not know upon what date Florence Cook approached William Crookes, but according to her own account she visited the scientist very shortly after 9 December, 1873. She wrote:

"I went to Mr. Crookes myself, without the knowledge of my parents or friends, and offered myself a willing sacrifice on the altar of his unbelief. It was immediately after the

[1] *See* pp. 124 ff.

31

unpleasant incident of Mr. Volckman, and those who did not understand said many cruel things of me."[1]

Crookes, who had been interested in spiritualism since 1869, was regarded as a meticulous investigator. According to Mr. H. M. Dunphy, he had already met Florence Cook at the house of Mr. J. C. Luxmoore on 28 October, 1873.[2]

What happened at that meeting we shall never know. It is probable that Crookes had heard of Florence's phenomena and expressed a wish to investigate them himself. To gratify curiosity was one thing, as Crookes expressed it, but to carry on systematic research was quite another. What he wanted and what he ultimately achieved was himself to "carry off the priestess from her shrine" and investigate her in his own house.

Thus the wishes of the scientist and the priestess appeared to coincide and, if a verdict were delivered in the priestess's favour, then the Volckmans, the Russells and the other critics could be forgotten. Towards this end Florence Cook directed all her skill, her energy, her resourcefulness and her charm.

---

[1] *L.*, 29 December, 1894, p. 629.
[2] "Modern Mysteries", *London Society*, February 1874, pp. 166 ff.

CHAPTER TWO

THE INVESTIGATION OF FLORENCE COOK
BY WILLIAM CROOKES

THE fact that Florence Cook threw herself on the mercy of William Crookes proves that she was almost desperate. She must have known that before her introduction to him he had been investigating the phenomena of D. D. Home, and had come to the conclusion that this medium's phenomena were undoubtedly genuine. If she were herself also genuine and the criticisms against her ill-founded and due to a misunderstanding of the laws of the spiritual world, then it might well be that she thought that William Crookes was the man to retrieve her reputation. If, on the other hand, she knew herself to be a fraud, then she may have thought that D. D. Home was one also and that if he had deceived William Crookes, then she, young, lithe and charming, might have the same good luck.

Perhaps, however, there might have been something more in it even than that. Maybe she thought that just possibly her charm, vivacity and pretty ways might affect the scientist as a man rather than as a cool, calculating observer of spiritual things. Anyhow, such a possibility should be borne in mind. Genuine or fraudulent, it could do no harm to think of such things; and a personal relationship of a friendly kind could only help her and clearly could not hurt anybody. What was all important was to restore her prestige so rudely shaken by Mr. Volckman and thus again bring her back into favour with Mr. Charles Blackburn, from whom she hoped to receive enough money to save her from becoming a professional medium, or worse still from having to take some poorly paid job. The stage was thus set for the most critical period of Florence Cook's life. Success meant the top of the tree: failure an ignominious retreat into obscurity.

One of the most remarkable features of the Crookes investigation was the manner in which he chose to deal with it. Hitherto no satisfactory explanation has been brought forward to account for it and I am not aware that any was offered by Crookes during his lifetime. Yet there must have been some compelling reason which forced him to record the story of the miracles he said he had witnessed in the pages of a cheap spiritualist paper rather than, as in the case of his previous work, within the covers of a learned journal or of a treatise written by himself. Indeed, when the story was reprinted in a book it was through the energy of the editor of another spiritualistic journal, and it was said that Crookes complained that it had been done without his knowledge or consent.

Another puzzling feature of Crookes's treatment and reports of his investigation of Florence Cook was that in the earlier days of his interest in spiritualism his approach to the subject was critical and scientific. In a paper contributed to the *Quarterly Journal of Science* in July 1870, for example, which was reprinted in his book.[1] he wrote:

"The spiritualist tells of tapping sounds which are produced in different parts of a room when two or more persons sit quietly round a table,

The scientific experimenter is entitled to ask that these taps shall be produced on the stretched membrane of his phonautograph.

The spiritualist tells of rooms and houses being shaken, even to injury, by superhuman power. The man of science merely asks for a pendulum to be set vibrating when it is in a glass case and supported on solid masonry.

The spiritualist tells of heavy articles of furniture moving from one room to another without human agency. But the man of science has made instruments which will divide an inch into a million parts; and he is justified in doubting the accuracy of the former observations, if the same force is powerless to move the index of his instrument one poor degree.

The spiritualist tells of flowers with the fresh dew on them, of fruit, and living objects being carried through closed windows, and even solid brick-walls. The scientific investigator naturally asks that an additional weight (if it be only the 1000th part of a grain) be deposited on one pan of his balance when the case is locked."

[1] *Researches*, etc., p. 6.

The words command respect, and had these standards of scientific evidence been applied by Crookes to his investigation of the mediumship of Florence Cook the position of the critic would have been untenable. In this connexion it is useful to examine the circumstances and substance of Crookes's first published observations upon the Katie King affair.

We know that Florence Cook had gone to Crookes very shortly after 9 December, 1873. His preliminary report[1] dated 3 February, 1874, said that he had hitherto tried to keep as clear of controversy as possible on the subject of spiritualism, but that in the case of Florence Cook he felt it right to depart from this rule if "a few lines" from him would "assist in removing an unjust suspicion which is cast upon another". He added "And when this other person is a woman—young, sensitive and innocent—it becomes especially a duty for me to give the weight of my testimony in favour of her whom I believe to be unjustly accused."

Crookes argued that so far no one had claimed to have seen Florence in the cabinet while Katie King was in the room. He declared, in my opinion rightly up to a point, that "the whole question" narrowed itself into this small compass.[2] He added that the proof must be absolute and not based upon the supposed integrity of knots and seals. He went on:[3]

"I was in hopes that some of those friends of Miss Cook, who have attended her *séances* almost from the commencement, and who appear to have been highly favoured in the tests they have received, would ere this, have borne testimony in her favour. In default, however, of evidence from those who have followed these phenomena from their beginning nearly three years ago, let me, who have only been admitted as it were, at the eleventh hour, state a circumstance which came under my notice at a *séance* to which I was invited by the

---

[1] *S.*, 6 February, 1874, p. 71. It was reproduced on pp. 102–4 of his *Researches*, etc.
[2] This was an over-simplification. Clearly it was the preliminary question to be settled, and the simple opening of the cabinet doors or curtains to show the entranced medium would have enabled it to be determined during the scores of "full form" séances which had taken place since the spring of 1873 before Crookes came on the scene at all. However, even the simultaneous visibility of the medium and the figure would in itself be no proof of genuine materialization, for one of the figures might be a human confederate.
[3] *Researches*, etc., pp. 103–4.

favour of Miss Cook, a few days after the disgraceful occurrence which has given rise to this controversy.

The *séance* was held at the house of Mr. Luxmore, [*sic*] and the 'cabinet' was a back drawing room, separated from the front room in which the company sat by a curtain.

The usual formality of searching the room and examining the fastenings having been gone through, Miss Cook entered the cabinet.

After a little time the form Katie appeared at the side of the curtain, but soon retreated, saying her medium was not well, and could not be put into a sufficiently deep sleep to make it safe for her to be left .

I was sitting within a few feet of the curtain close behind which Miss Cook was sitting, and I could frequently hear her moan and sob, as if in pain. This uneasiness continued at intervals nearly the whole duration of the *séance, and once, when the form of Katie was standing before me in the room, I distinctly heard a sobbing, moaning sound, identical with that which Miss Cook had been making at intervals the whole time of the séance, come from behind the curtain where the young lady was supposed to be sitting*.

I admit that the figure was startlingly life-like and real, and, as far as I could see in the somewhat dim light, the features resembled those of Miss Cook; but still the positive evidence of one of my own senses that the moan came from Miss Cook in the cabinet, whilst the figure was outside, is too strong to be upset by a mere inference to the contrary, however well supported.

Your readers, sir, know me, and will, I hope, believe that I will not come hastily to an opinion, or ask them to agree with me on insufficient evidence. It is perhaps expecting too much to think that the little incident I have mentioned will have the same weight with them that it had with me. But this I do beg of them—let those who are inclined to judge Miss Cook harshly, suspend their judgment until I bring forward positive evidence which I think will be sufficient to settle the question.

Miss Cook is now devoting herself exclusively to a series of private *séances* with me and one or two friends. The *séances* will probably extend over some months, and I am promised that every desirable test shall be given to me. These *séances* have not been going on many weeks, but enough has taken place to thoroughly convince me of the perfect truth and honesty of Miss Cook, and to give me every reason to expect that the promises so freely made to me by Katie will be kept."

This significant letter is worth careful scrutiny. In the first place it seems certain that the séance at Mr. Luxmoore's house, taking place as it did "a few days" after the Volckman episode, can hardly have been later than the middle of December 1873. An interval of some six weeks had therefore elapsed between this sitting and Crookes's letter of 3 February, 1874.[1]

During this period the "series of private séances" with Crookes and one or two friends, to which Florence was "now devoting herself exclusively", had clearly started, but had "not been going on many weeks". It is not unreasonable to assume, however, since Crookes confined himself to a detailed description of what occurred at a séance as early as the middle of December, that nothing more impressive had occurred in the interim than the incident at Mr. Luxmoore's house, which amounted to a moaning noise apparently coming from behind the curtain whilst the figure of "Katie King" was standing in front of it.

It seems clear that the form merely "appeared at the side of the curtain, but soon retreated", with the excuse that the medium could not during this sitting be put into a sufficiently deep sleep to enable her safely to be left. The impression is gained that the figure did not actually leave the curtain, "within a few feet" of which Crookes was sitting. In these circumstances it is hard to understand how Crookes could be so satisfied that the moaning he heard came from behind the curtain and not from Katie King. Whether Crookes knew that he was dealing with a medium who had been trained in the production of the "direct voice" by Herne and Williams, and was obviously capable of a simple ventriloquial effect such as this I do not know.

However, it seems that on the basis of this incident Crookes had already made up his mind that Florence Cook was not a fraud, at

[1] Loc. cit.

37

least, on this occasion. He had decided that she was "young, sensitive and innocent". The séance of 9 December was "a disgraceful occurrence". Crookes was thoroughly convinced "of the perfect truth and honesty of Miss Cook". He advised those who were inclined to judge Florence harshly to suspend judgment until he brought forward "positive evidence" which he anticipated would settle the matter.

Taking the above facts at their face value it would seem that Crookes was pre-judging the matter in favour of Florence Cook at a very early stage of the investigation, on a piece of evidence which was clearly valueless by the standards which he himself had advocated in his paper in 1870. It is also worth considering why the letter of 3 February was written at all, and why it was written to *The Spiritualist*.

One answer might be that Florence was understandably anxious to have something in print over Crookes's name at the earliest possible date following the upheaval of 9 December to impress Blackburn favourably and restore the allowance if this had been stopped. If this theory be right, we must ask why Crookes allowed himself to be persuaded to write the letter. If we assume, for a moment, that certain surrounding circumstances were such that he had little choice but to write it, uneasily and against both his better judgment and earlier pronouncements on how spiritualistic phenomena should be investigated, then it becomes easier to understand why Crookes sent his letter to a weekly paper and not to one of the scientific journals in which all his previous contributions to the literature of the subject had been published.

Before considering these circumstances in greater detail it will be convenient here to describe the investigations as Crookes recorded them and as other writers have mentioned them in the course of their reports, beginning with the private séances at Crookes's own house.

Apart from Crookes's own narrative, we have no information about what happened during the long series of sittings at his home at 20 Mornington Road, London, in the presence of "one or two friends"[1] as well as the scientist himself. In this lack of corroborative testimony they differed radically and perhaps significantly from those at the mediums's own home, when named believers

---

[1] *S.*, 6 February, 1874, p. 71.

were invited and glowing accounts by W. H. Harrison, Florence Marryat and others were contributed to the columns of *The Spiritualist*.

The dates in April and May 1874 of the Hackney sittings, moreover, were published in the same paper. All we are told about the dates of the Mornington Road séances is that over a period of six months from the middle of December 1873 Florence was a frequent visitor, staying "sometimes a week at a time",[1] and that on at least one undated occasion before 10 April, 1874, she gave a séance jointly with Mary Showers,[2] when the two materializations marched round Crookes's laboratory "with their arms entwined schoolgirl fashion, and in a strong light".[3]

The séances at Crookes's home, about which we know so little, seem to have continued to the end of the period of the Katie King materializations, overlapping the Hackney sittings, for Crookes said that "during the week before Katie took her departure [Florence] gave séances at my house almost nightly to enable me to photograph her by artificial light".[4] As the final Katie King séance took place at Hackney on 21 May, 1874, this last intensive week of activity at Mornington Road was evidently from 14 May to 21 May, 1874. This must have been a busy period for Florence Cook, for after a holiday in Paris with Charles Blackburn[5] in late April and her secret marriage to Edward Elgie Corner on 29 April she gave séances at Hackney on 30 April, 4 May, 9 May, 13 May, 16 May and 21 May, and sittings at Mornington Road "almost nightly" from 14 May to 21 May.[6]

[1] Op. cit., 5 June, 1874, p. 270.

[2] The teenage daughter of a military officer, who produced a variety of astonishing phenomena, including a full-form materialization "Florence", and other figures. She became a great friend of Florence Cook.

[3] *S.*, 10 April, 1874, p. 176.

[4] Ib., 5 June, 1874, p. 270.

[5] Ib., 8 May, 1874, p. 224. Blackburn said in his letter of 4 May that he had taken Florence to Paris for the restoration of her health and not for séances. It is quite clear from Florence's letter to Blackburn of 22 May signed "Florence E. Cook" that her marriage to Corner on 29 April was being concealed from him at this time. The return from Paris can scarcely have preceded the marriage by more than a few days.

[6] If it was required to show on a single sheet of paper that something decidedly odd was taking place at this time, the quoting of the dates and circumstances of these sittings would be sufficient. Why was it necessary for it not to be known that Florence was a married woman until after Crookes had published his final endorsement of her mediumship on 5 June, 1874? It is, moreover, impossible to believe that Corner would have agreed to his new bride devoting virtually every evening to spiritualistic séances immediately after her marriage unless there was some compelling reason for her to do so.

Now Crookes never said who the "one or two friends" at Mornington Road were. Indeed, the only person identified in his story as having been present, apart from Florence and Crookes himself, was the scientist's eldest son, "a lad of fourteen", who according to Crookes's narrative saw a phosphorus lamp "apparently floating about in space over Miss Cook".[1] But Crookes's account of the photographing of Katie King gives us two clues. According to Crookes the forty-four photographs were all taken at Mornington Road where the necessary apparatus, consisting of no less than five cameras and their accessories, was installed in the laboratory.[2] Nearly all these photographs and negatives were later destroyed,[3] but fortunately not before one or two had been published.[4] One of these, which has more recently been reproduced as the frontispiece of Harry Price's *Fifty Years of Psychical Research* (London, 1939), shows Dr. James Manby Gully (1808–83) holding the hand of the white-clad materialization, which had just emerged from the cabinet. Although Gully's name does not appear in any of Crookes's accounts it is clear that he must have been present during some of the Mornington Road sittings, and it seems very possible that it was he who operated the camera when the photograph was taken of Crookes arm-in-arm with Katie King.[5]

We know nothing of the relationship between Crookes and Gully, who was a prominent member of the British National Association of Spiritualists, his Presidential Address at the second Annual Conference in London being published in 1874.[6] He was

[1] *S.*, 3 April, 1874, p. 158.
[2] *S.*, 5 June, 1874, p. 270.
[3] *Psychic Science* (London, April 1934), p. 27, where it is said that "all the forty-four negatives taken by Sir William Crookes, O.M., F.R.S., were destroyed after his death by persons who considered that all memorials of his devotion to psychical research would damage his scientific standing". H. Wyndham, however, on p. 257 of *Mr. Sludge, The Medium* (London, 1937), writes that it was Crookes himself who had "subsequently destroyed these photographs and forbidden their reproduction" whilst Fodor remarks that Crookes "never allowed the circulation of the photograph in which he stood arm-in-arm with Katie King". (*Encyclopædia of Psychic Science*, London, 1934, p. 71.)
[4] Cf. E. E. Fournier d'Albe's *New Light on Immortality* (London, 1908), p. 232, *Encyclopædia of Psychic Science*, p. xlvi and *Psychic Science* (April 1934), p. 24. In each of these reproductions, incidentally, the face of Katie King appears to be absolutely identical with that of Florence Cook, photographs of whom were also published on p. 250 of *New Light on Immortality* and p. xlvi of *Encyclopædia of Psychic Science*.
[5] Crookes said that the "photographing operations" were "performed by myself, aided by one assistant", but the name of his helper was not disclosed. (*S.*, 5 June, 1874, p. 270.)
[6] *S.*, 7 August, 1874, pp. 64–5.

a bizarre character, who had achieved fame by reason of his hydropathic cures at Malvern, but we have no evidence to show that in 1874 Crookes was aware that Gully was then secretly engaged in activities that were to bring notoriety and disaster upon him when they were revealed two years later.[1]

The second clue lies in the anonymous article "Four 'Katie King' Photographs" which accompanied the four photographs reproduced in *Psychic Science*.[2] According to this account, these photographs were found amongst the papers of the artist F. W. Hayes (1848–1918) and were presented to the British College of Psychic Science by his son, Gerald Hayes. Each bears the caption "Copy of original photograph taken by Sir William Crookes. Made by Miss Kate Cook for F. W. Hayes. Katie King". The photographs are undated but the fourth has on the back the autographed inscription of the materialization Katie King and the signatures of those who were present at the séance, other than Crookes himself who took the photograph. They were Mrs. Helen Whittall, Dr. Gully and Kate S. Cook, who were, it seems, the "one or two friends" referred to by Crookes.

It is worth considering the declared purpose of the Mornington Road séances, as stated by Crookes himself. He wrote on 3 February, 1874, that his object was to make a systematic examination of the phenomena produced by the medium, over a long period of time, in order to ascertain whether or not the medium and the materialization were separate beings—though he was obviously prejudiced in favour of Florence already, and the "positive evidence" he promised to produce was bound to confirm his prejudice. It has already been shown that in his first account of 3 February, 1874, in which Crookes announced the programme of the proposed investigation, he had already decided that Florence

---

[1] In 1876 Gully's name was removed from all the medical societies of which he had been a member. During the inquest on the death by poisoning of Charles Bravo, a mystery which remains unsolved to this day, the widow, Florence Bravo, revealed that in 1873 she and Gully had been lovers. During her resultant secret miscarriage she had been attended medically by Gully. Gully's guilt, said *The Times*, lay in his violation of the responsibilities of his profession and in his abandonment of himself to a selfish intrigue, without the excuse of the passions of youth, with a woman many years younger than himself. Authoritative accounts of the case are contained in Yseult Bridges's *How Charles Bravo Died* (London, 1956) and John Williams's *Suddenly at the Priory* (London, 1957). Cf. also *The Gay Young Widow of Balham* (London, 1876) and *The British Medical Journal*, 7 April, 1883.
[2] April 1934, p. 25.

was "young, sensitive and innocent", that the Volckman exposure was "a disgraceful occurrence" and that he was thoroughly convinced of the *bona fides* of Miss Cook. In his second account of 30 March, 1874, Crookes endorsed this curious pre-judgment of the investigation by declaring that by this date he had obtained the "absolute proof" which he had sought.

Certainly astonishing things had been happening in Mornington Road. Crookes declared that during a séance there Katie King had been walking and talking amongst the unnamed sitters for some time and had then retired into the library, which was used as the cabinet. She invited Crookes to join her in the cabinet to assist Florence, who had partially slipped from the sofa on which she was lying entranced. Crookes declared that on two occasions during this sitting he saw the medium lying on the sofa during the materialization. The illumination was by means of a bottle containing phosphorized oil, and it was on this occasion that Crookes stated that his son aged fourteen saw the improvised lamp apparently floating in space over the entranced form of Miss Cook.

In his undated final letter[1] Crookes went further still in his declaration that proof had become available at Mornington Road that the medium and the materialization existed separately. The visual proof previously vouchsafed to him alone had been given to all the sitters, whilst the dim illumination of the phosphorus lamp had been replaced by electric light. He wrote:

"I prepare and arrange my library myself as the dark cabinet, and usually after Miss Cook has been dining and conversing with us, and scarcely out of our sight for a minute, she walks direct into the cabinet, and I, at her request, lock its second door, and keep possession of the key all through the *séance*; the gas is then turned out, and Miss Cook is left in darkness.

On entering the cabinet Miss Cook lies down upon the floor, with her head on a pillow, and is soon entranced. During the photographic *séances*, Katie muffled her medium's head up in a shawl[2] to prevent the light falling upon her face. I

[1] *S.*, 5 June, 1874.
[2] Whilst Crookes's explanation that the medium's face was hidden by a shawl at Mornington Road to prevent the photographic flashlight causing her discomfort, despite the fact that the curtain intervened, is not entirely implausible, it is curious that

frequently drew the curtain on one side when Katie was standing near, and it was a common thing for the seven or eight of us in the laboratory to see Miss Cook and Katie at the same time, under the full blaze of the electric light."

It seems incredible to us today that this declaration by Crookes that the sittings at Mornington Road had at last provided the complete proof of the separate existence of the medium and the materialization was not accompanied by statements from the other witnesses. In fact, as we have seen, he concealed the identities of the "seven or eight" persons[1] for whom it was "a common thing" to see Katie King and Florence Cook simultaneously in full light. Not a shred of corroborative evidence was offered in support of the published statement that the whole object of the investigation had been triumphantly achieved at Mornington Road. It is not un-reasonable to say that Crookes's accounts of what was supposed to have taken place were valueless as a scientific report, and that he must have known this himself.

Taking the evidence as a whole it seems likely that if the alleged materialization at Mornington Road was fraudulent, it was a simple imposture by Florence Cook clad in white drapery. What may have remained behind in the cabinet, to be glimpsed at a distance by the sitters in the dim light of the phosphorus lamp on the rare occasions when the curtains were opened by Crookes, was Florence's discarded frock and boots spread over a couple of cushions on the sofa with a bundled shawl in place of the head. It

no explanation is offered by Crookes as to why the shawl was similarly employed at Hackney where no photographs were taken. It is of additional interest to notice that according to Crookes's statement (S., 5 June, 1874, p. 270) only one photograph out of the forty-four depicted both the materialization and the medium and in this "Katie King" unfortunately concealed the head of the medium.

[1] It is possible that this number of persons was made up of Mrs. Whittall, Dr. Gully, Kate Cook and members of Crookes's family, amongst whom was his eldest son. It is reasonable to suppose that since Mrs. Crookes gave birth to a son, Lewis Philip, on 2 May, 1874, she would not herself take any active part in the séances. It is of interest that in a letter to a spiritualist journal headed "How 'Katie King' held a Crookes baby", Edith K. Harper said that Lady (then Mrs.) Crookes had told her that at a séance at Mornington Road the apparition had asked to see and to hold her three weeks old baby, and that this had been permitted. According to the writer Lady Crookes had remarked "I do not suppose that many babies have had such an experience as my son". (*The International Psychic Gazette*, June 1919, p. 158.) This "pretty story", as Miss Harper herself termed it, was of course published after Lady Crookes's death and forty-five years after the event it purported to describe. When Lewis Crookes was three weeks old, moreover, Katie King had already made her final departure.

will be recalled that only Crookes was admitted to the privacy of the cabinet.[1]

This was of course an advance on anything which had been previously attempted, for never before had the sitters at any of Florence's séances been given an opportunity, however brief and unsatisfactory, of seeing the interior of the cabinet whilst the materialization was outside it. Serjeant Edward W. Cox had put the matter pungently in his letter of 23 April, 1874,[2] when he had pointed out that under the earlier conditions experienced by him there was no evidence whatever to support the assertion of the materialization, which exactly resembled the medium "in face, hair, complexion, teeth, eyes, hands, and movements of the body", that the medium was in fact at that time entranced behind the curtain. He added, with reason, that the proof could easily have been established in a moment beyond all doubt by the simple process of opening the curtain, but that this essential test had neither been proffered nor allowed at the séances he had attended.

It is, incidentally, of some interest to notice that Crookes's insistence in his published accounts that the materialization at Mornington Road did not resemble the medium, a declaration which seemed designed to deny the theory of imposture, has no corroborative evidence to support it. Virtually all independent observers, such as Edward Cox and J. Enmore Jones, whose revealing testimony as to what went on at Hackney will be quoted later, were emphatic that the face and movements of the materialization at this period were identical with those of Florence Cook. It is perhaps of even greater interest to notice that those of Crookes's own photographs of Katie King which have been preserved, show a striking resemblance to the medium.[3]

---

[1] Crookes himself said "Katie instructed all the sitters but myself to keep their seats and to keep conditions, but for some time past she has given me permission to do what I liked, to touch her and to enter and leave the cabinet almost whenever I pleased. I have frequently followed her into the cabinet, and have sometimes seen her and her medium together."(*S.*, 5 June, 1874, p. 270.)

[2] *S.*, 15 May, 1874, p. 230. The letter, first sent to *The Spiritualist* and suppressed by Harrison, was finally printed after it had been published in *The Medium and Daybreak* on 8 May, 1874.

[3] Crookes's contradiction of his own testimony is very revealing. It was at the conclusion of his letter of 30 March (*S.*, 3 April, 1874, p. 158) that Crookes's principal comment upon the dissimilarity of the appearance of the figures was published. The photographs were not taken until the week of 14–21 May.

I do not believe that any confederate was employed during the mediumship of Florence Cook until the final Hackney sittings. It has been urged, and I think rightly, albeit on rather different grounds than those which are now being considered, that the employment of a confederate at Mornington Road would have been impracticable. Clearly it would have been most difficult to explain the necessity for the presence in the house of some friend of Florence, such as Mary Showers, who was, moreover, not to appear as a sitter during the séances. But, as has been indicated, I do not think that the idea of a confederate was ever contemplated at Mornington Road. It was probably hoped that the showing of an occasional glimpse of the dummy figure in a dim light to an uncritical audience would be sufficient to justify the account published in *The Spiritualist* on 3 April, 1874.

Moreover, Crookes may have thought that the publication of his second report would be sufficient to silence the critics and satisfy Florence's demands. At the conclusion of his letter of 30 March, 1874, he said that Florence's health was not good enough to enable the séances to continue, and that she would need an entire rest for some weeks before resuming the sittings, the results of which he hoped "to be able to record on some future day". This sounded rather like the preparation of the ground for allowing the matter to die a natural death, but unfortunately for Crookes outside circumstances were to dictate otherwise.

On 30 March, 1874, concurrently with Crookes's own letter, Edward Cox wrote to *The Spiritualist*[1] suggesting certain additional tests which might be applied to the alleged materialization which "should place beyond all question the fact that the medium was in the cabinet while the form was outside" such as marking the forehead of the medium with Indian ink. I have not been able to find any evidence to show that such a test was ever made, but the mere suggestion of it may have been disturbing in the extreme. Crookes's response was the letter, of which rather curiously only part was published on 10 April,[2] in which he described the joint appearance in his laboratory of the two materializations produced by Florence and Mary Showers, presumably relying upon the faulty concept that if one leaking bucket will not hold water it is

[1] *S.*, 3 April, 1874, p. 167.
[2] *S.*, Loc. cit.

possible that two will.[1] Cox's devastating reply was his letter of 23 April with the details of the glaring exposure of Mary Showers.[2] In this letter Cox hinted plainly at what he believed to be the truth of the matter, i.e. that the alleged materializations, exactly resembling as they did the mediums, were mere impostures and that only their discarded clothes remained behind in the cabinet.

It was probably directly as a result of Cox's criticisms, and the effect which these may have had on the occasionally suspicious Charles Blackburn,[3] that the decision was taken at this time to move the location of the séances to Florence's own home at Hackney, where the first sitting took place on 30 April. This may have been done because a satisfactory demonstration of the separate and simultaneous existence of the medium and the apparition, which would be convincing enough to persuade selected and docile spiritualists to publish glowing independent accounts, could only be produced with the help of a confederate. This could not be arranged in Crookes's house without arousing suspicion, but, as I hope to show, it was possible to do so at Hackney.[4]

To sum up, then, it would not be too much to say that as scientific reports Crookes's accounts of what was supposed to have taken place at Mornington Road were sufficiently valueless as to excite suspicion. There must have been some compelling motive which made Crookes act as he did when describing the sittings in

[1] It seems likely that the whole matter was under wide discussion and that embarrassing criticisms had been made which were never published. On p. 179 of *The Spiritualist* of 10 April, 1874, for example, H. Cholmondeley-Pennell quoted a letter from Crookes in which the latter had written "I have abundant reason to know that I was not deceived by a lay figure or a bundle of clothes", an insistence which may not have been without significance in the circumstances.

[2] The damaging effect of this letter is demonstrated by the fact that W. H. Harrison attempted to suppress it. It is, however, reasonable to suppose that it would be shown to Crookes and Florence when it was received. It was published in *The Medium and Daybreak* on 8 May and ultimately and reluctantly in *The Spiritualist* of 15 May, 1874.

[3] This is suggested by Crookes's letter to Charles Blackburn on 11 May, 1874, describing the séance at Hackney on 9 May. Referring to his having allowed the sitters to see both the materialization and the recumbent medium together by gas light he wrote: "A test like this, in a good light, and in the presence of good witnesses, ought to satisfy even Serjeant Cox." As the medium's head was "tied up in a red shawl" and clearly need not have been Florence Cook at all, the test was not convincing. The figure was undoubtedly a living person; when prodded, it made "sobbing, moaning noises" and its hand and foot moved. This improvement on the silent, inanimate figure seen dimly at a distance at Mornington Road may have been the whole point of the Hackney sittings.

[4] Dr. Ivor Tuckett said that until the Hackney séances " 'Katie' had never indisputably been seen simultaneously with the medium". (*The Evidence for the Supernatural*, London, 1911, p. 62.)

his own home. His accounts of what went on at Hackney were even more surprising, and it is to those that we must shortly turn.

During the period of the Mornington Road séances one isolated incident occurred which differed in pattern from the mysteriously vague events which were alleged to be taking place at Crookes's home. No other published independent account of Florence's activities during the period of her association with Crookes seems to have appeared apart from this one until the sittings at Hackney began. Mr. Cromwell F. Varley, F.R.S., the electrical engineer, was a convinced spiritualist who had known Crookes since the death of Philip Crookes in 1867. According to Crookes's biographer, it was Varley who persuaded Crookes to try and get into communication with his dead brother by means of spiritualism.[1]

Early in 1874 Varley devised a method of electrical control of a medium allegedly producing a full-form materialization. The object of the apparatus was to prove by electrical means (as opposed to the simpler procedure constantly suggested by Serjeant Edward Cox of drawing back the curtain to show the sitters the inside of the cabinet) that the medium was still entranced behind the closed curtains, whilst the materialized figure was walking and talking amongst the sitters. The proposed procedure was to place the medium in circuit with a two-cell battery, two sets of resistance coils and a reflecting galvanometer, the latter instrument being visible outside the cabinet during the whole of the séance.

Presumably Varley approached Crookes and suggested that the electrical test be applied to Florence, for Varley said in his report that he had lent the apparatus to Crookes, who had examined its workings at Mornington Road, using his son in place of the medium.[2] This suggestion, which may or may not have been welcomed by Crookes, probably occurred during February 1874, for the test sitting took place near the end of that month. Varley's report is undated, but it appeared on 20 March, 1874, and it stated that the experiment took place "about three weeks ago".[3] W. H. Harrison said that the experiments took place partly at the residence of Mr. J. C. Luxmoore and partly at Crookes's home,

---

[1] E. E. Fournier d'Albe, op. cit., p. 133.
[2] S., 20 March, 1874, p. 134. In a later account Varley said that it was Charles Blackburn who asked him to test Florence's mediumship. (*Psychic Facts*, London, 1880, p. 36.)
[3] Ib., p. 133.

whilst Varley said that all the experiments were carried out at Luxmoore's house at 16 Gloucester Square, Hyde Park, London.[1]

Florence was seated in an armchair, unbound and free to move, in the room serving as the cabinet, which was separated from the adjoining room by "thick curtains". Pieces of blotting paper, moistened with a solution of nitrate of ammonia were placed upon each of her bare arms and sovereigns in their turn were laid upon the two pieces of blotting paper, paper and coins being held in position by elastic bands. Platinum wires attached to the two sovereigns led to the battery, resistance coils and galvanometer, presumably connected in series, thus completing the electrical circuit.

In an editorial by W. H. Harrison the purpose of this apparatus was described.

> "All through the séance the current flowed through the galvanometer showing that the circuit was never for an instant broken, as it would have been had the wires been taken off the arms of Miss Cook: moreover had they been taken off and the ends of the wires joined together, the increased flow of electricity due to the removal of the electrical resistance caused by the body of the medium would instantly have increased the deflection very greatly: instead of this, there was a gradual and irregular decrease of deflection, caused chiefly by the gradual drying of the blotting paper."[2]

The drying of the blotting paper evidently had its effect, for according to Varley's account the galvanometer deflection of 220 divisions at the beginning of the séance at 7.10 p.m. showed a decreased reading of 146 by 7.48 p.m. This decrease was regular and progressive throughout the sitting apart from one or two surprising variations.

Varley's detailed account is of great interest, showing as it does precise times, galvanometer readings and his personal impressions of the events taking place. It was not until 7.38 p.m., twenty-eight minutes after the commencement of the sitting, that the form of Katie King emerged from the cabinet, and it is noteworthy that

[1] Ib., p. 134.
[2] S., 20 March, 1874, p. 133.

when the dim illumination of the room was momentarily increased so that Varley could look at the apparition his spontaneous comment, recorded by himself, was "You look exactly like your medium".[1]

While Katie King was out of the cabinet the galvanometer did not record "any variation exceeding one division on the scale", which would of course be accounted for by the steady decrease in deflection due to the drying of the blotting paper, but during the long period from 7.10 p.m. to 7.38 p.m., when the apparition was making her preparations to emerge, several variations occurred which Varley recorded in his account.

At 7.22 p.m. the patience of the sitters was rewarded by whispering by Katie King behind the curtains. At 7.25 p.m. the galvanometer suddenly dropped from 191 to 155 divisions. Varley wrote, "A fall of thirty-six divisions in one minute. Miss Cook has evidently shifted her position and has probably moved the sovereigns a little in so doing. No break of circuit, however." Varley's note of this occurrence seems to exemplify his attitude, which was that of an honest scientific man who was also an ardent spiritualist.

After this incident, which appears significant, the monotony was occasionally broken by a hand or arm being shown briefly through the curtains. Between 7.35 p.m. and 7.37 p.m., during one of these demonstrations, the galvanometer reading dropped from 152 to 135 and rose again to 156 divisions. Varley wrote, "Katie showed her hand and arm, galvanometer fell 17 divisions!" He added that the medium "seems to have moved much" and that this "looked very suspicious", but qualified this justifiable comment by remarking that after the figure had emerged from the cabinet the galvanometer remained quite steady. He said that "it did not fall more than one division; this neutralizes the doubt just expressed".

Varley's argument is hard to understand, for the purpose of the test was to show that if the medium released herself from the electrical control to perform as Katie King the galvanometer would indicate to the sitters the interruption of the electrical circuit. The fact that the galvanometer remained steady during the whole time that the figure was outside the cabinet clearly proved nothing, and should not have resolved the doubts which arose in

[1] *S.*, 20 March, 1874, p. 134.

Varley's mind when the galvanometer demonstrated that activity of some sort was taking place behind the curtains prior to the emergence of the figure. Varley added to his confusion of thought about the object of his test by his remark regarding the galvanometer reading at 7.42 p.m. when Katie King was outside the curtain writing her customary messages with pencil and paper for the sitters. He said, "At 7.42 she was actively writing, but the galvanometer did not vary one division. This, I maintain, clearly proves that Miss Cook was not only in the dark chamber while Katie was in sight, but also perfectly quiescent."

The spiritualists were delighted, and W. H. Harrison, speaking of Varley as "one of the greatest of electricians", said that had the medium "been freed in any way from the wires while entranced, it would have been instantly made known by the instruments outside".[1] Harrison added that Crookes had written to him and had said:

> "It will be impossible for you to put stronger language in my mouth when speaking of Miss Cook's perfect honesty, truthfulness, and perfect willingness to submit to the severest tests that I could approve of; and you can also state that, as far as the experiments go, they prove conclusively that Miss Cook is *inside* while Katie is *outside* the cabinet."

Harrison said that such "outspoken testimony" was "greatly to the honour of Mr. Crookes, who holds such responsible positions in the scientific world".

It will be recalled that Crookes's first report on Florence Cook was published on 6 February, 1874, and he then committed himself to the opinion that Florence was perfectly honest. In his second published account written on 30 March, 1874, he declared that he had obtained the "absolute proof" he had sought by virtue of the alleged fact that at Mornington Road, on entering the cabinet alone, he had seen the entranced medium on the sofa. *Nowhere in this long letter did he mention the electrical test,* Varley's full account

[1] S., 20 March, 1874, p. 139. Count Carl von Klinckowstroem declared that the only scientific document of value in the whole case was the report of the Varley experiment. (W. von Gulat-Wellenburg, Graf Carl von Klinckowstroem & H. Rosenbusch. *Der Physikalische Mediumismus*, Berlin, 1925, p. 141.) The same importance was insisted upon by Carl Kiesewetter, who in his *Geschichte des neueren Occultismus* (Leipzig, 1891) described the tests in detail, pointing out Varley's eminence in the electrical world of the time.

of which had been published only ten days previously, an omission which was repeated in his book and which is not easy to understand.

These facts would appear to indicate a desire on Crookes's part to draw a veil over Varley's experiments, a desire which existed as early as 30 March, 1874. Against this assumption Crookes's letter to Harrison enthusiastically acclaiming the success of the electrical test and published on 20 March in the same issue of *The Spiritualist*, has to be considered. Harrison did not give the date of Crookes's letter but it was clearly written some time before 20 March, 1874.

It seems that a possible explanation of this apparent contradiction may be that Crookes had not foreseen that Varley's account would be a detailed minute-by-minute record of the séance disclosing its several suspicious features and Varley's spontaneous, if temporary, doubts about them. It would no doubt be clear to Crookes that the unbiased reader of Varley's statement would be bound to reach the conclusion that something untoward was going on behind the curtains during the twenty-eight minutes which elapsed before Katie King came out of the cabinet. If Florence Cook had remained entranced and motionless in her chair behind the curtains the sudden movement of the galvanometer needle by 36 divisions at 7.25 p.m., for example, would clearly be inexplicable, as would the later deflection of 17 divisions, which Varley had first thought to be "very suspicious".

Crookes would know, moreover, that the contrasting immobility of the galvanometer needle during the period that the materialization was out of the cabinet would increase, and not ameliorate, the suspicions surrounding the curious antics of the galvanometer whilst the figure was preparing to emerge. Finally, Crookes was probably unpleasantly surprised to read Varley's published record of his expressed opinion that the alleged materialization exactly resembled Florence Cook.

It has been said in an earlier chapter that all the available evidence points to Crookes being favourably disposed towards Florence Cook by 3 February, 1874, at the latest, for that was the date of his first letter to *The Spiritualist*, when he pre-judged in her favour and without qualification the result of his supposed investigation of the medium. It was suggested that this letter was probably written uneasily by Crookes at the insistence of Florence who wanted a preliminary endorsement of her mediumship by him as soon as possible. If this assumption be justified, then in the almost incredible circumstances of Crookes and Florence being in collusion during the Varley experiment, the whole of the otherwise curious circumstances might be explained.

When Varley came forward with his idea, Crookes asked for the loan of the apparatus for examination at Mornington Road. Florence would need no instruction from Crookes as to how to release herself from two elastic bands, but she would need rehearsal in the fitting of another form of resistance across the platinum wires to replace that of her body. This could have been a resistance coil prepared by Crookes in the privacy of his laboratory at Mornington Road whilst the apparatus was in his hands, measured against Florence's body resistance. She was constantly at Crookes's home during this period and Crookes was, of course, thoroughly competent as regards electrical devices.

All Florence would need to do in the privacy of the cabinet would be to wrap the ends of the connecting wires from the resistance coil around Varley's platinum wires before removing the elastic bands from her wrists. She would then be free to assume her draperies before emerging as Katie King, having had twenty-eight minutes in which to carry out this simple operation. If all had gone well the galvanometer would presumably have remained steady apart from a probable momentary increase in the reading of the galvanometer whilst the two resistances were in parallel.

We can only speculate as to what did in fact occur but it would seem possible that in her excitement Florence bungled the operation and in some way managed, during her manipulation of the wires and connections to her wrists, accidentally to put the resistance coil in series in the circuit for a few seconds. This would have produced the abrupt galvanometer deflections which were observed and recorded by Varley. It is difficult to conceive of any other explanation which would account for the demonstration by the galvanometer that an additional substantial resistance had been momentarily introduced into the circuit.

Serjeant Edward Cox, in commenting briefly upon the electrical test, wrote:[1]

[1] S., 5 June, 1874, p. 273.

"I turn now to the electrical test invented by Mr. Varley and tried by Mr. Crookes. I am not electrician enough to form an opinion as to the validity of that test. It was tried by Mr. Crookes with Miss Cook, and satisfied him that she was personally within, while Katie was obviously without. He tried it with Miss Showers, and he informed me that it failed.[1] But I must confess myself unable to comprehend how a perfect test could fail. Either it proved Florence [Maple][2] to be Miss Showers, or it fails to prove that Miss Cook is not Katie. But in any event I return to my argument, that indirect evidence cannot and ought not to be accepted in such a case, when direct and positive evidence is easily to be procured."

Cox's reference to "direct and positive evidence" was, of course, to his constant and devastating suggestion at this period that if proof was required that the medium and the alleged materialization existed separately this could be simply and immediately accomplished by allowing the sitters to satisfy themselves by sight and touch that the entranced medium was still in her place during the appearance of the materialization.

[1] Cox amplified this comment on p. 23, S., 10 July, 1874. "At Mr. Crookes's the electrical test was tried twice by that gentleman, and proved by demonstration that Florence (Maple) then also was Miss Showers in person. Another test was tried by Mr. Crookes, in which the fingers of the spirit Florence were dipped in a dye, and the stain was found by him upon the fingers of Miss Showers."
[2] The name of the alleged materialization produced by Mary Showers.

CHAPTER THREE

THE FINAL "KATIE KING" SITTINGS

THE final sittings at which the alleged materialization Katie King appeared through Florence's mediumship took place at the Cooks' home in Hackney between 30 April and 21 May, 1874. The house, along with others in Eleanor Road, was destroyed by enemy action during World War II and prefabricated dwellings now occupy the site of the famous séances. One of the few records which remain of the rooms in which the sittings took place is contained in Dr. C. M. Davies's book *Mystic London*,[1] in which he described a séance which he attended during this period. He wrote:

> "We sat no longer in the subterranean breakfast room of Miss C's parental abode; but moved up to the parlour floor, where two rooms communicated through folding doors, the front apartment being that in which we assembled, and the back used as a bed-room, where the ladies took off their 'things'. This latter room, be it remembered, had a second door communicating with the passage, and so with the universe of space in general. One leaf of the folding doors was closed, and a curtain hung over the other. Pillows were placed on the floor, just inside the curtain, and the little medium, who was nattily arrayed in a blue dress, was laid upon them. We were requested to sing and talk during the 'materialization', and there was as much putting up and lowering of the light as in a modern sensation drama. The Professor acted all the time as Master of the Ceremonies, retaining his place at the aperture; and I fear, from the very first, exciting suspicion by his marked attentions, not to the medium, but to the ghost."

An important circumstance which this account revealed was that the location of the séance room had been moved from the

[1] P. 317.

lower floor, where all Florence's previous sittings at home had been held and where the corner cabinet was to be later used by Kate Cook, to an upper part of the house. Obviously this was done because the upper rooms were more suitable for the purpose for which they were to be used, and it might be asked what precisely that purpose included. From the account of Dr. Davies it would seem that the arrangement of the rooms could hardly have been more suitable for the secret introduction of a confederate to the bed-room which served as the cabinet. It had two doors, one communicating with the adjoining room and the circle of sitters, the other opening on to the corridor and the kitchen stairs, as Dr. Davies made clear in the latter part of his account. He said openly in his book that he suspected the presence of a confederate.

The first séance was held on Thursday, 30 April, 1874,[1] and those present were Crookes, W. H. Harrison, Thomas Blyton, G. R. Tapp and Charles Blackburn. Harrison, Blyton and Tapp might fairly be described as the "old guard" of the Dalston Association of Inquirers into Spiritualism who had consistently supported Florence Cook from the earliest days of her mediumship, and who were irretrievably committed to belief in the phenomena by their published articles and letters.

Charles Blackburn, in his letter of 4 May, 1874,[2] written from his home at Didsbury, near Manchester, described the sitting of 30 April and said that Florence lay on the floor of the bed-room, her head being covered with a red woollen shawl. It may well be significant so far as the purpose of the sitting was concerned, that Blackburn said that he was allowed to see Florence take up her position in the cabinet and that he then withdrew at request and closed the curtain. In a few minutes the sitters heard the alleged spirit voice talking to the medium followed by silence. The materialization ultimately appeared through the curtains wearing her customary white dress "and evidently devoid of stays; this Mr. Crookes proved, as he stood close to her and was allowed to feel. She had a white head-dress, as usual, all very plainly seen by the gas light."

Blackburn asked if he might kiss the materialization and Katie King's cheek, "warm and soft as velvet", was offered to him.

[1] Florence had secretly married Edward Elgie Corner the day before.
[2] S., 8 May, 1874, pp. 224–5.

Blackburn then asked if he could see the medium in the cabinet. He was given the bottle of phosphorus oil by Crookes and followed the white-clad figure into the bed-room. Blackburn said that he saw the medium still lying on the floor in the same clothing as when she entered the cabinet. He placed his hand on the red shawl which covered the medium's head and a painful moan was emitted by the figure. He passed his hand down from neck to waist and to the medium's boots to the accompaniment of further moans. There seems to be no doubt from Blackburn's account that he was convinced that the figure lying on the floor of the bed-room with its face disguised by the shawl was a human being.

There seems also no doubt that the persuasion of Blackburn on this point was the whole purpose of this sitting and that this was successfully accomplished. He returned to his home in Manchester between 30 April and 4 May, presumably unavoidably because of his large business interests, and never saw Katie King again. Before he was next able to come to London she had made her final appearance after announcing her imminent departure at the next sitting on 4 May. Assuming fraud, once Blackburn had expressed his satisfaction with what he had seen and heard on 30 April it might well have been decided not to tempt Providence unnecessarily, and to bring the dangerous sittings to an end as soon as this could reasonably be done, once a sufficient number of independent accounts of the miracle had been published by docile and credulous spiritualists. The published accounts support such a suspicion.

On Monday, 4 May, 1874, a further séance was held. On this occasion the sitters were Crookes, Harrison and Tapp, Mrs. Amelia Corner (another trusted Dalston supporter), Mr. and Mrs. Earl Bird, Mr. and Mrs. Whithall, Mr. B. W. Pyecock and Miss Belsey. Blackburn had, as has been said, returned to his home near Manchester. No details of this séance were recorded by W. H. Harrison in his account in *The Spiritualist* of 8 May, apart from the names of the sitters and the single fact that on 4 May Katie King announced that she would very shortly return to the spirit world.

She said that the reason for her departure was "to make way for recognisable spirit faces" which, if she was fraudulent, was probably a paving of the way for what we know later to have occurred, i.e. Florence's prudent retreat from the dangers of the full-form materialization and her return later in 1874 to the feeble anti-climax of the Punch and Judy cupboard, which she had used two years earlier, with its advantages of no risk and no necessity for a confederate.

If Katie King was to continue to delight the spiritualists she could now only do so acceptably with an entranced medium not only visible to the whole company in a good light, but with a medium who was capable of being prodded and of producing moans. There could be no return to an inanimate silent bundle of clothes to be occasionally seen only at a distance in a dim light nor, worse still, to the earlier conditions where the curtains remained closed and the medium was never visible at all during the appearance of the figure.

The third séance of the series took place on Saturday, 9 May, 1874, and the account of it by Benjamin Coleman, another ardent spiritualist and supporter of Florence Cook, was published on 15 May, 1874.[1] Coleman did not list the names of the sitters but merely mentioned that a party of eight or ten ladies and gentlemen known to Miss Cook and her family formed a congenial and harmonious circle which was best calculated to secure the most perfect results. His story confirmed the other descriptions of the arrangements whereby Florence's bed room was used as the cabinet whilst the audience sat in a parlour adjoining the bedroom. The latter room was lighted by gas which was partially raised and lowered at intervals by Crookes who conducted the whole proceedings.

Coleman said that Florence Cook wore her ordinary blue dress in which she lay down on the floor of the bed-room with a red worsted shawl thrown over her head. He described the apparition, which appeared "ten or fifteen minutes" after the drawing of the curtain, dressed in white as usual, as "a supple flexible-limbed young woman of graceful and childlike habits". Coleman gave the enthusiastic published endorsement which was doubtless expected of him:

> "During the evening she frequently went behind the curtain to look after her medium, as she said, and once whilst

[1] S., pp. 234–5.

she was there, Mr. Crookes raised the curtain, and he and I and four others who sat by me saw at one and the same time the figure of Katie, clad in her *white dress*, bending over the sleeping form of the medium, whose dress was *blue*, with a red shawl over her head. This incident was repeated with an increased amount of gaslight, which went streaming into the inner room, and thus the fact is at length established that both the living form of Miss Cook and the spirit form of the materialized Katie were seen by Mr. Crookes, myself, and others twice on the evening of 9th day of May last."

The séance of 9 May was obviously regarded as an important one, and Crookes wrote to Blackburn on 11 May to describe the impressive details. His letter revealed, among other things, that the sitters other than the Cooks, Harrison, Tapp, Coleman, Mrs. Corner and himself had consisted of Dr. and Mrs. Speer, Mrs. Ross-Church [Miss Florence Marryat] and Mrs. and Miss Kislingbury, all of whom were enthusiastic spiritualists. It is of some interest to notice that with the exception of the small Dalston group the circle of sitters at the Hackney séances appears generally to have been composed of different persons on each occasion. It might be suggested that had the sittings been intended as a critical investigation it would have been preferable for Crookes to have arranged for the same persons to have sat throughout the series, with the advantage of increasing experience of the events they were examining. On the other hand, if the séances were a mere demonstration, then clearly the constant changing of the sitters had much to commend it. A larger number of convinced spiritualists would be available to vouch for the final wonders of Florence's mediumship and, more importantly perhaps, one of the first rules in the psychology of conjuring was being observed. The same trick was not being repeated before the same audience.

Crookes's letter of 11 May is of great interest, for in it the existence of the second door to the cabinet mentioned by Dr. Maurice Davies was confirmed. Crookes wrote, "Before she went into the back parlour, now used as a cabinet, I examined the room and fastened the window and side door myself." As Crookes was the impresario and organizer of the séances, the conditions would clearly have been less vulnerable to criticism if an independent person had locked and sealed the side door, but this was not to be. Here is another example of the distinction between an exhibition and a scientific inquiry. The critic might have sought a similar improvement in the conditions of the séance of 30 April, when it was unfortunate that Crookes was evidently the only person present on sufficiently familiar terms with Katie King to be allowed to satisfy himself, by feeling, that she was not wearing corsets.

Whilst Benjamin Coleman's published account of the séance of 9 May was no doubt regarded as very satisfactory by Florence and her friends, it was evidently thought necessary for Crookes himself to describe the details of the sitting in glowing terms to Blackburn in his unpublished letter of 11 May. It is possible that Crookes had little choice in the matter and that it was Florence who decided that such a testimonial, addressed directly to her benefactor, was desirable. However that may be, Crookes's letter, like his published accounts, cannot fail to suggest to the reader, incredible as it may seem, that if the séances were fraudulent he must have been fully aware of the fact, and that complicity on his part would have made the employment of a confederate a simple matter.

"Katie exacted no conditions from me, but gave me permission to move about, look into the cabinet and touch her as I liked, except when she specially asked me not. I occupied my usual position standing close to the side of the curtain where she appeared. The rest of the sitters were arranged round the room, holding hands.

For about an hour and a half Katie was coming out at frequent intervals, and several times she walked into the room resting on my arm. Once appearing reluctant to come away from the curtain I put my arms round her and gently drew her some paces forward. During this time I had many opportunities of looking into the cabinet and I saw Florrie lying on the floor each time. Several times I opened the curtain sufficiently to let the gas light shine full on Florrie and Katie when they were both in the cabinet together.

I was very desirous that this should be seen by all the others, and when Katie was standing at the side talking to me, I drew the curtain away and called attention to the fact that Florrie could be seen lying down. Katie stood rather in the

59

light so I asked her to move a little on one side so as to let the others get a better view. This she did, but soon asked me to close the curtain.

Florrie's head was tied up in a red shawl, so I asked Katie to go and arrange her dress so that one foot and one hand should be visible. Katie at once complied and I looked in the whole time she was doing this. When she had arranged Florrie's dress as I had requested, Katie came to the curtain, and asking me to hold it on one side, invited the sitters to look in, allowing those at the side to move forward, so as to get a better view of Florrie and herself.

Katie then walked up to Florrie's side and leaned over her, in full view of all present. She touched Florrie on the head, and I then heard Florrie make one of her sobbing, moaning noises; at the same time I saw her foot and hand move. I was leaning right in the cabinet at this time, and, being within a few feet of Florrie, could not have been mistaken."

As Serjeant Edward Cox wrote on 1 June, 1874:[1]

"If the face was hidden under a shawl the proof fails entirely, for it is impossible for any of the persons present to say certainly that Miss Cook herself was lying there. All that is proved by this experiment is that while a form precisely resembling Miss Cook in face and figure was outside the curtain, a body wearing her dress, or a dress like hers, was lying inside the curtain. But there is no proof whatever that it was Miss Cook's body. The concealment of the face by the shawl raises indeed a very strong presumption to the contrary."

The next séance was on 13 May. The independent sitters invited by Crookes were Mrs. MakDougall-Gregory, Mr. and Mrs. Jas. Mankiewicz, Miss Katherine Poyntz, Mr. S. C. Hall and Miss Florence Marryat. The latter lady, although not one of the "old guard" from Dalston, had become one of Florence's most ardent supporters. She could, moreover, be relied upon to write columns of eulogistic and inaccurate rubbish about spiritualism and her friends Professor Alfred [sic] Crookes and Florence Cook.

[1] S., 5 June, 1874, p. 273.

No details of this séance known to me are available which distinguish its results from those of the sitting of 9 May.

In her account published on 29 May,[1] Miss Marryat said that "on that occasion [13 May] we had the benefit of mutual sight also, as the whole company were invited to crowd round the door whilst the curtain was withdrawn and the gas turned up to the full, in order that we might see the medium, in her blue dress and scarlet shawl, lying in a trance on the floor, whilst the white-robed spirit stood beside her". It seems fairly evident that the séance of 9 May was repeated for the benefit of a new group of spectators, and that Miss Marryat was relied upon on this occasion to give it the necessary publicity.

The séance of 16 May was attended by yet another group of independent spiritualists, notably M. Gustave de Veh (enthusiastically described in The Spiritualist as a friend of Prince Sayn-Wittgenstein-Berleburg, and one of the leading spiritualists in Paris), Mr. M. E. Boulland, Mr. Henry Bielfield, Mr. J. Enmore Jones and his sons Rupert and Arthur, his daughters Alice and Emily and his mother Mrs. Jane Jones. Crookes's choice of Mr. Enmore Jones was not a fortunate one, for this gentleman was evidently unfavourably impressed with the conduct of the séance. His testimony is important, for he was a convinced spiritualist and a believer in Florence Cook. In his letter of 17 May he wrote:[2]

"Last night the medium was in her bed-room, was unbound, and was entranced lying on the floor. The leader stood in front of the awning, and made himself very active every time that 'Katie' appeared; stooping down to, or with face almost touching the face of 'Katie'; physically, and unscientifically, hampering all her movements, so as in several instances to compel the spirit with her hand to knock the face away from her, though done in a playful manner; reminding me of a fussy mesmeriser, who suddenly finding himself in office, desires to show himself off to the audience. The result of the mannerisms of the awningkeeper, and the crowded state of

[1] S., pp. 258-9.
[2] The Medium and Daybreak, 22 May, 1874, p. 327. The critical remarks of Mr. Jones are especially noteworthy when viewed in the light of what is known about him. He was the godfather of Kate Jencken's mediumistic baby (see p. xiii) and held the eccentric idea that "all nations were, and are, more or less controlled by ghosts". Cf. his Theological Ghosts (London, 1875), p. 7.

the room, reduced the whole séance to principally that of 'Katie' showing herself at the awning, and busying herself with dividing bunches of flowers and giving to each visitor. I trust that at future séances the leader, whoever he may be, may not be a familiar half-showman and half-playactor, on more than respectful terms with the ghost; but let the spirit have 'sea-room', for her own advantage and that of the visitors.

I was much struck with the strong resemblance the spirit had to the medium last night, even to the colour of the face; the mannerism of action also was the same, the voice was similar when joining with the sitters while singing in the bedroom behind the awning. To those who had not seen 'Katie' under other and test conditions the impression must have been that 'Katie' was Miss Cook, and Miss Cook 'Katie' in a state of undress."

Mr. Enmore Jones's word-picture of Crookes is very curious and suggestive. It would more appropriately describe the behaviour of a man whose judgment was temporarily impaired by a foolish infatuation than that of a scientist conducting a serious experiment. Moreover, his comment regarding the likeness of Katie King to Florence Cook does not leave any room for doubt that on this occasion there was complete justification for Serjeant Cox's comment upon the same point. He said:[1]

"When I saw them they were not merely resemblances; they were facsimiles. I had carefully noted the shape of the eyebrows, which cannot be altered, and they were the same in the medium and the form. The hands were identical. The movements of the body were precisely similar."

Whether or not the contents of Mr. Jones's critical letter of 17 May were reported to Crookes and Florence before its publication on 22 May I do not know. It is, however, possibly significant in this connexion that only one more séance was held, on 21 May, and that no independent persons were invited to this sitting apart from Miss Florence Marryat. W. H. Harrison wrote:[2]

[1] S., 5 June, 1874, p. 273.
[2] S., 29 May, 1874, p. 258.

"The farewell *séance* was held on Thursday last week, and Katie had emphatically stated that she intended to give it only to the few tried friends now in London, who for a long time had been fighting her medium's battles with the public; and, notwithstanding many solicitations, she made but one exception, by inviting Mrs. Florence Marryat Ross-Church. The other spectators were Mr. William Crookes, Mrs. Corner, Mr. W. H. Harrison, Mr. G. R. Tapp. Mr. and Mrs. Cook and family, and the servant Mary."

The closing scene of this final sitting was described by Crookes in an undated letter[1] published on 5 June, 1874. He wrote:

"Your readers may be interested in having Mrs. Ross-Church's, and your own accounts of the last appearance of Katie, supplemented by my own narrative, as far as I can publish it. When the time came for Katie to take her farewell I asked that she would let me see the last of her. Accordingly when she had called each of the company up to her and had spoken to them a few words in private, she gave some general directions for the future guidance and protection of Miss Cook. From these, which were taken down in shorthand, I quote the following: 'Mr. Crookes has done very well throughout, and I leave Florrie with the greatest confidence in his hands, feeling perfectly sure he will not abuse the trust I place in him. He can act in any emergency better than I can myself, for he has more strength'. Having concluded her directions, Katie invited me into the cabinet with her, and allowed me to remain there to the end.

After closing the curtain she conversed with me for some time, and then walked across the room to where Miss Cook was lying senseless on the floor. Stooping over her, Katie touched her, and said, 'Wake up, Florrie, wake up! I must leave you now.' Miss Cook then woke and tearfully entreated Katie to stay a little time longer. 'My dear, I can't; my work is done. God bless you,' Katie replied, and then continued speaking to Miss Cook. For several minutes the two were conversing with each other, till at last Miss Cook's tears prevented her speaking. Following Katie's instructions I then

[1] Ib., p. 271.

came forward to support Miss Cook, who was falling on to the floor, sobbing hysterically. I looked round, but the white robed Katie had gone. As soon as Miss Cook was sufficiently calmed, a light was procured and I led her out of the cabinet."

Miss Florence Marryat contributed an account to the same periodical:[1]

"On the 21st, however, the occasion of Katie's last appearance amongst us, she was good enough to give me what I consider a still more infallible proof (if one could be needed) of the distinction of her ideality [sic. identity?] from that of her medium. When she summoned me in my turn to say a few words to her behind the curtain I again saw and touched the warm breathing body of Florence Cook lying on the floor, and then stood upright by the side of Katie, who desired me to place my hands inside the loose single garment which she wore and feel her nude body. I did so thoroughly. I felt her heart beating rapidly beneath my hand; and passed my fingers through her long hair to satisfy myself that it grew from her head, and can testify that if she be 'of psychic force', psychic force is very like a woman.

Katie was very busy that evening. To each of her friends, assembled to say goodbye, she gave a bouquet of flowers tied up with ribbon, a piece of her dress and veil, and a lock of her hair, and a note which she wrote with her pencil before us. Mine was as follows: 'From Annie Owen de Morgan (alias Katie King) to her friend Florence Marryat Ross-Church, with love. Pensez à moi. May 21st, 1874.' I must not forget to relate what appeared to me to be one of the most convincing proofs of Katie's more than natural power, namely that when she had cut, before our eyes, twelve or fifteen different pieces from the front of her white tunic as souvenirs for her friends, there was not a hole to be seen in it, examine it which way you would."

Miss Marryat altered this story in her book.[2] She said that when

[1] S., 29 May, 1874, p. 259.
[2] There is No Death, pp. 142–3.

Katie King invited her into the cabinet she dropped her white garment and "stood perfectly naked before me. 'Now,' she said, 'you can see that I am a woman.' Which indeed she was, and a most beautifully-made woman too; and I examined her well, whilst Miss Cook lay beside us on the floor."

According to Miss Marryat's account, she evidently claimed that it was she and not Crookes who was in the cabinet when Katie King disappeared. She continued:

> "Instead of dismissing me this time, 'Katie' told me to sit down by the medium, and, having brought me a candle and matches, said I was to strike a light as soon as she gave three knocks, as Florence would be hysterical on awaking, and need my assistance. She then knelt down and kissed me, and I saw she was still naked. 'Where is your dress, Katie?' I asked. 'Oh that's gone,' she said; 'I've sent it on before me.' As she spoke thus, kneeling beside me, she rapped three times on the floor. I struck the match almost simultaneously with the signal; but as it flared up, 'Katie King' was gone like a flash of lightning, and Miss Cook, as she had predicted, awoke with a burst of frightened tears, and had to be soothed into tranquillity again."

Miss Marryat added that the sitters sealed up in envelopes the pieces of Katie King's dress which they had received as souvenirs and took them home, only to find on opening the envelopes that the pieces of fabric had disappeared into thin air. The testimony of Crookes himself about the cutting of pieces from Katie King's dress is worth recording. In 1911 Mrs. C. W. Earle in one of her books quoted *verbatim* a letter written to her by Lord Lytton on 22 September, 1891, in which the latter described some of the wonders experienced through the mediumship of Florence Cook as told to Lord Lytton by Crookes.[1] Lytton wrote of Crookes that he was "a very intelligent and singularly accurate minded man, most cautious and conscientious in his statement of facts". Crookes had told Lytton that he cut large pieces from the dress of the materialized form of Katie King and no sooner were they cut out than the holes thus made in the dress closed up under his eyes.

---

[1] *Memoirs and Memories* (London, 1911), pp. 381–5. For an amusing paragraph ridiculing this phenomenon see *Punch*, 15 August, 1874, p. 65.

Miss Marryat's account was mentioned with approval by Crookes in his own description of the final séance in which he referred his readers to Miss Marryat's letter in the previous issue which he said his own narrative supplemented.[1] It is worth recording that Crookes later disclaimed much of Miss Marryat's account of the séance,[2] saying that "there is not a word of truth in it".

The testimony of Miss Florence Marryat can, I think, be disregarded. She included a quite fantastic account of the mediumship of Florence Cook in her book *There is No Death*. The lack of accuracy of this careless and imaginative narrative (which was reviewed on 12 September, 1891, by *The Athenæum* under "Novels of the Week"!) is exemplified by the fact that throughout Miss Marryat referred to William Crookes, whom she claimed to know well, as Alfred Crookes. In the entry under her name in the *Dictionary of National Biography*[3] it is said with restraint:

> "*There is No Death*, published in 1891, gives a detailed account of the various mediums with whom she came in contact, and of the séances she attended. Although it bears evident marks of the author's sincerity, it is difficult to believe that a large element of fiction does not enter into the volume."

In addition to the account of the cutting of material from the dress of the materialization, Miss Marryat said that she saw Katie King, subjected to the heat of three gas burners, slowly collapse like "a wax doll melting before a fire". According to her story the figure "sank lower and lower on the carpet like a crumbling edifice, at last there was nothing but her head left above the ground—then a heap of white drapery only, which disappeared with a whisk, as if a hand had pulled it after her, and we were left staring by the light of three gas burners at the spot on which Katie King had stood".

Crookes's attitude towards Miss Marryat's accounts in 1874 was to refer his readers to them without qualification, with the comment that his own narrative supplemented them. In these circumstances it was not perhaps unreasonable for later writers to

[1] *S.*, 5 June, 1874, p. 271.
[2] *Journal* of the Society for Psychical Research, 1906, XII, p. 265.
[3] London, 1901, Supplement, Vol. III, pp. 141–2.

have assumed that he meant what he said. Thus in 1906 these incidents were described in the columns of *Annales des Sciences Psychiques*[1] as if Crookes had witnessed them himself. Whether Crookes was experiencing a chill of disillusionment by 1906 in contrast with his enthusiasm of 1874 is a matter which will be discussed later.

Little more need be said regarding the writings of Miss Marryat, who declared in her book[2] that Katie King frequently materialized in order to get into bed with Florence whose husband had told Miss Marryat that he felt as if he had two wives and was never sure which was the earthly Florence. Miss Marryat's testimony is important only because of its connexion with the curious behaviour of Crookes, who recommended his readers to it in 1874 and declared at least some of it to be quite untrue in 1906.

It is unfortunate that Crookes's disclaimer in 1906 seems to have passed virtually unnoticed by contributors to the literature of spiritualism, who continued to place reliance upon Miss Marryat's testimony. Thus the late Sir Arthur Conan Doyle quoted[3] *verbatim* Miss Marryat's fantastic account of the spirit melting in the heat of the gas burners. One of the least serious of his contradictions of Crookes's own testimony was his account[4] of how the spirit "Katie King" regaled Crookes's children with stories of her adventures on the Spanish Main during her earthly life two hundred years before as Annie Morgan, a pirate's daughter. Crookes, on the other hand, in his account said that the materialization used to collect his children around her and amuse them by recounting anecdotes of her adventures in India.[5]

One point which requires discussion is Crookes's insistence, in his final letter,[6] that the appearance of the materialized form differed markedly from that of the medium. He said:

"I have the most absolute certainty that Miss Cook and

[1] March 1906, pp. 140–1 (English Edition, April 1906, pp. 213–14).
[2] Op. cit., p. 140.
[3] *The History of Spiritualism*, (London, 1926), I, pp. 248–9. Charles Richet had also included this story on p. 646 of *Traité de Métapsychique* (2. éd. Paris, 1923).
[4] Ib., p. 247. Doyle added that on one occasion "Katie King" nursed Mrs. Crookes's three weeks old baby.
[5] *Researches*, etc., p. 110.
[6] *S.*, 5 June, 1874, pp. 270–1.

Katie are two separate individuals so far as their bodies are concerned. Several little marks on Miss Cook's face are absent on Katie's. Miss Cook's hair is so dark a brown as almost to appear black; a lock of Katie's which is now before me, and which she allowed me to cut from her luxuriant tresses, having first traced it up to the scalp and satisfied myself that it actually grew there, is a rich golden auburn.

On one evening I timed Katie's pulse. It beat steadily at 75, whilst Miss Cook's pulse a little time after, was going at its usual rate of 90. On applying my ear to Katie's chest I could hear a heart beating rhythmically inside, and pulsating even more steadily than did Miss Cook's heart when she allowed me to try a similar experiment after the *séance*. Tested in the same way Katie's lungs were found to be sounder than her medium's, for at the time I tried my experiment Miss Cook was under medical treatment for a severe cough."

In a previous comment about the Mornington Road sittings in his letter of 30 March, 1874,[1] Crookes had said that the materialization and the medium differed in height (which Volckman had merely observed as "tip-toeing by the young lady as if to alter her stature"), that Florence had a blister on her neck which was "rough to the touch" and wore ear-rings, whilst the materialization's neck was "perfectly smooth both to touch and sight" and her ears were not pierced. It is noteworthy that he said nothing at all on this earlier occasion about what obviously was the most remarkable difference at Hackney, i.e. the luxuriant auburn tresses of Katie King and the contrasting shorter and darker hair of Florence Cook.

It is reasonable to suppose that the explanation of this earlier reticence about the striking colour and quality of Katie King's hair was that it was, for some reason, first revealed at Hackney. This assumption is supported by the fact that without exception, all photographs of the materialization which I have seen show her to be wearing a white head-dress, usually tight fitting, which effectively concealed everything but her face. It may be added that in every

[1] S., 3 April, 1874, p. 158.

one of the photographs, again without exception, the face of Katie King strongly resembled that of Florence Cook.[1]

It will be obvious that the alleged differences at Mornington Road depended entirely upon the testimony of Crookes himself. He did not say whether he felt Katie King's pulse and tested her lungs at Mornington Road or at Hackney; but there is, in any event, no corroborative testimony whatsoever on these points. Crookes's insistence that the figures were dissimilar, despite the evidence to the contrary of his own photographs and the testimony of virtually all independent observers, was clearly designed, whether honestly or dishonestly, to rebut the constant suggestions by Volckman, Cox and others that the materialization was an imposture by Florence Cook.

Whilst the smaller points of difference mentioned by Crookes can clearly be dismissed as having no evidential value, it is impossible to set on one side the contrast of the length and colour of the materialization's hair at Hackney. The luxuriant auburn tresses were observed by persons other than Crookes, and indeed a considerable amount of the hair would seem to have been cut off and distributed to the delighted circle on 21 May. Indeed, one of these souvenirs was even sent to Charles Blackburn on 22 May. I found a lock of auburn hair, which seems to have been artificially curled, amongst the Blackburn correspondence at the Britten Memorial Library.

We have now to examine a very peculiar situation. Before the Hackney sittings the hair of the materialization was consistently concealed by a head-dress, and in his comments upon the differences of appearance between the figure and the medium Crookes made no remark upon what later was advanced as the most striking difference of all. At Hackney the head-dress was removed and it was seen that Katie King had luxuriant auburn hair, which was cut

[1] The places and dates of the publication of a number of Katie King photographs have already been recorded earlier. Four reproductions were additionally published in the issue of *Two Worlds* of 20 April, 1957, accompanied by a photograph of Florence Cook with the caption "Here is the medium, Florence Cook, who bears no resemblance to the materialization". This is misleading, for the photograph is in fact a reproduction of one taken about 1893 in Usk, when the medium was twenty years older. As photographs of Florence Cook as she was in 1874 were available, the choice of this later picture as a comparison, in which she had naturally much altered in appearance, is somewhat disingenuous. In this connexion the reader may find it of interest to compare the two photographs of Florence Cook in this book.

off and distributed to the sitters, and was totally unlike that of Florence Cook.

When we examine the accounts of the Hackney séances it would seem that even there the materialization's hair was not always visible, for it is reasonable to suppose that it was so striking that when it was seen it would be the subject of recorded comment. Thus, it is obvious that the luxuriant auburn tresses were not in evidence on 13 May when Mr. Enmore Jones remarked upon the strong resemblance the spirit had to the medium "even to the colour of the face" and on the identical voice and mannerisms, with the comment that the unbiased observer would simply have concluded that Katie King was Florence Cook "in a state of undress". He could hardly have failed to notice it if the figure had "long hair of a light auburn or golden colour, which hung in ringlets down her back and each side of her head, reaching nearly to her waist", which was evidently the case at the final séance of 21 May.[1]

Assuming Florence was fraudulent, the difference in the hair might have been accounted for by the medium and her confederate at Hackney changing places on occasions, but prolonged scrutiny of the evidence has convinced me that such a theory is untenable. In the first place, despite the fact that the independent sitters were changed at every séance, the risk of detection would have been much increased by such a transposition. Secondly, it is difficult to suppose that the confederate would have consented very willingly to parting with a substantial quantity of her hair. Thirdly, it is clear from the account by Benjamin Coleman of the sitting of 9 May that the materialization on that occasion, whilst displaying the auburn tresses, nevertheless strongly resembled Florence Cook. Coleman said that the materialization and the medium were "much alike in features".

Again, assuming for the sake of argument that Florence was a fraud, then the luxuriant auburn tresses may have been an ordinary theatrical wig, worn by the medium during one or two séances at Hackney, and specially at the final sitting of 21 May. The purpose of this deception, if it were so, may have been twofold; to make the final effort in the series of similar stage-by-stage attempts to increase the impression that the materialization and the medium were different individuals, and to enable the spectacular hair-

[1] *S.*, 29 May, 1874, p. 258.

cutting ceremony to be staged on 21 May without inconvenience. It seems significant that Crookes thought it necessary to say that before cutting off the hair for distribution to the spectators he "first traced it up to the scalp and satisfied myself that it actually grew there"[1] and that Florence, in her letter to Blackburn of 22 May, 1874, said, in curiously similar terms, "It really grew on her head, for Mr. Crookes felt the hair right up to the skin of the head." Neither could have been at greater pains to insist, virtually in so many words, that the materialization was not wearing a wig, and it seems very odd, to say the least, that both thought it necessary to do so.

The rôle of the confederate who lay on the floor of the bed-room, clad in one of Florence's dresses and with a shawl over her head, would not be an onerous one. The friend, suitably dressed, would obviously be in the house before the sitters arrived, probably in the kitchen quarters, and would secretly enter the bed-room by the side door after the curtains had been drawn. She would take up Florence's position on the floor, thus leaving the medium free to play the part of the materialization. The insistence that the sitters sang hymns during this period would obviously cover any noise inadvertently made.

The interval of as much as "ten or fifteen minutes" which according to Benjamin Coleman elapsed between the closing of the curtain and the emergence of Katie King would be ample for Florence to assume her white robes and wig or head-dress. Whether she took off her frock I do not know. We need not accept Crookes's unsupported statement that he satisfied himself by feeling that she was not wearing corsets. Indeed, in the photo-graph of Crookes arm-in-arm with Katie King which forms the frontispiece of this book and which it is said Crookes tried to suppress, the figure seems to be wearing a frock underneath its white robe, an assumption which is supported by the suggestive bulkiness of its waistline.[2]

After an interval of nearly ninety years it is only possible to speculate upon the identity of the confederate, if indeed, one existed. She must have been a young woman of about Florence's

[1] S., 5 June, 1874, p. 271.
[2] Though an alternative explanation for this might have been that Florence was pregnant, which might also explain her secret marriage (see note 1 on p. 55).

age, and whilst no doubt she received payment for her trouble she must have been someone who would in no circumstances have revealed the secret.

It does not seem to have been Kate Cook. She was certainly involved in the Mornington Road séances, but it is probable that she was amongst the visible sitters at Hackney. Amongst the papers in the Britten Memorial Library is a pencilled message, presumably written by Katie King during the final séance, which supports this assumption. It reads:

"To Kate S. Cook with Katie's love and best wishes for her future. May 21, 1874."

The confederate may have been Caroline Corner, who at the relevant time was Florence's sister-in-law. It is noteworthy that whilst Caroline with her mother had been a constant sitter at Florence's earlier séances before the Mornington Road era she was conspicuously absent from the Hackney sittings. Mrs. Amelia Corner attended several of them as a member of the old Dalston group. In the days when the spectators were not allowed to see the inside of the cabinet at all, great emphasis had been placed upon the fact that Florence was searched before the séances and, as has been previously pointed out, this duty seems usually to have fallen to Mrs. and Miss Corner. If Florence was a fraud and these searches were purposefully superficial then obviously Caroline was already involved and would have been a suitable person to act as a trusted confederate.

It is, however, more likely that the confederate was Mary Showers. She had been Florence's partner in the joint materialization in Crookes's laboratory, and, as we shall see later, it was highly likely that Mary Showers was a fraudulent medium and if so, had been in collusion with Florence Cook. If these assumptions be justified it would seem that Mary Showers was the ideal confederate. She was already addicted to trickery, she had helped Florence before in deception and she was in no position to betray any secrets without involving herself.

When discussing the problem of the auburn hair we saw that Crookes had verified that it grew on the head and Florence's letter to Blackburn confirmed it. The dual insistence on this fact appeared odd at first sight, but on further consideration was it so odd?

Supposing Florence Cook was a completely fraudulent medium and that Crookes knew it and was actively supporting her in her performances, thus helping her to persuade Mr. Blackburn to continue his allowance to her? What conceivable motive could Crookes have had to countenance, aid and abet so gigantic an imposture? What could have inspired him to enter into collusion with an uneducated London girl and help her to gain her ends through so shameful a deception? Let us see if contemporary writers can shed any light on so extraordinary a mystery.

CHAPTER FOUR

DOUBTS ABOUT KATIE KING

THERE were so many suspicious circumstances in the early history of Florence Cook's mediumship that it is not easy for the critical reader to rid his mind of the growing conviction that Florence was a fraud and that her sitters and supporters were being deceived. The testimony of so many spiritualists and writers like Florence Marryat convey no sense of conviction. Persons like these have been telling similar stories ever since the rise of modern spiritualism and time and again exposures have shown that their beliefs had no foundation in fact.

It is true that writers like Sir Arthur Conan Doyle have tried to explain away such unpleasant revelations, but their attempts will not persuade any reasonable and well-informed person that the exposures were not just what they seemed. But even among the spiritualists of the 1870s there were a few who had not entirely given way to blind credulity and who were still able to recognize signs of deception when they saw them and to realize clearly how such deception was to be avoided. It is true that the spiritualist press, just as today, did its best to suppress their views, but in this it was not entirely successful. Indeed, where doubts were expressed by independent journalists who were also inclined to believe in certain forms of spiritualism, its efforts to silence them failed altogether.

Perhaps the most eminent of those who were intensely interested in the spiritual manifestations but who, at the same time, retained a certain amount of critical acumen was Serjeant Edward William Cox (1809–79). His involvement in the last stages of the story of Crookes and Florence Cook is of such importance that it must be dealt with in some detail. Cox, who was a barrister of the Middle Temple and a serjeant-at-law, was the Recorder of Falmouth from 1857 to 1868, and of Portsmouth from 1868 until his death. He was the proprietor of the *Law Times* from 1843 to 1879, and was also a psychical researcher of distinction.

Cox and Crookes were closely associated on the most friendly terms in the investigation of the mediumship of D. D. Home and Crookes's other work in connexion with spiritualism before the advent of Florence Cook. There seems to be little doubt, however, that Cox had very good reason to believe that Florence was a fraud and that in consequence there was a cooling of their relationship. Cox, the elder of the two men, seems to have acted with dignity, and it is noteworthy that in his book he wrote in the highest terms of Crookes's earlier work and contented himself with the omission of any reference to Florence Cook.[1]

Shortly after Florence's mediumship began to attract attention, another girl of about the same age, Mary Showers, started to produce the same sort of phenomena, including "spirit faces" and a full-form materialization calling itself Florence Maple. It may be significant that Mary and her mother were also members of the Dalston Association of Inquirers into Spiritualism and that they were friends of the Cooks and of Mrs Amelia Corner and her daughter Caroline.

Mary Showers is important to this inquiry because of a letter from Crookes published in part on 10 April, 1874,[2] a letter, incidentally, which was not reproduced in Crookes's book and was the only one to be omitted so far as I am aware. The extract from Crookes's letter quoted by the editor, which was undated, read as follows:

"You can mention that Miss Cook's 'Katie' has been walking about in my laboratory along with Miss Showers's 'Florence' with their arms entwined schoolgirl fashion, and in a strong light. 'Katie' has also materialized and spoken when I have been in the cabinet with Miss Cook, holding her hand; but, being dark, I could see nothing except lights here and there, one of which settled on my coat-sleeve."

It seems from this curious letter that by April 1874 Crookes was willing to write about these incredible materializations as if they

[1] *The Mechanism of Man* (London, 1879), Vol. II, pp. 444–56. Lord Rayleigh, in his Presidential Address to the S.P.R. delivered seven days after Crookes's death, also referred with approval to the scientist's life and work in psychical research, discussing in some detail the experiments with D. D. Home and Mrs. Jencken, but omitted any mention of Florence Cook. (*Proceedings*, S.P.R., XXX, pp. 275–90.)
[2] *S.*, p. 176.

were accomplished facts without offering a shred of corroborative evidence. This communication is one of the few indications available to us of what was going on during the series of private séances at Crookes's house to which Florence was exclusively devoting herself.

It is of course of great interest to know that on occasions Florence brought Mary Showers with her to do a joint materialization, for it is plain that if there were supposed to be two entranced mediums in the cabinet and two materializations walking around the laboratory arm-in-arm, both Florence and Mary were genuine or both were fraudulent. In this connexion it is helpful to consider an account by Serjeant Cox, who had some experience of both the mediums. It is important to record that the letter from which the following quotation is taken was written on 23 April, 1874, and sent by Cox to the editor of *The Spiritualist*. W. H. Harrison refused at first to publish it, whereupon Cox wrote to the editor of *The Medium and Daybreak* on 4 May explaining what had happened. His letter and the original communication were published there on 8 May, being finally published in *The Spiritualist* on p. 230 of the issue of 15 May, 1874:

"I have seen the forms of Katie [King] and Florence [Maple] together in the full light, coming out from the room in which Miss Cook and Miss Showers were placed, walking about, talking, playing girlish tricks, patting us and pushing us. They were solid flesh and blood and bone. They breathed, and perspired, and ate, and wore a white head-dress and a white robe from neck to foot, made of cotton and woven by a loom. Not merely did they resemble their respective mediums, they were facsimiles of them—alike in face, hair, complexion, teeth, eyes, hands, and movements of the body. Unless he had been otherwise so informed, no person would have doubted for a moment that the two girls who had been placed behind the curtain were now standing in *propriâ personâ* before the curtain playing very prettily the character of ghost.

On that occasion there was nothing to avoid this conclusion but the bare assertion of the forms in white that they were not what they appeared to be, but two other beings in the likeness of Miss Cook and Miss Showers; and that the real ladies were at that moment asleep on the sofa behind the curtain. But of this their assertion no proof whatever was given or offered or permitted. The fact might have been established in a moment beyond all doubt by the simple process of opening the curtain and exhibiting the two ladies then and there upon the sofa, wearing their black gowns. But this only certain evidence was not proffered, nor, indeed, was it allowed us—the conditions exacted from us being that we should do nothing by which, if it were a trick, we should be enabled to discover it.

This and similar exhibitions have been advanced as proofs of positive materialization, and it is said, 'You have seen, heard, touched the spirit forms'. True, I have seen two forms, and they were material forms beyond all question. But they exactly resembled the ladies, and not the slightest proof was given or allowed to me that they were not the ladies themselves, as they appeared to all of us to be.

But I have had one piece of evidence that goes far to throw a doubt over the whole. At a sitting with Miss Showers a few days ago, the curtain, behind which the form of Florence [Maple] was exhibiting her face, was opened by a spectator ignorant of the conditions, and a peep behind the scenes was afforded to those present. I am bound, in the interests of truth and science, to say that I, as well as all the others, beheld revealed to us, not a form in front and a lady in the chair, but the chair empty, and the lady herself at the curtain wearing the ghost head-dress, and dressed in her own black gown! Nor was she lying on the floor as some have surmised. When the head was thrust out between the curtain the eyes were turned up with the fixed stare which has been observed in the supposed Florence [Maple], but the eyes rapidly assumed their natural position when the exposure was made, and the hands were forthwith actively employed in trying to close the curtain, and in the struggle with the inspecting lady the spirit head-dress fell off. I was witness to it all, and the extraordinary scene that followed—the voice crying out 'You have killed my medium!'—an alarm which, by the bye, was quite needless, for she was neither killed or injured beyond the vexation of the discovery. She said in excuse that

G

she was unconscious of what she had done, being in state of trance.'

That this damaging incident caused consternation amongst the friends of Florence Cook is shown by the efforts of W. H. Harrison to suppress it. The account by Cox of the joint performance by Mary Showers and Florence Cook, coupled with the previous account in April by Crookes, meant that the integrity of the two young mediums could not be considered separately. If Mary was a glaring fraud, a question about which Cox's statement seemed to leave little doubt, then clearly Florence's mediumship could not conceivably have been genuine.

The spiritualists did their best. Mrs. Amelia Corner wrote a letter on 18 May which was published[1] under the heading "Miss Showers and Florence Maple seen at the same time" to say that during a recent séance, now described for the first time, she and her daughter Caroline had entered the cabinet and had seen both the medium and the materialization together. As Mrs. Corner and Caroline were the two ladies who always made themselves responsible for the searching of Florence Cook before her séances, and who often performed a similar duty for Miss Showers, it seems possible that their testimony was not entirely disinterested. It is also worth remembering that Caroline's brother, Edward Elgie Corner, had married Florence Cook as recently as 29 April, a fact which was being kept secret until Crookes had published his final endorsement of Florence's mediumship in *The Spiritualist* of 5 June. So it may have seemed desirable at this vital period for those concerned to make as united an effort as was possible in the circumstances, which could be the explanation of a very opportune letter from the Dalston Association of Inquirers into Spiritualism published in the same issue of *The Spiritualist* as the communication from Mrs. Corner. It was signed by Thomas Wilkes, formerly the President of the Association, who said that he was as fully satisfied as to the truth and sincerity of Mrs. and Miss Showers as he was of his own existence.[2]

Cox was not to be silenced, and in a moderately worded letter

[1] *S.*, 22 May, 1874, p. 247.
[2] *S.*, 22 May, 1874, p. 248. It will be recalled that in Florence Cook's autobiographical account of her early mediumship she said that the second spiritualist she met was Mr. Wilkes.

dated 1 June, 1874,[1] which discussed the final Katie King séances and to which I shall refer later in some detail, he wrote:

"I am aware that improbability is no answer to facts; but in estimating the amount of evidence necessary to establish the fact, we must take into account the circumstances that tell against it, and therefore demand the more jealous scrutiny of this investigation. Having witnessed this strange phenomenon, I am bound to say that it is surrounded with extraordinary features of doubt and suspicion. I will name some of them.

1. All the prescribed conditions are such as facilitate trickery, if designed, and to prevent, and not to promote inquiry. Friends are posted on either side of the curtain, as if to exclude a too curious eye. If any strangers are present, hands are to be held. The singing usually invited diverts attention, and prevents the intent ear from perceiving movements behind the curtain. The hand of the 'spirit' is not to be held, only opened to a hasty touch. Visitors not known to have the firmest faith are placed in a semicircle, and conditioned not to rush forward or grasp. A considerable time elapses before the form appears. The sitting is not closed and the curtains withdrawn so that all may see, for a long time after the form has retired. None are admitted behind the curtain until the most perfect confidence is placed in their previously assured faith. Even the few thus favoured were not admitted at once but by slow degrees—thus far tonight—a little further another night—as trial proved the extent of their inquisitorial purposes or powers.

2. This unquestionable likeness of the form to the medium. When I saw them they were not merely resemblances; they were facsimiles. I had carefully noted the shape of the eyebrows, which cannot be altered, and they were the same in the medium and the form. The hands were identical. The movements of the body were precisely similar."

Cox's views are of the greatest possible importance because (a) he knew Crookes intimately and had worked with him in previous research, (b) he had been an eyewitness of the alleged materializa-

[1] *S.*, 5 June, 1874, pp. 272–4.

tions on a number of occasions and (c) he almost alone amongst those concerned in the affair understood what constituted evidence. His impressions, coupled with the revelation that he had positive information regarding the fraudulence of the "spirit forms", are contained in a long letter to D. D. Home written on 8 March, 1876,[1] after the tumult had died down:

> "The great field for fraud has been offered by the production and presentation of alleged spirit-forms. All the conditions imposed are as if carefully designed to favour fraud if contemplated, and even to tempt to imposture. The curtain is guarded at either end by some friend. The light is so dim that the features cannot be distinctly seen. A white veil thrown over the body from head to foot is put on and off in a moment, and gives the necessary aspect of spirituality. A white band round head and chin at once conceals the hair, and disguises the face. A considerable interval precedes the appearance— just such as would be necessary for the preparations. A like interval succeeds the retirement of the form before the cabinet is permitted to be opened for inspection. This just enables the ordinary dress to be restored.
>
> While the preparation is going on behind the curtain the company are always vehemently exhorted to sing. This would conveniently conceal any sounds of motion in the act of preparation. The spectators are made to promise not to peep behind the curtain and not to grasp the form. They are solemnly told that if they were to seize the spirit they would kill the medium. This is an obvious contrivance to deter the onlookers from doing anything that might cause detection. It is not true. Several spirits have been grasped, and no medium has died of it; although in each case the supposed spirit was found to be the medium. That the detected medium was somewhat disturbed in health after such a public detection and exposure is not at all surprising. Every one of the five mediums who have been actually seized in the act of personating the spirit is now alive and well. There need be no fear for the consequences in putting them to the proof.
>
> But I have learned how the trick is done. I have seen the

---

[1] D. Home. *Lights and Shadows of Spiritualism* (London, 1877), pp. 326 ff.

description of it given by a medium to another medium who desired instruction. The letter was in her own handwriting, and the whole style of it showed it to be genuine.

She informs her friend that she comes to the *séance* prepared with a dress that is easily taken off with a little practice. She says it may be done in two or three minutes. She wears two shifts (probably for warmth). She brings a muslin veil of thin material (she gives its name which I forgot). It is carried *in her drawers*! It can be compressed into a small space, although when spread it covers the whole person. A pocket-handkerchief pinned round the head keeps back the hair. She states that she takes off all her clothes except the two shifts, and is covered by the veil. The gown is spread carefully upon the sofa over the pillows. In this array she comes out. She makes very merry with the spiritualists whom she thus gulls, and her language about them is anything but complimentary.

This explains the whole business. The question so often asked before was—where the robe could be carried? It could not be contained in the bosom or in a sleeve. Nobody seems to have thought of the drawers.

But it will be asked how can we explain the fact that some persons have been permitted to go behind the curtain when the form was before it, and have asserted that they saw or felt the medium. I am sorry to say the confession to which I have referred states without reserve that these persons knew that it was a trick, and lent themselves to it. I am, of course, reluctant to adopt such a formidable conclusion although the so-called 'confession' was a confidential communication from one medium to another medium who had asked to be instructed how the trick was done. I prefer to adopt the more charitable conclusion that they were imposed upon, and it is easy to find how this was likely to be. The same suspicious precautions against detection were always adopted. The favoured visitor was an assured friend; one who, if detecting trickery, would shrink from proclaiming the cheat. But one was permitted to enter. A light was not allowed. There was nothing but the 'darkness visible' of the lowered gas rays struggling through the curtain. I have noted that no one of them was ever permitted to see the face of the medium. It was always 'wrapped

81

in a shawl'.[1] The hands felt a dress, and imagination did the rest. The revealer of the secret above referred to says that, when she took off her gown to put on the white veil, she spread it upon the sofa or chair with pillows or something under it and this was what they felt and took for her body!

The lesson to be learned from all this is that no phenomena should be accepted as genuine that are not produced under strict test conditions. Investigators should be satisfied with no evidence short of the very best that the circumstances will permit. Why accept the doubtful testimony of one person groping in the dark when the question can be decided beyond dispute once and for ever by the simple process of drawing back the curtain while the alleged spirit is outside and showing the medium inside to the eyes of all present?"

This letter is one of the most significant documents in the history of the materializing mediums of the 1870s. It seems extremely unlikely that Cox, a Recorder at Quarter Sessions for over twenty years, could have invented the story of the confidential communication he had seen, and it is therefore worth some speculation regarding its origin. Who were the mediums who respectively wrote and received the letter?

It seems from the contents of the letter (a) that the two mediums must have been intimate friends for one to write so compromising a letter to the other; (b) that the two mediums must have been producing the same sort of phenomena for the advice to be of value; (c) that the writer of the letter must have been more experienced in fraudulent mediumship than the recipient; and (d) that the recipient had probably given a séance either at Cox's house or one at which he was present if the opportunity was to arise for the letter to be accidentally lost by the medium and later found by Cox.

In the periodical literature of the time is to be found no mention of any mediums who satisfy these conditions other than Florence Cook and Mary Showers. They were in fact the only women

[1] The reader may attach significance to this reference to a shawl as indicative of the strong probability that the anonymous medium to whom Cox was referring was Florence Cook. He will remember that in the account of the Hackney sittings the face of the medium was always "wrapped in a shawl". In Crookes's own description of the Mornington Road séances, moreover, he said that the face of the medium could not be seen "because of the shawl". (S., 5 June, 1874, p. 270.)

materialization mediums with whom Cox was in any way closely connected, and it seems very probable that the letter was written by Florence Cook to Mary Showers and inadvertently left behind at Cox's house by the latter during a sitting. The hasty changing of clothes was a feature of these materialization séances; and in these circumstances it is not difficult to imagine a letter being accidentally dropped from a pocket.

The matter can usefully be carried a little further without our speculations becoming wildly fanciful. It seems clear from the text of the letter, despite Cox's charitable refusal to accept it as a fact, that the writer of the letter was assuring the recipient that one of the persons who would be at the sitting was "an assured friend" who would not reveal any trickery if he detected it. This friend, moreover, was in a privileged position and was allowed to enter the cabinet.

Was this letter one that was written by Florence Cook to Mary Showers about the joint séance they were to give at Crookes's house, and was part of its purpose to assure Mary that they need not fear exposure because there was to be an "assured friend" who would be in control of the proceedings? We have only Crookes's account, without dates, names of sitters or any corroboration, of what transpired during the series of séances at 20 Mornington Road, and it would seem that the company may have consisted at least partly if not wholly of his family. Possibly it was only in the presence of a particularly docile audience and a singularly sympathetic director of ceremonies that the two "materializations" could confidently march around the room "with their arms entwined schoolgirl fashion and in a strong light".

It is curious that Cox, convinced of the truth of the rest of the letter, found it difficult to accept what appears to have been the positive statement that there was "an assured friend" in a privileged position who would refrain from any exposure of trickery. The presence of such a confederate at the sitting was, it would seem, an integral part of the explanation of how the spurious phenomena were accomplished. Cox's reluctance to believe in such a possibility would, however, be explicable if the writer of the letter was Florence Cook. In these circumstances he would know that the alleged confederate, the "assured friend", could be none other than Crookes himself, his former friend and colleague. Whilst there can be no doubt that Cox was bewildered by Crookes's championship of Florence Cook, he might still find it impossible to believe that a man for whose earlier work he had nothing but respect could have stumbled so far into the morass as to be capable of deliberate deception.

Whether Cox ever revealed to Home the actual identity of the writer of the letter we do not know. Cox, as a distinguished jurist, would obviously have regard to the law of libel. It is, however, noteworthy that Home later revealed to Camille Flammarion, the astronomer and psychical researcher, that it was within his knowledge that Florence Cook's mediumship was based on skilled trickery.[1] What was the basis of Home's knowledge we do not know. Serjeant Cox was often in correspondence with him and it may well be that he later told Home who the two mediums were. It is hardly likely that Home would keep this knowledge to himself. He probably told others besides Flammarion, and the passage in his book[2] where he says that Crookes's experiments with Florence Cook gave "undeniable certainty" may have been written before he had received Cox's letter or had been told who had written it.

At this date it is probably impossible to determine whether Cox had any suspicions as to the identity of the "assured friend". From his previous association with Crookes it would have seemed to be impossible that his distinguished colleague could have ever become an accomplice to a couple of fraudulent mediums. Yet he must have known something of Crookes's peculiar behaviour at the various séances, at which Florence Cook was the medium, for an account of it had been published in the Rev. Maurice Davies's book, *Mystic London*,[3] in 1875.

[1] Camille Flammarion. *Mysterious Psychic Forces* (Boston, 1907), p. 343.
[2] D. D. Home, op. cit., p. 350.
[3] It seems certain that the author was in fact recounting his own experiences. In his earlier book *Unorthodox London* (London, 1873), pp. 337–43, he described in different phraseology what seems to have been an identical séance at Florence Cook's home at which he was a sitter. The wording of this chapter "Spirit Faces" in *Unorthodox London* is identical with that of an earlier article of the same title which was published in the *Daily Telegraph* of 10 October, 1872, by "Our Own Commissioner". From this it is reasonable to suppose with some certainty that the Rev. C. Maurice Davies was the contributor to the *Daily Telegraph* and that his account of his experience with Florence Cook was included word for word over his own name in his earlier book in 1873. As I have said, the phraseology was altered in *Mystic London* in 1875 but the events described were the same. Why the author in his later book ascribed the experience to "a friend who shares my interest in these matters" is a circumstance for conjecture.

In a vivid description of a séance with Florence Dr. Davies did not hesitate to reveal the identity of the medium and continued:

"In one respect the physiognomy did interest me, for I read that the medium was pretty—mediums, according to my experience being generally very much the reverse—and I found that report had certainly not misrepresented the young lady in this respect. Her name is now public property, so I need not veil it under the pseudonyms of Miss Blank or Asterisk, or anything of that sort. Miss Florence Cook, then, is a trim little lady of sweet sixteen and dwells beneath the parental roof in an eastern suburb of London." (p. 309.)

In the chapter which followed dealing with the experiments with Crookes, Florence Cook was cautiously reduced to "Miss C" and Crookes, whose name was not divulged, was introduced to the reader in the following words:

"It was to me personally a source of great satisfaction when I learnt that Miss C had been taken in hand by a F.R.S. —— whom I will call henceforth the Professor . . . ." (p. 314.)

The chapter ended with these suggestive words, for which no explanation was given:

"I am free to confess the final death-blow to my belief that there might be 'something in' the Face Manifestations was given by the effusive Professor who has 'gone in' for the Double with a pertinacity altogether opposed to the calm judicial examination of his brother learned in the law,[1] and with prejudice scarcely becoming a F.R.S.
I am quite aware that all this proves nothing. Miss S [howers] and Miss C [ook] may each justify Longfellow's adjuration:
'Trust her not, she is fooling thee;'
and yet ghosts be as genuine as guano. Only I fancy the 'wave' of young ladies will have to ebb for a little while; and I am exceedingly interested in speculating as to what will be the next 'cycle'. From 'information I have received', emanating

[1] Edward W. Cox.

85

THE MEDIUM AND THE SPIRITUALIST

from Brighton, I am strongly of opinion that babies are looking up in the ghost market, and that our next manifestations may come through an infant phenomenon." (p. 319.)[1]

The statement by Dr. Davies that Mr. Crookes had "gone in" for Florence Cook's "double" could bear only one interpretation and that was that, in the language of today, he had "fallen for" Florence Cook herself. That Davies had some grounds for his suspicion apart altogether from what he had himself observed can be shown when we read the account of Katie King in Crookes's letter to *The Spiritualist* of 5 June, 1874. It was in this extraordinary document, which describes the final appearance of Katie at Hackney, that he wrote:

> "But photography is as inadequate to depict the perfect beauty of Katie's face, as words are powerless to describe her charms of manner. Photography may, indeed, give a map of her countenance; but how can it reproduce the brilliant purity of her complexion, or the ever-varying expression of her most mobile features, now overshadowed with sadness when relating some of the bitter experiences of her past life, now smiling with all the innocence of happy girlhood when she had collected my children round her and was amusing them by recounting anecdotes of her adventures in India?
>
> > 'Round her she made an atmosphere of life,
> > The very air seemed lighter from her eyes,
> > They were so soft and beautiful, and rife
> > With all we can imagine of the skies;
> > Her overpowering presence made you feel
> > It would not be idolatry to kneel.' "

The fact that Crookes brought himself to describe the materialization in such terms and to have his eulogy printed in a popular spiritualistic journal must, it seems, point to one conclusion only, namely that he was infatuated with Katie King and that he was prepared to throw all caution to the winds. Moreover, if as now might be assumed, Katie King was simply Florence Cook then

[1] Possibly referring to young Ferdie Jencken, the mediumistic baby of the former Kate Fox. *See* p.xiii and cf. A. L. Underhill, *The Missing Link* (New York, 1885), pp. 464 ff.

it becomes clear that Crookes had fallen in love with her. Mr. J. N. Maskelyne, therefore, can hardly be blamed when in his book *Modern Spiritualism* (London [1876]) he said that "The 'scientist' who writes like this—and clasps the beautiful and substantial spirit in his arms—is much too far gone for 'investigation'!" (p. 145.)

It would have been difficult for the reader of 1876 to place any construction upon Maskelyne's remark that Crookes was "much too far gone", other than that the scientist was clearly infatuated, a conclusion reinforced by Davies's statement that the marked attentions paid by Crookes to Katie from the very first excited suspicion.[1]

There seems to have been no doubt that Florence Cook was extremely prepossessing. Even Davies commented upon her pretty appearance, and additional evidence is provided by Prince Emile Sayn-Wittgenstein-Berleburg (1824–78) who had Florence to stay with him in Germany. He described Katie King as a ravishing and poetic apparition, an antique statue who had descended from her pedestal to become for an hour the most gracious and attractive young woman of whom it was possible to dream.[2]

If the suspicions of the authors cited above were justified, then the decision of Florence Cook to throw herself at the feet of Crookes and leave it to him to make the great decision as to the genuineness of her mediumship can be understood. But she can hardly have thought that her physical attractiveness was sufficient to overcome the scientist and bring him into subjection. It had to go further than that and Crookes must be persuaded to become her lover. Is it possible or even conceivable that such a plan was brought to fruition? Does the story of Crookes's life provide any clues to deciding this important question? And if nothing emerges from such a study how is it then possible to explain the relations between Crookes and Florence and his apparent belief in the genuine character of her incredible phenomena in the face of all the devastating criticism that even then had been levelled against it? If the "assured friend" was not Crookes, then who was he?

[1] Op. cit., p. 318.
[2] *Souvenirs et Correspondance* (Paris, 1888), vol. II, pp. 417 ff.

CHAPTER FIVE

THE CHARACTER OF WILLIAM CROOKES

THE theory that Crookes's relations with Florence Cook went beyond a simple infatuation which led him, perhaps, to overlook evidence against her mediumship and to support her in her fight with her detractors has never been considered very seriously. Crookes was a distinguished, gifted and ambitious man and it seemed preposterous to imagine that he would be foolish enough to risk his reputation and position for the fleeting satisfaction of an affair with a girl over twenty years younger than himself and a medium whose honesty had been questioned. William Crookes and his wife were considered a devoted couple, with a family of ten, who enjoyed an exceptionally long married life together and it seemed therefore highly unlikely that the scientist, an affectionate husband and father, would have embarked on a passionate love affair with a girl of eighteen, or over, however accommodating and attractive she might have been.

These are considerations to which due weight must be given, but other possibly relevant facts must not be neglected.

When Crookes's career is looked at as a whole it would seem that 1874 was the turning point in his life as a scientist. His biographer[1] in discussing the rationalist version as opposed to the spiritualist explanation of Crookes's entry into and curiously abrupt abandonment of the "debatable land" of alleged supernormal phenomena said:

"He probably in the end suspected that all was not well, and in 1874 he decided to have done with the matter for ever. Having publicly committed himself to raps, levitations and 'materializations' he did not like to retract. But he abruptly closed a rather unfortunate chapter in his career and made amends by an unparalleled devotion to pure science which soon brought forth abundant and refreshing fruit."

[1] E. E. Fournier d'Albe, op. cit., pp. 175–6.

Although d'Albe maintained that following the Katie King episode Crookes "closed that chapter" the facts do not support this supposition as we shall see later. For a better appreciation of Crookes and his achievements it will be useful to summarize briefly the main events of his life.

He was born on 17 June, 1832. Starting with no scientific tradition and a very modest education at a private school, Prospect House, Weybridge, Crookes studied chemistry at the Royal College of Chemistry under Professor A. W. von Hofmann, whose assistant he became in 1851. He had no university training and the degrees he received in later life were honorary ones.

In 1854 he was appointed an assistant in the meteorological department of the Radcliffe Observatory, Oxford, and in 1855 he obtained the position of teacher of chemistry at the College of Science, Chester, which he also held for one year. He married Ellen Humphrey of Darlington on 10 April, 1856, and after his marriage he made London his home, devoting his energies initially to the development of photography and editing first the *Liverpool Photographic Journal* and in 1857 the *Journal of the London Photographic Society* of which organization he also became secretary. These appointments launched him into the editorial career which he followed for the rest of his life. From the chemical laboratory at his house in Mornington Road he began in 1858 the analytical and consultative work which was to be his other main activity.

In 1859 Crookes became the proprietor and editor of the weekly *Chemical News*. In 1860 he unsuccessfully applied for the vacant professorship of chemistry at the Royal Veterinary College. He discovered the new element thallium in 1861 and largely on account of his work in this connexion he was elected a Fellow of the Royal Society in 1863. In 1864 he became the editor of the *Quarterly Journal of Science*. From 1864 to 1868 he interested himself in such widely different projects as the treatment and prevention of cattle plague and the employment of sodium amalgam for the extraction of gold and silver from ore. None of these ventures was particularly rewarding or remunerative and the sodium amalgam process in particular was a disappointment.

The years 1868 and 1869 marked a lull in any outstanding events in Crookes's scientific career. He suffered from ill health but he began the writing of books on aniline colours and on beetroot sugar and continued to edit the *Chemical News* and to contribute articles to the *Quarterly Journal of Science* on a variety of subjects.

The Royal Astronomical Society urged the British Government to arrange for several eclipse expeditions in 1870 when the track of totality would cross Spain and North Africa. The important spectroscopic observations made in the United States during the total solar eclipse of 7 August, 1869, had been described by Crookes in the *Quarterly Journal of Science* for January 1870. William Huggins, of the wealthy brewing family, who had become a distinguished astronomer, invited Crookes to join one of these expeditions which set sail on 6 December, 1870, for Oran where they arrived on 16 December. The expedition was a failure, owing to the overcast sky, Crookes arriving back in London on 5 January, 1871.

This is a very brief summary of William Crookes's career before the period from 1870 when he actively interested himself in spiritualism. It was not until after 1874, as d'Albe wrote, that

"Crookes closed that chapter, regretfully perhaps, but fully determined to devote all his strength to ultimate problems of a nature open to accepted scientific methods.

And then came that wonderful chapter of researches in high vacua, leading to 'radiant matter', the Radiometer, and the 'Crookes tube', which incidentally solved the problem of electric lighting, and is now universally represented by the electric lamp found even in humble homes.

Here we find Crookes at the very height of his career. He was, indeed, the outstanding discoverer of the day and of his generation. Working mostly alone and apart in his great laboratory, he wrested many a secret from Nature and laid bare his hard-won treasures before an astonished world. For the next thirty years honours fell thick upon him from all sides. The presidency of the Chemical Society, of the Institution of Electrical Engineers, of the British Association for the Advancement of Science, and finally of the Royal Society fell to him in succession, thus giving him some of the most coveted distinctions open to science in England. The knighthood conferred upon him in 1897 was but the Royal assent to the full measure of recognition already earned and received."[1]

[1] Op. cit., p. 5.

It has been argued that Crookes may have been disturbed by the criticisms of his scientific colleagues regarding his interest in spiritualism, and that this was the reason for his temporary withdrawal from involvement in the subject about 1874, but this is not in accordance with the facts. In his book on his spiritualistic work Crookes reproduced the correspondence with his critics and the articles by himself and others which had appeared in the scientific journals at the time Crookes's work with the medium D. D. Home was under fire.

The final and most severe attack, to which he retaliated violently and with which the Council of the Royal Society ultimately became involved, came from Dr. W. B. Carpenter, F.R.S., in March 1872. Crookes was victorious, and the letter from the Secretary of the Royal Society of 18 April, 1872, ended the controversy. It was also the final item on the last page[1] of the section of Crookes's book dealing with this aspect of his connexion with spiritualism. It is clear, therefore, that if the attitude of the scientific world in itself was going to cause him to disengage himself from spiritualism, he would have done so in 1872 or earlier.

During the period of the séances and his close contact with Florence in 1873 and 1874 Crookes was nearly forty-two years old, and there is nothing unusual for a man of this age to be attracted to a pretty, pleasant and compliant woman much younger than himself. Moreover, Crookes's biographer, E. E. Fournier d'Albe, indicated here and there in his book that the scientist's family life may not have been so completely satisfactory as is generally supposed. He wrote, for example, of Lady Crookes:[2]

> "She had been a devoted wife and had borne him ten children. Of these, seven survived childhood and one—the second girl—died at the age of 13. Henry, the eldest son, was his mother's favourite, but Crookes considered none of his children as being up to his own standard, with the exception of Bernard, and his friends were disposed to agree with him. In addition to her activities as a mother Lady Crookes was a wise and intelligent companion and friend in all Crookes's affairs, and in the earlier days she frequently acted

[1] *Researches*, etc., p. 80.
[2] Op. cit., pp. 383-4.

91

as his secretary and amanuensis. She was a great talker and on many occasions, it is said, she ruled the conversation to the total extinguishment of her rather retiring husband, and kept it on a level far below the high altitudes which her guests expected from the presence of a world-famous savant."

The final sentence is revealing despite its restraint, the implication behind these and other hints of a similar nature being that Lady Crookes, who had married the youthful scientist in the days of his obscurity, had not entirely kept pace with her husband's ambition and achievements.

During the years preceding 1874 Crookes's attitude towards even mild criticism was one of almost violent intolerance. He reacted immediately to any comment which he considered to be adverse to his interests by a resourceful and often bitter defence of his position. This aspect of Crookes's character may be one of the more significant features of the case, and it may be desirable to record one or two episodes which adequately illustrate it.

On 18 July, 1862, after Crookes had failed in his application for the appointment of Professor of Chemistry at the Royal Veterinary College, he wrote the following letter to P. Squire, a member of the Council of the Pharmaceutical Society:

"I have just heard that someone, interested in my non-success, has circulated a report amongst the Council of the Pharmaceutical Society, that I am a very litigious and quarrelsome fellow, having, in fact, no less than three law suits connected with the *Chemical News* in hand at the present time. I take the very earliest opportunity of denying this in the most emphatic and absolute manner . . . It is also reported that my manner as a teacher is unpopular. My testimonials from those who have known me longest in that capacity afford the best evidence that this is not the case.

I am unable as yet to trace these reports to anything definite, and am consequently not in a position to give a more particular contradiction to them: but I am proud to say that there is no single incident in my career which will not bear the strictest scrutiny."[1]

[1] E. E. Fournier d'Albe, op. cit., p. 82.

Crookes's actions following the death of his brother in 1867 were not in his own defence, but they illustrate better than any other single incident his readiness to enter the fray without regard to what the repercussions might be. Philip Crookes died on 22 September, 1867, of yellow fever when engaged on a cable laying expedition to Havana. Crookes blamed the commander of the expedition, F. C. Webb, for his brother's death on the grounds of negligence and sent a circular letter to his employers, the Directors of the India Rubber, Gutta Percha and Telegraph Works Company, referring to Webb in the most critical terms. The commander of the expedition instituted proceedings for libel against Crookes. Webb's solicitors gave Crookes the opportunity to withdraw and to apologize, which he refused to do. The case was tried at the Court of Queen's Bench on 12 December, 1868. Crookes lost the case, the libel being proved and an apology was made on his behalf by his solicitors. It was incidentally this incident which put Crookes into close touch with Mr. Cromwell F. Varley, F.R.S., who was interested in spiritualism and who persuaded Crookes to try to get into communication with his dead brother by spiritualist methods.

On 4 November, 1871, Crookes wrote to the editor of the *English Mechanic* regarding his former friend John Spiller, who had publicly stated that he knew how the medium D. D. Home worked the accordion under the table during Crookes's experiments with him. This letter is of great interest, for it showed that Crookes reacted angrily to criticisms of his investigation of spiritualism as well as to those directed at other aspects of his life and work. He wrote:[1]

> "Allow me to give an unqualified denial to the rumour. It is utterly false . . . It is much to be regretted that the author of these reports does not come forward, and state honestly what he has to say, in preference to setting rumours afloat behind my back, and prompting his friends, under fictitious signatures, to make false accusations against my honour and veracity. It is a cowardly, un-English trick and one which I can scarcely believe Mr. Spiller would be guilty of."

[1] E. E. Fournier d'Albe, op. cit., p. 226.

H

The earlier part of Crookes's book on spiritualism deals with his investigation of those mediums in whom he interested himself, including D. D. Home, before the séances with Florence Cook in the early part of 1874. The latter part of the book is devoted exclusively to Florence Cook. It is in the earlier section that Crookes demonstrated rather clearly his intolerance of criticism, and his extreme readiness to reply to it in his psychical research activities other than those connected with Florence Cook. The following extracts are sufficient to document the point made:

> "But with reference to myself he has further mis-stated and distorted the aim and nature of my investigations . . . so that I feel constrained to protest against his manifest unfairness, prejudice, and incapacity to deal with the subject and my connexion with it." (p. 46.)
>
> "The review is so full of perverse, prejudiced, or unwarranted mis-statements, that it is impossible to take note of them all." (p. 53.)
>
> "This spiteful statement is utterly false." (p. 55.)
>
> "I forbear to characterize with fitting terms the spirit of this attack upon a scientific worker; it is enough that I have proved that in ten distinct instances the reviewer has deliberately calumniated me." (p. 61.)
>
> "For six months past false and injurious reports concerning me and my recent investigations have been assiduously circulated in scientific circles." (p. 67.)

Against this background it seems curious and sharply out of character that Crookes seems to have made no attempt whatever to defend himself against the provocative comments which were made in print as early as 1875 regarding his possible emotional involvement with Florence Cook, or with the allegedly materialized form of Katie King. It will be remembered that John Nevil Maskelyne remarked in print in 1876[1] on "the 'gush' upon her loveliness" in which Crookes had indulged in describing Katie King in his letter to *The Spiritualist*, and Maurice Davies had said what he thought about it all in very suggestive terms.

[1] *Modern Spiritualism* (London, 1876), p. 145. Cf. William Marriott, the conjurer, who, writing in 1910, drew renewed attention to Crookes's behaviour in "walking and talking with a young woman for two hours, after holding her in his arms and presumably kissing her". (*Pearson's Magazine*, June 1910, xxix, p. 609.)

Some of these statements were close to being libellous and must have infuriated Crookes. He remained silent. The fact that one of them came from an avowed opponent of spiritualism is not material. What is important is the fact that then and later he made no comment on the extraordinary incidents which he himself had allowed to be published for anyone to read, and which had been criticized in a way which quite clearly indicated his emotional involvement with Florence Cook. Yet many years later he was still insisting on the accuracy of his story. For example, on the occasion of his Presidential Address before the British Association at Bristol in 1898 he said that no incident in his scientific career was more widely known than the part that he took in certain "psychic researches". He went on to say that he had "nothing to retract" and that he adhered to his already published statements. His only regret was that there was a certain crudity in his early expositions. Nearly twenty years later he is recorded in a published interview as saying almost the same thing, stating that he had never had any occasion to change his mind on the subject and was perfectly satisfied with what he had said.[1]

The fact that Crookes's published views in later life were couched in these unqualified terms, which after reading this chapter the reader may consider were entirely typical of him, does not in itself offer any proof either way as to whether what he said was sincere or not. His enthusiastic endorsement of the mediumship of Florence Cook over twenty years previously had been published in permanent form in his book on his researches, and had been in terms, as has been shown, which made it abundantly clear to the reader that Crookes could not have been deceived by the medium. According to Crookes, for example, he had actually been inside the cabinet with the medium and the materialization on the occasion of the final disappearance of Katie King, with the key of the locked side door in his pocket. Either Florence was genuine or Crookes was her accomplice. That fact was as plain in 1898 as it had been in 1874.

[1] *The International Psychic Gazette*, December, 1917, pp. 61–2. The interview was with the editor, John Lewis, on 7 November, 1917. It would seem that after Florence's death Crookes's assertions became even bolder and more positive. He is said to have reiterated to Mr. Lewis that he had seen Katie King and Florence Cook together on many occasions, and that he never had any occasion to suspect Florence of cheating, adding, "I am quite sure of it".

In earlier years, at the end of 1874, without the buttress of his knighthood, his honorary degrees and his Presidencies of learned societies, Crookes had adopted a different attitude. Doyle himself, the greatest champion and most uncritical exponent of spiritualism in its history, wrote:[1]

"Without going to the length of subterfuge, he did unquestionably shirk the question. He refused to have his articles upon the subject republished, and he would not circulate the wonderful photographs in which the materialized Katie King stood arm-in-arm with himself. He was exceedingly cautious also in defining his position."

Benjamin Coleman, who had been Crookes's colleague during the séances at Hackney in April and May 1874 said ruefully at the end of that year that Crookes would not answer letters from him about the Katie King materializations. He said that Crookes "did not reply to me on these points, as I expected he would have done, nor has he ever broached the subject since". Coleman, an ardent spiritualist, added that as a Fellow of the Royal Society Crookes might think it "wiser to be silent" and that this "might excuse his studied reticence",[2] although he did not attempt to explain why this silence and reticence had so curiously replaced Crookes's published eulogies of only a few months earlier.[3]

According to Moncure D. Conway[4] Crookes had met Professor John Tyndall, F.R.S., at the Royal Institution during this period, and when spiritualism was mentioned "Mr. Crookes was silent,

[1] Sir A. C. Doyle, op. cit., Vol. I, pp. 255–6. The remark that Crookes refused to allow his letters to *The Spiritualist* to be published in book form is an over-simplification by Doyle of what occurred, which in fact followed the pattern of the odd contrast in Crookes's attitude in earlier years and in successful later life. The first edition of *Researches in the Phenomena of Spiritualism* in 1874 was published without Crookes's consent. According to him he did not hear of it until it appeared. (*The International Psychic Gazette*, loc. cit.) But the book was reprinted in 1903, and 1904 and again in 1926 when his son, Mr. B. H. Crookes, stated that at the time of his death his father was preparing yet another edition.
[2] *S.*, 18 December, 1874, p. 298.
[3] Crookes's attitude at this period would seem to be established beyond doubt by a letter written by him to the medium D. D. Home on 24 November, 1875, quoted by Mrs. Home on p. 218 of *D. D. Home. His Life and Mission* (revised edition, London, 1921) in which he said, "I am so disgusted with the whole thing that, were it not for the regard we bear to you, I would cut the whole Spiritual connexion, and never read, speak, or think of the subject again".
[4] *Autobiography, Memories and Experiences* (London, 1904), Vol. II, p. 332.

and it seemed to give so much pain that he [Tyndall] concluded never to mention the subject again."

Much has been made of the fact that Crookes was offered the Presidency of the Society for Psychical Research in 1897 and that this would hardly have occurred if the Council of that organization had thought that Florence Cook was a fraud. It seems that this is hardly conclusive. After the Sitwell exposure in 1880, to be detailed later, the members of the Council could hardly have supposed Florence to be genuine with any certainty. Probably the truth of the matter is that they preferred not to think too precisely about the matter at all. It had all happened twenty-three years previously and the important fact was that Crookes was by now an eminent man of science, ideally suitable as a President and figurehead to succeed the Earl of Balfour and Professor William James.

There can be little doubt that Crookes enjoyed fame and would accept the offer of the Presidency of the Society with alacrity, for he seems to have obtained satisfaction from being and having been the President of many learned and other organizations.[1] Indeed, as his biographer records,[2] Crookes did not hesitate to denigrate his own son in a letter to Professor Sylvanus Thompson, when he thought that his hoped-for election as President of the Royal Society might be in jeopardy because of a dispute between Henry Crookes and Sir James Dewar, the head of the Research Laboratory at the Royal Institution.

Although from what we know of William Crookes he was in many ways a somewhat strange character, nothing decisive emerges from what we have learnt about his life with the exception of his reiterated statements regarding the truth and accuracy of his reports concerning his experiences in psychical research. Indeed, in some cases this seemed unnecessary. Why, at the British Association Meeting in 1898, did he think it desirable to state that he had nothing to retract? Did he think that his position with regard to Florence Cook was now so firmly established that nothing could shake it? Many of the documents and letters had been

[1] Crookes had been President of the Royal Society, the British Association for the Advancement of Science, the Chemical Society, the Institution of Electrical Engineers, the Society for Psychical Research and of a society called "The Ghost Club", which even Sir Oliver Lodge thought was of "exceedingly small importance and a superstitious body". See Sir Oliver Lodge, Letters, (London, 1932), p. 82. The members addressed each other as "Brother Ghost".
[2] E. E. Fournier d'Albe, op. cit., pp. 392–4.

destroyed and he may have thought that nothing could be discovered which would reveal that what was thought even in the 1870s might have been the truth. Nobody could know for certain what were the details of his infatuation with Florence Cook. He naturally would never reveal them and Florence Cook was getting on and would surely keep silence. What Sir William Crookes and the world did not know was that years before her death Florence Cook *had* spoken to another partner in her sexually adventurous life. And that partner himself spoke too.

CHAPTER SIX

LATER REVELATIONS
ABOUT WILLIAM CROOKES

IN JUNE 1922 a gentleman called at the offices of the Society for Psychical Research and asked to see the Research Officer, who at that time was Dr. E. J. Dingwall. He gave his name as Francis G. H. Anderson and said that he thought it his duty to reveal in the strictest confidence what Florence Cook had told him when they were having an affair many years before. He said that Florence was quite irresistible, that he had never met any other woman so well versed in the art of love and that her enthusiasm and pleasure made her an ideal companion. One night, he continued, she told him, rather to his astonishment, that her mediumship (concerning which he knew very little) was fraudulent and that she had had an affair with William Crookes, the famous séances being used for cover purposes. He then instructed Dr. Dingwall to tell no one of his statement, but to put the secret document in a file which was to be opened only when instructions were given.

Dr. Dingwall himself was not much surprised at what Mr. Anderson had told him. He had never believed in Florence Cook, and that she had been having an affair with Crookes seemed indicated by the contemporary documents. But there was no proof, and Mr. Anderson did not say enough to satisfy him as to the truth of the story.

In 1949 Mrs. K. M. Goldney (Organizing Secretary of the Society for Psychical Research) telephoned Dr. Dingwall to say that a Mr. A had just told her full details concerning an alleged love affair between Florence Cook and Sir William Crookes. Did he know anything about it? To this question he replied by another, "Was Mr. A Mr. Anderson?", to which Mrs. Goldney said, "Yes, but how did you know?". Dr. Dingwall then told Mrs. Goldney that he had known of the story for twenty-seven years but had had instructions to tell no living person. Thereupon Mrs. Goldney said that Mr. Anderson had told a much fuller story together with other facts all, or nearly all, of which could presumably be verified.

On 23 November, 1949, Mr. Anderson made his longer and more detailed statement to Mrs. K. M. Goldney. Notes of this narrative were taken by her and on 4 December, 1949, Mr. Anderson visited the S.P.R. rooms and dictated and signed a statement in the presence of Mrs. Goldney, Dr. E. J. Dingwall and Mr. W. H. Salter. These two enlarged accounts were placed in the Society's files. They were designated as confidential because in 1949 both Mr. and Mrs. Anderson were still alive. According to Mrs. Goldney there is no reason to doubt the general accuracy of Mr. Anderson's testimony. She knew him very well, and he was her neighbour from 1937 to 1947. It is true that when he made his more detailed statement in 1949 he was seventy-nine years old, but according to Mrs. Goldney his mental capacity at the time was exceptional for a man of his age. He was in fact still teaching Latin, Greek, French and English at a London coaching establishment. During the 1939–45 war he was a master in one of England's most famous public schools in place of a younger man away on military service.

Mr. Anderson was an Englishman of considerable education and intellectual attainment, and formerly held a distinguished appointment in the government service in India. He said that in 1893 he became the lover of Mrs. Elgie Corner, formerly Florence Cook, on the occasion of a visit to her house. Mr. Anderson discussed with Florence her famous séances with Sir William Crookes in 1874 and, according to him, she told him that the phenomena were fraudulent and that Crookes knew that they were. He and Florence were, however, having a secret affair and the forty-one-year-old scientist was infatuated with the beautiful eighteen-year old medium.[1] Because of his infatuation he had to endorse her mediumship publicly and protect her from exposure at the séances.

Mr. Anderson's account must of course be considered in some detail. In the winter of 1892, according to him, he was a graduate of Balliol College, Oxford (he took a first in Greats earlier that year), and was preparing for the appropriate examination for government service in India. His mother was moderately interested

---

[1] During the relevant period Lady Crookes would be in advanced pregnancy. Her last child, Lewis Philip, was born on 2 May, 1874.

in spiritualism and was introduced to Florence Cook by Miss Florence Marryat. Florence Cook was a guest of the Andersons at their home in Portishead, Somerset, and invited Francis Anderson to pay a return visit to her house, Usk Vale, Llanbadoc, near Usk in Monmouthshire. This he did in January 1893.

At the time time of his stay at Usk Anderson was twenty-three years old. Florence, according to Anderson, was between thirty-five and forty years of age. She was married to Captain Edward Elgie Corner who was away from home at the time. Her two daughters, one aged seventeen and one a little younger, were living with her. In Anderson's opinion, Florence was "a very attractive woman". He said that she "was the most beautiful little thing, with a lovely skin—quite exceptional". She soon made it clear to her young guest that she would be willing to have an affair with him. According to Mrs. Goldney's notes Anderson said:

> "She was very highly sexed, and I can remember the scene of how it all started as if I saw it now. There was a large hall with a staircase leading upstairs and bending to form a sort of square as it ascended, so that one looked down into the hall from above. In the drawing-room was a piano at which the daughter was practising. Mrs. Corner told her she must practise well, and she would leave the door open so that she could verify that she was doing so.
>
> She came to me in the dining-room downstairs and said 'I know what you want, I think,' and went upstairs. Shortly she leant over the banisters and called to me 'Frankie, Frankie—come up'. I went up and she called me into her room and I found her very much undressed on the bed. And so it all began!"

The liaison continued for nearly a year, with meetings in Usk and elsewhere, until Anderson left for India at the end of 1893.

He declared that Florence told him of her former relationship with Sir William Crookes, how she had been his mistress, and how they had gone to Paris together.[1] She openly admitted that her mediumship had been fraudulent.

[1] An unpublished letter of Crookes of 15 September, 1874, reveals that Florence Cook did accompany him on at least one journey to the Continent, although according to him the fact that they did travel together was a matter of convenience.

"She used to keep a light burning at night in the bed-room, and told me that she did so because she had so often impersonated spirits and pretended these manifestations at séances that she became afraid that possibly there might have been such things, which might have a spite against her for her deceptions, and she had consequently a dislike of being in the dark.

She told me that she had done all this in collusion with William Crookes (I am not sure whether he had at that time been knighted)[1] and that she had been for some time his mistress; and that the materialization and assumption of earthly life by 'Katie King' (who was herself) was just a device by which she had been able to live in Crookes's house,[2] under his wife's nose, without exciting too much suspicion. For the same reason, she said, she had been over to Paris with Crookes on several occasions."

Anderson thought it possible that Crookes became sexually entangled with Florence before he discovered that she was a fraud, and was then too much involved either to expose her or break off the liaison. He was under the impression that Crookes "got money for Florence by means of the séances", a circumstance which later investigation has shown to be virtually certain, although this would not in itself mean that the sittings were necessarily fraudulent.

It is of the greatest importance that in his signed statement Anderson included a few sentences relating to another story told to him by Florence which had nothing to do with Crookes and of which no notice appears to have been taken until now. According to him, Florence said bitterly that living in another house near Usk were her two sisters, Kate and Edith, who by means of fraudulent séances had persuaded a wealthy old man named Blackburn to leave money to them in his will. Anderson said that during his intimacy with Florence she used to describe the details of her sisters' frauds upon Blackburn.

Anderson concluded his statement with the following paragraphs:

[1] Crookes was knighted in 1897.
[2] It is true that she did stay at Crookes's house. He said, "During the last six months Miss Cook has been a frequent visitor at my house, remaining sometimes a week at a time". *Researches*, etc., p. 109.

"At the end of 1893 I went out to India and never saw her again. I have retained to this day a couple of photographs of Florrie, which I am presenting with this statement to the Society for Psychical Research. I also have a photograph including myself and the Corner family, but I have not this by me.

This statement has been dictated to my friend of many years standing, Mrs. K. M. Goldney, for the files of the S.P.R., but I made a similar statement to the Society many years ago, thinking it would be in the interests of truth and psychical research that my testimony should be on record in such a well-known case."

As has been said, there seems to be no reason to doubt Anderson's veracity. The circumstantial details of his story are convincing. If his narrative were fictitious, moreover, it seems impossible to understand his motive in telling such a story twice to officers of the Society for Psychical Research in 1922 and 1949. Also, investigation has shown that the broad factual outline of Anderson's narrative was correct. It is, for example, surprising that despite her life having been almost wholly spent in the heart of London where she ultimately died, Florence Corner was temporarily living in a house near Usk in rural Wales in 1893. The extremely curious circumstances surrounding her unlikely sojourn in Monmouthshire, a part of the British Isles with which she had no family or other connexions so far as I am aware, will be dealt with in a later chapter.

Although Anderson was almost certainly telling the truth, the real problem is whether Florence herself was doing so. In this connexion it will be remembered that apart from a critical revelation regarding her sister Kate, which will be discussed later, Florence's testimony was broadly confined to two statements. She said (a) that her mediumship, like that of her sister, was fraudulent and (b) that she had been Crookes's mistress during his association with her in 1874.

Whether Florence's mediumship was genuine or fraudulent, it is not easy to understand her motive for declaring to Anderson in 1893 that her phenomena were accomplished by means of trickery, when we know that she continued to give sittings as late as 1904.

It might be argued that several mediums have made sensational confessions of this kind, possibly motivated by exhibitionism, and have afterwards retracted them, and Florence knew that Anderson was probably going to India in less than a year and could not in any event have spread the story without involving himself in a scandal. This argument could be extended to include the further suggestion that the story of her love affair with Crookes was also untrue, and that she boasted of a liaison with the scientist which existed only in her imagination in order to impress Anderson with the desirability of her charms at a time when she was endeavouring to seduce him. It might be suggested that the plausibility of her declaration that she had been the mistress of Sir William Crookes would be increased if she said that her séances were fraudulent and that the scientist's infatuation was such that he was willing to become her accomplice.

These are contentions to which some weight must be given, and this aspect of the matter will receive more detailed consideration later. It is, however, reasonable to say on the basis of Anderson's statement, that he became Florence's lover before her revelations regarding Crookes were made. After the beginning of the affair in Usk, the circumstances of which have been quoted on an earlier page, Anderson returned to Oxford on 20 January, 1893. The lovers "desired to meet again" and did in fact do so at intervals throughout the whole of the year 1893. It was after this statement in his signed account that Anderson went on to describe later hotel assignations in other towns where "in this intimacy" Florence told him that "she had done all this [trickery] in collusion with William Crookes". Anderson, moreover, made it abundantly clear in his narrative, as he had done in 1922, that Florence was adept in the arts of love and irresistibly attractive to him, making it difficult to imagine that any stories of Florence's previous conquests were necessary to induce him to become her lover.

However this may be, there can be little doubt of the invalidity of any theory that if Florence Cook's mediumship was fraudulent then Crookes was unaware of it and published his reports mistakenly but in good faith. The genuineness or otherwise of the phenomena and Crookes's integrity as an investigator are inextricably entangled. It is perfectly clear from Crookes's published accounts that if Florence were a fraud he could not have failed to have been aware of it. Many of the séances were held at Crookes's own house during stays by Florence of as long as "a week at a time" when she brought with her "nothing but a little handbag, not locked". Crookes said that there was "absolutely no opportunity for any preparation even of a less elaborate character than would be required for enacting Katie King". He added that he himself prepared his library as the dark cabinet and that after dinner Florence would walk directly into it and commence the sitting.[1]

Crookes was thus the impresario who chose the sitters, controlled the séances and was allowed inside the cabinet. He said himself:[2]

> "During the time I have taken an active part in these *séances*, Katie's confidence in me gradually grew, until she refused to give a *séance* unless I took charge of the arrangements. She said that she always wanted me to keep close to her, and near the cabinet, and I found that after this confidence was established, and she was satisfied I would not break any promise I might make to her, the phenomena increased greatly in power and tests were freely given that would have been unobtainable had I approached the subject in another manner. She often consulted me about persons present at the *séances* and where they should be placed, for of late she had become very nervous, in consequence of certain ill-advised suggestions that force should be employed as an adjunct to more scientific modes of research."

Crookes's description of the departure of Katie King at the close of the séance of 21 May, 1874, when he was actually inside the cabinet with the medium and the materialization has already been quoted. For him to have been an innocent dupe in the circumstances he himself described would surely have been a complete impossibility.

A choice between only two possible alternatives seems inescapable. Either Katie King was a genuine materialization, or Crookes was shielding the fraudulent medium from exposure, and publicly

---

[1] *S.*, 5 June, 1874, p. 270.
[2] Ib., p. 270.

endorsing phenomena which he knew to rely upon imposture and trickery. If the latter seemingly incredible circumstance happened to be the truth, as Florence said it was, then a violent sexual relationship between them seems to be the most likely explanation. It is indeed difficult to conceive of any other motive which would have induced Crookes to behave in such a way. Such a hypothesis would involve our considering the possibility of Florence Cook having set out deliberately to seduce Crookes after her exposure by William Volckman on 9 December, 1873, following a number of other embarrassing incidents, when her allowance from her wealthy spiritualist patron was in jeopardy.

It seems that much light would be thrown upon the whole matter if Florence's secondary narrative about her sister Kate and the wealthy Mr. Blackburn could be shown to be true. If this part of Florence's story was found to be factual, then the likelihood of the whole of her account being true would be greatly increased.

It is indubitably of great significance that during the intimacy of her relationship with Anderson, Florence evidently told him how the frauds practised by her sister on Blackburn were accomplished. As we shall see later when investigating the career of the hitherto almost unknown Kate Cook, the phenomena produced during her mediumship precisely duplicated those of her famous sister in every particular. Three alternative explanations of this circumstance seem to offer themselves.

The first is that Florence, despite the fact that she declared to Anderson that she was a fraud, was in fact a genuine medium, whilst Kate was able later to duplicate every one of her sister's genuine manifestations by means of trickery and did so with Florence's knowledge. The second possibility, which has at least the advantage of offering a unified explanation, is that both Florence and Kate were genuine materializing mediums, and that Florence was lying to Anderson about herself and Kate. The third alternative, which is also a unified one, is that both the sisters were frauds and that Kate copied the earlier tricks of Florence with which she was completely familiar.

Fortunately, we can make use of additional evidence relating to the Crookes–Cook affair which has also been recorded from another quite independent source. Mrs. Eileen Garrett, the President of the Parapsychology Foundation of New York, wrote to me on 9 April, 1960, to say that a statement of some significance had been made to her in earlier years by M. H. A. Jules Bois, the French poet, dramatist and novelist. Some years before his death on 2 July, 1943, at the age of seventy-two, he had been introduced to Mrs. Garrett by the late Mrs. Padraic Colum, the wife of the Irish poet. M. Bois was then an elderly man and a Roman Catholic, whose conscience was disturbed lest he should die without revealing the information he possessed to a sympathetic psychical researcher.

His story was that whilst in England as a very young man he had had a love affair with Mrs. Elgie Corner, formerly Florence Cook. She was much older than he. During the affair Mrs. Corner told M. Bois that the séances in 1874 had been fraudulent and that she and Sir William Crookes had used them to cover up their sexual liaison.[1]

The importance of this information is that it provides some independent corroborative evidence which confirms the story of Mr. Anderson. The statements of Mr. Anderson and M. Bois, both distinguished in their particular fields, regarding what they were told by Mrs. Corner, support each other, and it would be unreasonable in these circumstances to doubt the general truth of either. The real problem to be solved, however, if this is still possible at this distance of time, is whether the apparently incredible story told to both of them by Florence Cook could conceivably have been true.

We can now follow the story of the Cook family down the years. If it can be shown that there is not the slightest possibility that Mr. Anderson could ever have known of the facts revealed unless Florence had told him, then his whole testimony can be viewed in a new light. In order to examine this it will be necessary to draw upon a mass of new information recently discovered by the author. This material substantiates Mr. Anderson's assertion, and

---

[1] P. Joire on p. 474 of *Psychical and Supernormal Phenomena* (London, 1916) and Dr. A. da Silva Mello, on pp. 392–3 of *Mysteries and Realities of This World and the Next* (London, 1960) both quote Jules Bois as having declared "without the slightest doubt" that Florence Cook was fraudulent. The original comment may have been that which appeared in *Conferencia* (5 September, 1909), and which was quoted by Gustave Le Bon in his "La Renaissance de la Magie", (*Revue Scientifique*, 26 mars, 1910), p. 395. It was the subject of comment in *Annales des Sciences Psychiques*, 1–16 juin, 1910, p. 163, and a letter was sent to Bois inviting him to amplify his statement. He refused to do so, saying, possibly significantly, that he would publish a statement at a later date. Crookes was still living at the time.

discloses in addition details of financial transactions on the part of the Cook family which not only provide explanations of hitherto obscure events, but raise the curtain on one of the most fascinating intrigues in the spiritualistic world, which has never been suspected until now.

CHAPTER SEVEN

THE LATER MEDIUMSHIP
OF FLORENCE CORNER

WHEN Charles Blackburn opened his letters at his home at Didsbury on the morning of 23 May, 1874, he was no doubt very much surprised to hear from Florence that he, her generous patron, was never to see Katie King again. Florence presumably thought that it would be prudent for her to make the sudden disclosure before the account was published that the materialization séances had been abruptly and finally concluded in Blackburn's absence. Her letter, written on 22 May, ran as follows:

"Katie has gone! I need not tell you how grieved we all are. Some people cried last night. I am told she was lovely. She cut off pieces of her hair for every one present and sent you a piece. It really grew on her head for Mr. Crookes felt the hair right up to the skin of the head. I am so sorry she has gone. I am dreadfully lonely without her."

Florence added that she was not at all well and was "very much used up and nervous", which was probably true and quite understandable in the circumstances. The strain of the preceding weeks, her position balanced on a knife-edge between success and disaster, must have been very considerable, and we do not know what difficulties and anxieties she may have faced during the crisis in her affairs which had resulted in the secret marriage with Elgie Corner on 29 April. It is of some interest that although she had been a married woman for nearly a month, her letter to Blackburn of 22 May was signed "With best love, I am, ever yours affectionately, Florence E. Cook". She evidently considered that one revelation at a time was enough, doubtless because she felt that it would be prudent to keep her marriage a secret from Crookes until his final endorsement of her mediumship was safely in print on 5 June.

We can only speculate on the attitude of Captain Corner and

the probable reason for the secret marriage of 29 April, 1874. No child was born to Florence during 1874 so that there was no obvious reason for a hurried marriage. In any event, the delayed announcement of the marriage to 19 June clearly demonstrated that no circumstance of this kind entered into the matter.[1]

It is possible that the secret marriage was a compromise to satisfy Corner's jealous infatuation on the one hand and the absolute necessity on the other for Florence to be able to pose as a single woman to Crookes until the Hackney séances were over. There is evidence to show that the Hackney séances were swiftly brought to an end as soon as they had served their purpose by the simple expedient of Katie King announcing sadly during the séance of 4 May, 1874, that she must shortly bid good-bye to her earthly friends and return to the spirit world. It seems to be significant that this occurred only four days after her marriage to Corner to be followed by the rapid succession of séances ending on 21 May.

It may be that Corner, with every justification, was exceedingly suspicious of Florence's association with Crookes and insisted upon the marriage, however inconvenient the time may have been. It is probable that he was in a position to make such a demand, for if Florence was a fraud he was clearly aware of it from the part he had played at the Volckman exposure even if he was not involved earlier. Florence may have argued that if the allowance from Blackburn was to be secured it was essential that Crookes did not become aware that Corner was her husband until after the publication of his final report on the Hackney sittings. She may well have added that the money would be of benefit to Corner as well as herself, and from our later study of his character we may reasonably suppose that he would not be indifferent to such a suggestion.

Even after this deception Crookes endeavoured to rehabilitate

---

[1] It is possible that a reason for the secret marriage might have been that Florence discovered that she was pregnant in April 1874 and subsequently had a miscarriage. Such a theory would pose the question as to who was responsible for Florence's condition in view of the fact that since Corner, a mariner, was in England in December 1873 and April 1874 it was highly probable that he was away at sea during the vital intervening months. I doubt the theory myself, on the grounds that in such a difficulty Florence would be likely to preserve her ability subsequently to say that she had been married as early as April, and would not have burnt her boats by signing herself "Florence E. Cook" in a letter to Blackburn as late as 22 May.

the attractive Florence in the eyes of her patron. He evidently had some temporary success. In an undated letter in the summer of 1874, after her marriage had been belatedly revealed, Florence was able to write to Blackburn signing herself "Corner", thanking him for his "kind letter and most welcome enclosure this morning". On 15 September, 1874, Crookes wrote to tell him that "all her friends, myself not the least, are very grateful to you for your kindness to her. I have reason to know that your last act of generosity was peculiarly acceptable to her."

This letter happened to be an unfortunate one and may be significant as an example of the curiously unscientific approach by Crookes to his investigation of Florence Cook, displaying as it did an attitude which could hardly have contrasted more sharply with his earlier and more careful work with D. D. Home. Florence had brought the full-form Katie King materializations to an end on 21 May, 1874, when the alleged spirit bade farewell to her earthly friends amidst the tears of the spiritualists. The possible truth of the matter is that the final series of sittings at Hackney were arranged to meet the constant challenges from critics that the medium and the alleged materialization had never previously been satisfactorily visible at the same time. This was finally accomplished only when the séances took place in Florence's own home where her bedroom, with its convenient second door to the passage, could be used as the medium's cabinet. In these conditions, the assistance of a confederate with the disguise of a shawl over her head allegedly to protect her eyes from the light, to imperson-ate the recumbent medium in the cabinet, would have enabled Florence independently to appear to the company as Katie King. If the materialization were accomplished in this way, it was clearly not free from the risk of discovery sooner or later; another Volck-man might precipitate an even greater disaster. Once Crookes's endorsement was safely in print there was no advantage to be gained by continuing it, even on the assumption that the possible confederate was willing to proceed.

In this connexion, it is of considerable significance that the subsequent sittings with Crookes after May 1874 relapsed into an anti-climax of "spirit faces" in an aperture in the Punch and Judy corner cupboard in the breakfast-room in the basement of the Cooks' house at Hackney. One possible advantage of these elementary sittings, which, as we know, had been a feature of Florence's early mediumship two years previously was that a fraudulent medium could produce without assistance the simple effects of the allegedly materialized faces and an occasional hand and arm at the aperture in the upper part of the cupboard door. All she had to do was to stand on the chair inside the cabinet. It was in connexion with one of these sittings resumed later that Crookes, in his unpublished letter to Blackburn of 15 September, 1874, made an observation which seems to reflect oddly upon his critical faculty. He said of a "psychic arm" produced by Florence in these dubious circumstances, "I asked if I might take hold of the hand. Permission being given I felt it all over, squeezed it and traced it along the wrist, arm, etc. It seemed to be a projection from Mrs. Corner's shoulder."

In his letter of 15 September Crookes remarked to Blackburn that "Whilst Mr. Corner was in London very little could be done", which may well have been true. The presence of Florence's husband in London can hardly have been an insuperable obstacle, however, to the sittings as such, for Crookes went on to say:

> "Mr. Corner is not coming back to London before he goes abroad. He expects to be away for several months, and has given me the fullest permission to experiment to my heart's content with his wife provided I do not allow strangers to be present, and do not publish her name."

Corner left London on 7 September, 1874, and by the middle of the month Crookes and Florence went abroad together. Florence was on her way to Wiesbaden to visit her admirer Prince Sayn-Wittgenstein-Berleburg, and Crookes, finding that he had business to transact in Brussels, accompanied her on part of her journey.[1] "I expect Mrs. Corner here this evening," Crookes wrote, "to tell me the final arrangements, but it is pretty well settled, and we leave London on Friday evening and travel all evening via Harwich, Antwerp and Brussels."

[1] It is possible that these adventures of Florence's during Corner's first voyage after their marriage were the reason for his taking steps in the future to keep her out of mischief. However that may be, it is noteworthy that in January 1875 Florence was on board Corner's ship in Antwerp (S., 15 January, 1875, p. 36). They were back in England in February but in December 1875 Corner took his wife with him on a voyage to Shanghai, (S., 17 December, 1875, p. 300).

This incident is mentioned because of its possible connexion with what seems to have been Blackburn's ultimate hostility towards Florence and Crookes. Blackburn himself had taken Florence to Paris in April 1874, shortly before her secret marriage to Captain Corner on 29 April. According to Blackburn's letter to W. H. Harrison of 4 May this vacation was arranged by him "specially for the restoration of Miss Cook's health,[1] and not for séances".

One of the fragments preserved in the Britten Memorial Library was the only surviving portion of a letter from Crookes to Blackburn dated 21 November, 1874, which may have been his final and unsuccessful attempt to procure Blackburn's continued financial support for Florence and the Cooks. It reads "or say you will agree to join . . . extent you will assist with . . . decide upon going into the . . . Believe me, very truly yours, William Crookes". That it was unsuccessful is demonstrated by the fact that it was at the end of 1874 or at the beginning of 1875 that Florence wrote what may well have been her final letter to Charles Blackburn.[2] The points in it which are important can conveniently be listed. The letter from Blackburn to which it was a reply has been destroyed, probably because of its intimate nature, but fortunately Florence quoted Blackburn in several places before replying to his criticisms.

The significant facts revealed by this letter seem to be as follows:

(1) Florence said that she felt "extremely hurt at the way you have written to me".

[1] Florence's health did not seem to benefit either from the trip to Paris with Blackburn or from her marriage to Corner. In his letter to Blackburn of 15 September, 1874, Crookes wrote "Mrs. Corner is not at all well. The last three months have played sad havoc with her good looks and health." It is true that she seems to have had differences with her husband very early in their marriage.

[2] Although Florence was unpopular with Blackburn after 1874 her husband seems to have made a successful endeavour to remain in favour with everybody. Captain Corner was a beneficiary to the extent of £800 under the terms of the last codicil of Blackburn's will, signed a few hours before his death on 15 January, 1891, whilst Florence received nothing whatever. The reader will find that Corner possessed the knack of generally being in the right place at the right time. Thus, in December 1890 and January 1891, when Blackburn was dying in London and Florence was looking after Eliza Blackburn in Wales, Corner contrived to be with Kate Cook at Blackburn's house in Ladbroke Grove, Kensington Park. One of the witnesses of the eighth codicil of Blackburn's will, dated 27 December, 1890, was "E. Elgie Corner, Master Mariner, Oakfield, nr. Usk". When Blackburn died on 15 January, 1891, Corner supplied the particulars of the death, at which he was present, to the Registrar.

(2) She said that there were differences between her husband and herself even after a few months of marriage, which was attributed to her interest in spiritualism.

(3) She said that any quarrel between Crookes and Blackburn was no direct concern of hers.

(4) She said that Blackburn had made "Mr. Crookes's shortcomings the excuse to say unkind things to me".

(5) Blackburn had said that Crookes had been "paying for sittings under the rose", which Florence vehemently denied.

(6) Blackburn had declared that she had lost the power to materialize, which she said was "an utter absurdity".

(7) Blackburn had said that she was dependent upon Crookes for successful séances, which she denied.

(8) Blackburn had accused her of having "a weak nature", to which she had replied saying that if she became "really roused and made a stand no one can turn me from my purpose".

Florence made a valiant attempt at the end of her letter to salvage something of her previous relationship with Blackburn, begging him to "write and tell me that all this is at an end" signing herself "with love, I am, yours affectionately, F. E. Corner". She was, however, unsuccessful. Blackburn's suspicions could not be removed. The old days of "your loving medium, Florrie" had gone forever.

It is of some interest to notice that these events, hitherto unrecorded in the literature, seem to have marked the end of Crookes's active connexion with the Cook family so far as can now be ascertained. Crookes may have been discarded by Florence because he was no further use to her, for evidently his testimonial regarding her mediumship had ceased to be of any value so far as Blackburn and money payments were concerned. And whatever else they may have been, there is no doubt that Florence and her sister, Kate Cook, were practical women of the world who required either payment in money or other adequate consideration for any favours they might bestow.

A final point of interest is that although the mediumship of Kate Cook, which was about to begin, precisely duplicated that of her sister, Crookes seems to have taken no interest in her whatsoever, which is rather curious if Crookes had any real belief in the genuineness of Florence Cook.

It is impossible now to do more than speculate upon these intricate motives and personal relationships ninety years after the events which formed their background, but the general picture seems fairly clear. The evidence that Florence did conceal the fact of her marriage for a time is abundant, and was even the subject of comment by Crookes's biographer. It is impossible to avoid the conclusion that she had a compelling reason to do so. The announcement was made, without any indication of the date of the ceremony, on 19 June, 1874.[1] The secrecy of the marriage seems to be also indicated by the fact that the names of the two witnesses, W. S. Richards and Elizabeth Goodwin, recorded on the certificate, appear nowhere else in the story.

As we have seen earlier, the Hackney sittings were temporarily successful in that Blackburn continued to pay out money to Florence throughout the summer of 1874. Séances of some sort had to take place to justify these payments, and as we have seen, a retreat was made to the breakfast-room in the basement where the manifestations were reduced to the safety of "spirit faces" and an occasional "psychic arm" in the old Punch and Judy cabinet. It certainly seems rather odd that Crookes was willing to act as impresario at these sittings, to send Blackburn reports which tried to put the best face on these puerile phenomena, and to thank him on at least one occasion for his continued generosity to Florence.[2]

Such behaviour by a scientific man, who in earlier years had discoursed with unassailable logic upon the evidential standards demanded by psychical research, is not easy to understand. It seems difficult to explain, except on the assumption that Florence was still Crookes's mistress during this period, that he had made the best of her marriage to Corner and was anxious for the liaison to continue on any terms, and that Florence was still willing to bestow her favours provided that services were rendered in return.

Whether this theory be well founded or not, it is certain that Crookes and Florence were seeing each other apart from séances

---

[1] S., p. 294.
[2] It is to be noted that Anderson recorded that he had the impression that Crookes was instrumental in obtaining money for Florence for her séances.

during this period. In an undated letter to Blackburn after her marriage had been revealed, signed "Florrie Corner" and thanking him for a "most welcome enclosure" in his letter to her, Florence remarked, possibly tactlessly in the circumstances, that she was dining with Crookes that night.

The passions and intrigues of 1874 gradually subsided, and Crookes, with whom Florence probably broke off her association when his usefulness as her guarantor had become valueless, devoted himself henceforward mainly to his laboratory and to material success. It seems possible, indeed, that the enforced sublimation of the violent passions aroused by Florence Cook may have been responsible in part for the single-minded diligence which produced Crookes's most valuable work, which was undoubtedly accomplished between 1874 and his death in 1919, and the honours which later crowded upon him.

Florence, whose married life with Corner was evidently not happy, became a professional medium with a new familiar, "Marie", and her place in the fortunes of the Cook family was overshadowed by her sister, Kate, whose mediumship was now beginning and on whom the hopes of Mr. Charles Blackburn began to centre.

CHAPTER EIGHT

THE MEDIUMSHIP OF KATE COOK

K ATE SELINA COOK was not at any time a well-known medium. She gave no public sittings in the usual sense of the word, and was mentioned only infrequently in the periodical literature of her day. She never made the mistake of seeking publicity or of offering herself for alleged scientific investigation. So far as I am aware, she never sought fees from individual sitters at her séances. They were her guests, and were in no position to suggest embarrassing "test conditions". She is remembered in the published literature, when she is remembered at all, as a younger sister of the famous Florence Cook. Her life and mediumship are, however, of great interest and importance to the student of the "golden age" of spiritualism in the latter part of the nineteenth century, for in her chosen single objective Kate was extremely successful. That aim, probably stimulated in the early days by her mother, was the extraction of money and property on a substantial scale from the wealthy Charles Blackburn.

Kate Cook was born on 22 January, 1859, at Cobham in Kent. Between 1859 and 1867[1] the family moved to their home in Hackney, London. At the beginning of 1875, when her mediumship was hastily and opportunely discovered to fill the breach caused by the loss of Blackburn's favours by Florence, Kate was sixteen years old. I have not been able to discover any published photograph of her[2] but it is reasonable to suppose that she would resemble her sister Florence, whose considerable physical attractions were not in dispute in the literature or elsewhere. Alfred Russel Wallace described Kate as "a very pretty, little, lively girl".

Her correspondence shows Kate to have been possessed of some

[1] Edith Cook, the youngest of the three sisters, was born at 6 Bruce Villas on 14 August, 1867.
[2] See the account of the transparent photographs in the door at Broad Oaks, Benenden, Kent, on p. 163.

117

strength of personality, intelligence and power of expression. She was also resourceful in answering awkward questions about her mediumship, as we shall see. In 1880, for example, Blackburn complained with not unreasonable suspicion that when the alleged materialized full-form of Lillie Gordon was standing close to him he could "hear her bowels growling". The explanation he was offered was not lacking in logic of a kind. She pointed out to him that as much had been made of the fact that the spirit's heart could be heard beating, it was surely reasonable for it to possess other organs which might, on embarrassing occasions, also be audible.

On the other hand Kate showed no originality whatsoever in the alleged phenomena she produced, and appears to have been content that the development of her mediumship should follow that of her famous sister in all details. One possible explanation is that the phenomena of both sisters were devised and stage-managed by their mother.[1] In the early days of Florence's mediumship in 1871, Mrs. Cook, who was a member of the Dalston Association of Inquirers into Spiritualism, may have received suggestions and advice from her associates, and especially from W. H. Harrison, who, like the Dalston Association, was receiving financial support from Charles Blackburn. Harrison, we know, had attended Florence's séances, filled his columns with eulogies of her activities and consistently endeavoured to suppress the communications of even the mildest of Florence's critics.

In February 1875, however, after the Crookes imbroglio, Harrison seems to have had a revulsion of feeling regarding Florence. In his lecture "Spirit People", delivered to the Dalston

---

[1] In more material matters it is noteworthy that when in later years the Cook family virtually took possession of Blackburn's various households, Mrs. Cook was recorded as the official occupier in the directories of the period. Thus, although Blackburn owned and lived in a large and fashionable house, 105 Elgin Crescent, Notting Hill, London, during the years 1884–7 his name is nowhere listed as the occupier. It was Mrs. Emma Cook. When Blackburn bought his country house Oakfield, Llanbadoc, near Usk in Monmouthshire in 1889, Mrs. Emma Cook was shown as the occupier in local directories until her death in 1901. It is indicative of how closely Mrs. Cook kept her hand on the financial reins that although Kate Cook became the owner of Oakfield and its contents in 1891 under the terms of Blackburn's will Mrs. Cook continued to be the named occupier until her death in 1901. A curious and partial departure from this pattern occurred when Blackburn moved in January 1888 from Elgin Crescent to another large house in the same district, 34 Ladbroke Grove, Notting Hill, which he also owned and where the Cooks lived with him until his death in 1891. In this instance he and Mrs. Emma Cook were named as joint occupiers.

Association of Inquirers into Spiritualism on 25 February, 1875,[1] Harrison significantly omitted any reference whatsoever to Florence, who had been one of the most famous mediums of her time, and to whom he had given immense publicity in his periodical until June 1874.[2] In 1877 Harrison added a positive and damning criticism by saying, with obvious reference to the mediumship of Florence Cook, and especially to the final series of séances with Crookes at Hackney, that he had never seen an alleged materialized spirit form which did not precisely resemble the medium unless this occurred at the medium's house.[3] If in fact, as seems probable, Harrison was disillusioned by 1875 and was not prepared to give further help to Mrs. Cook at that time by devising and publicizing a new programme of mediumship for her younger daughter, then there would seem to be an adequate explanation for the phenomena produced by Kate precisely following the pattern of Florence Cook's mediumship.

The first account I have been able to find of Kate Cook's mediumship is by Dr. Alfred Russel Wallace, who described a séance at Hackney "last evening" in a letter dated "December 1875" to Miss A. Buckley.[4] At this date Kate was still living in Hackney with her family. The phenomena consisted of the spirit faces in what appears to have been the familiar and original Punch and Judy corner cupboard used by Florence in earlier days. Wallace said that the faces had a considerable likeness to that of the medium. Kate was described as "a very pretty, little, lively girl". The account of the séance would have precisely fitted one of Florence's early sittings in 1872.

How the Cooks managed to bring Blackburn back into the Hackney orbit is a matter for conjecture. He knew the family well, of course, and Florence had been to Paris with him as we have seen. He was partial to young and pretty mediums, and it may well

[1] Published as a book, *Spirit People. A Scientifically Accurate Description of Manifestations recently produced by Spirits, and simultaneously witnessed by the Author and other Observers in London* (London, 1875). The preface is dated 25 June, 1875. The book was No. 1 of a series *The Spiritualist Library* published by W. H. Harrison.
[2] In December 1875 Harrison and *The Spiritualist* ran into financial difficulties, and it is noteworthy that the Cooks were not among the eighty-two spiritualists, including Charles Blackburn with a donation of £50, who subscribed money to assist him in his "heavy pecuniary loss", (*S.*, 17 December, 1874, p. iv).
[3] *S.*, 28 December, 1877.
[4] James Marchant. *Alfred Russel Wallace: Letters and Reminiscences* (London, 1916), Vol. II, pp. 193–5.

be that his quarrel with Florence was as much due to personal matters and her association with Crookes as to his suspicions regarding the doubtful nature of her mediumship. If there had been any emotional relationship between Blackburn and Florence, then it may be possible that Blackburn was caught "on the rebound" by Kate. It is, however, surprising that he allowed himself to be deceived by Kate, despite his occasional expressed suspicions, over such a long period and by virtually the identical effects used by Florence. The fact remains, however, that he did.

The answer to this riddle may, perhaps, be found in the character and circumstances of Charles Blackburn himself. In 1875 he was a wealthy Manchester businessman of sixty-three, contemplating retirement, and an ardent and generally credulous spiritualist. Emma Hardinge Britten writing of him as early as 1879 said:

> "Family cares and bereavements have thickened around this worthy gentleman's path of late, and compelled his withdrawal from the scenes in which he has so long and faithfully laboured, but he carries with him into his retirement a philosophy which will be a quenchless light in the darkest hour of trial, whilst he leaves behind him 'on the sands of time' footprints of good, that can never be erased from the grateful memories of men or the imperishable records of eternity."[1]

Few biographical details of Blackburn are extant. Brief obituaries appeared in *Light*,[2] and *The Medium and Daybreak*[3] but we have practically no information about him of any real value except that which has been gleaned from his will, from those of his letters which have been preserved, and from the spiritualist journals of his day. He seems to have been forgotten in his native city of Manchester.

The family cares and bereavements mentioned by Mrs. Britten

---

[1] *Nineteenth Century Miracles* (Manchester, 1883), pp. 218–19. The fact that Mrs. Britten's material on Blackburn was compiled some four years or more before her book was published is shown by her reference to him as one of the eleven vice-presidents of the British National Association of Spiritualists. Blackburn resigned from his vice-presidency and his seat on the Council of the Association early in 1879, and later in the same year relinquished his membership altogether. See *The Spiritualist* of 21 March, 1879, p. 135 and 15 August, 1879, p. 83.
[2] 24 January, 1891, p. 43.
[3] 23 January, 1891, p. 54.

almost certainly refer to tragedies which are disclosed in Blackburn's will and its many codicils. He was a widower. Two of his four children, William and Ellen, had died. He was evidently estranged for some reason from his surviving son Henry, and his only other child, Eliza, was an inmate of Brook House Asylum, Clapton, by 1884 at the latest.[1] In these circumstances it is easy to understand that despite all that had happened, this lonely and unhappy widower would be vulnerable to the thrills of Kate's mediumship and to the other blandishments of the Cooks.

The first letter from Kate Cook to Blackburn I have been able to find in the Britten Memorial Library is dated 14 October, 1876, and said that the face of her control or spirit form, who was to be known as "Lillie Gordon", had made an appearance in the cabinet. This letter, like the rest of Kate's correspondence until June 1877 when the family moved to 53 Eleanor Road, was written from 6 Bruce Villas, Eleanor Road, Hackney, and was addressed to Blackburn at his house at Didsbury, Manchester.

On 25 November, 1876, Kate said that an attempt was to be made to photograph Lillie but whether this experiment was successful is not stated in the correspondence. On 8 April, 1877, which is the date of the next letter which has been preserved, Kate said that Lillie was now producing "spirit writings". It is noteworthy that the last mentioned letter was on notepaper which had the addition of Kate's monogram, an idiosyncrasy which was strongly reminiscent of one of Florence's habits in her correspondence with Blackburn in earlier days and seems to be another example of an idea borrowed by Kate from her sister.

Blackburn does not seem to have been present at many of these earlier séances and seems to have been content to receive thrilling accounts from Kate regarding the marvels which were allegedly taking place in Hackney. Kate's early letters give no indication of

[1] The name of the asylum and the fact that Eliza was an inmate was disclosed in the second codicil of Blackburn's will dated 14 August, 1888. However, Eliza was there as early as 12 January, 1884, when "Lillie Gordon" wrote to Blackburn to describe a visit made by her to Brook House in invisible spirit form, where she had seen Eliza excited, improperly dressed and under restraint. If Mrs. Britten's reference to Blackburn's "family cares and bereavements" included an allusion to the breakdown of Eliza's mental health this could clearly be put as early as 1879. The last account available of Eliza whilst still sane is a description of a séance with Blackburn and Kate at Didsbury on 23 February, 1879, reported in a letter from Blackburn dated 24 February and published in *The Spiritualist* of 28 February, p. 102. Whether the final loss of Eliza's sanity was due to her participation in spiritualism is a matter for conjecture.

the names of any sitters apart from her family, and there seems to have been nothing to prevent her accounts being either wholly or partly fictitious.

On 24 April, 1877, Kate wrote to Blackburn to say that Lillie Gordon had finally shown herself as a fully materialized figure, thus completing the cycle of phenomena which Blackburn had found so intriguing in the case of Florence. This letter was of additional interest as the earliest communication I have been able to find which mentioned money matters. It could be regarded, perhaps, as a tiny straw in the wind. Kate thanked Blackburn for the ten shillings he had sent and for some theatre tickets which she said would "make a change" for her. In her letter of 9 June, 1877, when Kate and her parents and Edith had moved to 53 Eleanor Road, Hackney, and had "got a little of the confusion over", Kate introduced into the correspondence a touch of the sentimentality which was later to prove so effective. She said that Lillie Gordon had asked her to send her love to Blackburn.

The earliest example of "direct writing" from Lillie Gordon herself to Blackburn in the Britten Memorial Library is dated 22 December, 1877. It was written in faint pencil on printed note-paper from 53 Eleanor Road, bearing the monogram KSC. Presumably Blackburn must have visited Hackney for a séance at this time for it is difficult to believe that even Kate had the audacity to send a letter from the spirit world through the post to Manchester! Unfortunately all the Lillie Gordon letters were over-written in ink for some reason by their previous custodian. The writing bears some general resemblance to that of Kate Cook but in the circumstances it is not possible to offer any firm opinion as to the authorship of the letters.

The letter from Lillie of 22 December, 1877, was also significant in that it thanked Blackburn for his great kindness to Kate and Emma Cook, "You have indeed done a great deal for them. I am sure they both fully appreciate your goodness. I can answer Katie will do everything she can to please you." It is noteworthy that Lillie said that she must emphasize at this early stage that she was not Kate Cook masquerading as a spirit whatever people might say. She added with obvious truth and probably unconscious irony that obviously she must know best on this subject. The first reference to Eliza Blackburn, who was to become a figure of tragic importance in the developing drama, occurred in this letter. Lillie wished Mr. Blackburn and his dear daughter all the happiness they so well deserved.

During the years 1878 and 1879 the séances continued with alleged full-form materializations of Lillie Gordon. The practice of holding most of the sittings in the absence of Blackburn seems to have been continued, "weekly reports" as he called them being sent to him at Didsbury.[1] In the main the sitters at this period appear to have been confined to the Hackney family circle of Kate, Edith and Mrs. Cook with an occasional friend.

One of these sittings, which took place on 11 September, 1879, is worth describing because of the picture it gives of the puerile phenomena and the credulity of the single independent sitter on this occasion, who was doubtless chosen to impress Charles Blackburn. The guest was Mr. J. F. Adrian Cateau van Rosevelt, who described himself in his account of the séance[2] as a Member of the Privy Council of Dutch Guiana and a Knight of the Order of the Netherlands Lion (Orde van den Nederlandschen Leeuw), a civil order for public services (he had spent over forty years in the Dutch colonial service). The other sitters were Kate, Edith Cook and their mother. The séance took place in the dark.

Mr. Rosevelt felt hands stroking his face and head, and an iron ring which he had brought with him touched his left hand several times. He said that these manifestations were, according to them, also experienced by Mrs. Cook and Edith. Lillie Gordon explained that the tactile phenomena were produced by spirits of a lower order than herself, who assisted her in her mission, conversed with her in spirit language and obeyed her commands.

Mr. Rosevelt, possibly tactlessly, asked if he could meet some of his departed relatives, but Lillie said that as she was unfortunately not acquainted with them she could not presume to invite them to the séance. By way of compensation for this disappointment he did, however, receive a piece of direct writing from the spirit world:

"My dear Mr. Rosevelt,
I am much pleased to see you again. I hope you will be

[1] Cf. "Spirit Drapery", by Charles Blackburn, *S.*, 17 January, 1879, p. 26.
[2] "Spiritual Phenomena in London" by J. F. A. Cateau van Rosevelt, *S.*, 3 October, 1879, p. 157.

satisfied by what I have shown to you, and more and more you will be convinced of the truths of Spiritualism. I hope to see you often here.

Your friend,
Lillie Gordon."

Mr. Rosevelt was both convinced and grateful. He concluded his account in the following words:

> "It will scarcely be necessary to remark how much I feel obliged to Miss Kate and her excellent mother, Mrs. Cook. Indeed, I have not words enough to express my gratitude to this respectable family, the more so as this sitting, and the former one in March were given me without any self interest, and only for the sake of the grand truth of Spiritualism.
>
> All I have read before of the experiences of Messrs. Crookes, Wallace, Varley, Cox, Zöllner, and other eminent and scientific men, I have now witnessed myself, and I thank the Almighty for the great blessing in having it proved to me that there is an existence for man beyond the grave, and that those we once loved are not lost, but will be met by us again."

Sometimes Blackburn visited London for a séance, staying at the Holborn Viaduct Hotel. Once at least Kate was entertained at Didsbury as "a little change from London" when the sitters were mostly confined to Kate, Blackburn and his daughter Eliza,[1] although it seems that once during this visit a number of Blackburn's male acquaintances from Manchester and district were entertained to a séance.

In March 1879 Blackburn began to entertain temporary but very real suspicions that he was being hoodwinked. He was evidently present during manifestations by Lillie Gordon at a dark séance, and discovered one day to his consternation that Kate Cook's chair was empty. His letter has not been preserved, but the replies which both Kate and Lillie Gordon thought it expedient to make on 8 April, 1879, are among the unpublished papers in the Britten Memorial Library.

[1] "Séances with a Modified Cabinet. Slate Writing Manifestations" by Charles Blackburn. *S.*, 28 February, 1879, p. 102.

Kate wrote with restraint that whilst Blackburn probably did not mean to offend her, his accusations had quite hurt her feelings. She said that she was surprised that he should doubt her after all the "good proofs" which Lillie Gordon had given, and was affronted by an unchivalrous suggestion by Blackburn that her sudden illness at the séance after the incident of the empty chair was the result of drinking too much wine. Kate was probably relying upon Lillie's supporting letter to heal the breach, pending the "test materialization séance" with the Fletchers which had been arranged to take place in a few days and which it was hoped would resolve all Blackburn's doubts.

Lillie Gordon's letter, dated 8 April, 1879, exemplified the flavour of her alleged direct writings to Blackburn, apart from the understandable absence in this instance of the customary endearments.[1]

"Katie asks me to write to you to give an explanation about an empty chair. I can give no explanation because Katie's chair was not empty. All I say is that in the dark you must have mistaken your position. I never moved her or gave orders that she should be moved. I am so sorry that you should doubt my word or Katie's. I thought I had done even more than enough to remove all doubts. I am afraid you do not understand Katie's delicate organization. Can you not see that by exciting her mind by your doubts you render her more likely to be attacked by evil influences?

Katie has shown me your letter and I must ask you to forgive me if I now put things too plainly. I notice in it you say 'I shall stop payment'. To Katie's highly sensitive nature this sounds like unkindness although I am sure you do not mean it so. Katie notices every word you write or say, her feelings are easily wounded, one such speech does more harm to her than I can undo.

You must not feel angry with me for writing thus, think when you read this that I am beyond your world and have

---

[1] Blackburn's letters to Lillie were by this time sentimental, were usually addressed to "My own dearest Spirit Lillie" and were concluded by the sending of Blackburn's "best Love and Kisses". Lillie's replies were generally in similarly endearing terms. The tragedy of this childish nonsense is that the correspondence with Lillie Gordon seems to have become Blackburn's principal interest during the last decade of his life.

such opportunities for studying human nature as it is impossible for you yet to have. I love my medium dearly, knowing her imperfections as well as her perfections. She has a sincerely affectionate nature though outwardly she may appear cold. A word or two of affection or praise is everything to her. She is not well just now, I know she suffers a great deal more than she tells you.

Write and tell me that your doubts are at rest and we shall be friends not only in the present world but when we are together in the bright pure home that is waiting for all those who live doing their duty faithfully."

It is possible that Kate's wish to set Blackburn's doubts at rest was the reason for her arranging to have a "test séance" with the American mediums, John William and Susan Willis Fletcher at their residence at 4 Bloomsbury Place, London. This séance was described enthusiastically by Blackburn as "An 'Absolute Test' Materialization Séance"[1] although the results appear to have depended entirely upon the good faith of the Fletchers. It is of some interest that the only letter ever contributed to *The Spiritualist* from Captain E. Elgie Corner which I have been able to trace was dated 17 March, 1879,[2] and appears to have been designed to guarantee the *bona fides* of the Fletchers, possibly in readiness for the all-important séance which was being arranged for Blackburn's benefit the following month. Kate Cook's association with the Fletchers is of importance for she had already participated with them in a séance on 22 February, 1879.

John William Fletcher (1852–1913) was an American clairvoyant and trance medium. His principal control was "Winona", the alleged spirit of an Indian girl. With his wife Susan, who was also a medium, Fletcher came to London in 1877. There are many references to him in the spiritualist literature of the day.[3] In 1881 the Fletchers were overtaken by disaster. Mrs. Fletcher was convicted at the Central Criminal Court to twelve months hard labour for being concerned with her husband in unlawfully obtaining in 1879 a quantity of jewellery and other property by means of

---

[1] *S.*, 18 April, 1879, pp. 186–7.
[2] *S.*, 21 March, 1879, p. 141.
[3] *See*, for example, Florence Marryat, op. cit., and especially Susan E. Gay's *John William Fletcher: Clairvoyant* (London, 1883).

false pretences from a Mrs. Juliet A. T. H. Hart-Davis.[1] At the time of the trial Fletcher was in America, and never returned to England to share his wife's fate. During his later years he became a palmist in New York. In June 1913 the police raided his premises with a warrant for his arrest. He collapsed and died of heart failure. It is of interest to see some of the amusing testimony offered in court which throws considerable light on what may well have been typical of behind-the-scenes activity during spiritualist séances of those days and of the almost unbelievable credulity of the sitters.

The best account of the case, from the point of view of the student of spiritualism, was published in the London *Daily News* of 29 January, 1881.[2] The testimony which is significant so far as we are concerned, was given by Mr. James Maddocks, a house decorator of Southwark, who had been a confederate of the Fletchers in the production of fraudulent phenomena. Maddocks said in evidence that he had been introduced to the Fletchers some three years previously by his brother-in-law, Mr. Poole of Lambeth, who was interested in spiritualism. At that time Mr. and Mrs. Fletcher were obtaining about thirty shillings for each séance, a substantial sum in those days. On occasions their earning capacity was doubled by the useful expedient of giving separate séances simultaneously in different rooms in their house. In January or February 1879, when Maddocks had known the Fletchers for about a year, he agreed to assist in the production of fake phenomena, and a rehearsal took place at the Fletchers' house in Bloomsbury Place, London, on 19 February, 1879, in readiness for a séance later the same day to which, as Fletcher had put it, he "had some titled people coming who would believe anything". In the event, it would seem that this encouraging remark was not without a foundation of truth.

The equipment to be used by Maddocks during the séance, at which all the company were to hold hands in a circle in complete darkness, consisted of a small bottle of phosphorus oil to produce spirit lights, a white handkerchief to place over his head to

---

[1] Mrs. Fletcher's prison diet was, she stated, supplemented by the spirits who, on one occasion, brought her a large bunch of juicy grapes. She was very popular, one of the wardresses, writing to her after her release, addressing her as "My dear darling baby". Perhaps it was she who brought the grapes.
[2] Reprinted in *S.*, 4 February, 1881, pp. 50–2, from which the account is taken.

impersonate a spirit, a false beard and a musical box. In addition a pasteboard tube was to be used through which the spirit was to speak with the "direct voice". Maddocks was to be represented to the other sitters as a "sceptical gentleman" who was to sit between the two Fletchers presumably as an insurance against trickery. When the candles were extinguished Maddocks was to be secretly released from the circle to be free to produce "phenomena". The *pièce de résistance* was reserved for the end of the séance when it was arranged that Mrs. Fletcher would call upon the spirits to produce a spectacular manifestation to conclude the proceedings. The responsibility for this lay with Maddocks who, under the cover of darkness, was secretly to place the coal scuttle on the table.

The following is a *verbatim* account of part of Maddocks's testimony in court as to what occurred at the séance:

"*Counsel:* How many people came to the séance?

Maddocks: Five or six besides Mr. and Mrs. Fletcher.

Counsel: What was done?

Maddocks: I sat near the end of the table with Mr. Fletcher on my right and Mrs. Fletcher on my left, and the rest of the company sat round the table, joining hands. Mr. Fletcher put the lights out. They were candles. He then released my hand, and I got up and went to the musical box. It was a very large one and the winding up made a noise.

Counsel: Did the people say anything?

Maddocks: Yes; they said 'How marvellous! What power the spirit has!'
[Loud laughter.]

Counsel: What happened then?

Maddocks: One of the gentlemen said 'I can feel the spirit draw me'.

Counsel: What else happened then?

Maddocks: The tube was used to tap the guests with. On touching some of them with it they said 'Thank you, dear spirit' and others said 'Oh, I am so nervous, don't touch me'.
[Laughter.]

Counsel: Who used the tube?

Maddocks: I did sometimes, and when I was standing up using the tube, I accidentally trod on some matches. They ignited and showed my face. I thought the people would discover who I was, and I sat down, but to my surprise a lady said she recognised me as the spirit of her uncle or cousin, I forget which, and was highly delighted. [Loud laughter.]

Counsel: And then you did something with the coal scuttle?

Maddocks: Yes. Mrs. Fletcher asked the spirits to do something, and I placed the coal scuttle on the table, and then I took one of the candles from the candlestick and touched them all round with that.

Counsel: Did the table move at all?

Maddocks: Oh, yes, we pushed the table backwards and forwards.

Counsel: Did you use the phosphorus?

Maddocks: Yes, I walked about the room with a bottle of phosphorescent oil to show the spirit lights, and Mrs. Fletcher made some small lights. I showed a phosphorescent light about the size of a half-crown."

This séance was said to have lasted about one and a half hours. Maddocks then gave evidence regarding a second séance which took place a few days later on 22 February, 1879, also at the home of Mr. and Mrs. Fletcher. Whether Blackburn was present at this sitting is not known.

"*Counsel:* At that séance was there a medium called Kate Cook?

Maddocks: They called her Miss Cook. I do not know her Christian name.

Counsel: And did you all sit round the table as before?

Maddocks: Yes, Miss Cook sitting next to me and Mr. Fletcher on her right. When the lights were put out Miss Cook took her hand from me and took the cork out of a phosphorus bottle which she had so as to admit the air and make it luminous, and she got up and went to the other side of the room and put a piece of muslin over her face.

Counsel: What was her appearance then?

Maddocks: She did what they usually do. She appeared as a spirit, and I believe she spoke, but I could not tell what she said.

Counsel: And the John King business, was that done in a similar way?

Maddocks: Yes, and the musical box.

Counsel: Was there the same enthusiasm on the part of the people?

Maddocks: Oh, yes.

Counsel: Were there some flowers?

Maddocks: Yes, Mr. Fletcher bought a few pennyworth in the Tottenham Court Road and threw them on the table, and they were supposed to come from the spirits.

Counsel: I believe you did not come here voluntarily?

Maddocks: No, sir.

Counsel: And you gave no information to the police, but the police came to you?

Maddocks: I gave no information whatever."

It was on this evidence of fraud that the magistrate, after an adjournment to 19 February, 1881, committed Mrs. Fletcher for trial at the Central Criminal Court where she was found guilty and sentenced to one year's imprisonment with hard labour. It is against this background of events in February 1879 that the reader can decide whether the "test materialization séance" arranged for Blackburn's benefit by Kate and the Fletchers two months later in April 1879 was likely to be genuine or fraudulent.

This digression in 1879 from the progressive account of Kate Cook's mediumship is not inappropriate, for it was probably about this time, after Kate had met Blackburn's daughter, Eliza, at Didsbury during the same year, that the medium decided that there was another way in which she could strengthen her hold upon her wealthy patron. The embarrassment of the "empty chair" and more especially the threat to "stop payment" must inevitably have caused the Cooks the greatest possible concern. Possibly

Kate and her associates reached the anxious conclusion that to ensure the golden future to which she and her family looked forward, spiritualism, like patriotism, was not enough. If such a decision was taken, it was shrewder than could have been foreseen. In the following year an event occurred in the career of Florence, to whom we must briefly return, which was to strike a severe blow at the prestige of physical mediumship in the eyes of all but the devotees of spiritualism.

CHAPTER NINE

KATE COOK AND CHARLES BLACKBURN

ALTHOUGH Florence Cook had lost the confidence of Charles Blackburn she was, as will be shown, still friendly with her family and probably watched her sister Kate's moves to replace her with somewhat cynical indulgence. She may have thought that the plans being prepared by Kate and her mother were mainly directed towards spiritualism and Blackburn's belief in it, rather than to the more subtle idea of influencing the old man through the position of his mentally defective daughter, Eliza, and the necessity of providing for her future. Thus, in a sense, Florence was left to her own devices and, deprived as she was of the "assured friend", she had to make the best of it by sitting professionally in public circles and running the risk of exposure unless she was extremely careful. She did not want the same thing to happen to her as had happened to her friend Mary Showers in the middle of 1874 when, at a sitting at which Serjeant Cox and his daughter were present, the latter, not realizing the "rules", opened the curtains when the full-form of Florence Maple was standing between them, which so upset Mary who was posing as the ghost that her head-dress fell off and it was seen that the chair on which she was supposed to be sitting was unoccupied.[1]

In spite of all her care disaster awaited her. This was the seizure of the materialized full-form, Marie, who had succeeded Katie King as Florence's familiar, by Sir George Sitwell.[2] This experience of his father is described in the autobiography of Sir Osbert Sitwell and much space was devoted to it in the newspapers of the times. The séance was held at the headquarters of the

---

[1] See the spiritualistic press of the period in April and May 1874, especially the letters from Cox, Mrs. Showers and Florence Cook herself.

[2] Cf. F. Podmore, *Studies in Psychical Research*, p. 23. The editor of *The Spiritualist* defended Florence on the somewhat desperate grounds that "grasping one of the forms and finding it to be the medium proves nothing" (*S.*, 16 January, 1880), whilst the editor of another periodical went so far as to say that he had "no difficulty in arriving at the conclusion that on the occasion of the recent seizure Mrs. Corner [i.e. Florence Cook] was completely guiltless of deception". (*Spiritual Notes*, February 1880.)

British National Association of Spiritualists in London, and at an
earlier sitting "certain appearances, notably the fact that the spirit
wore stays, excited some suspicion in the minds of the visitors,
and the next time they presented themselves at the door of the
temple of Spiritualism they were accompanied by Mr. J. C. Fell,
M.I.M.E., the editor of a scientific journal, and his wife".[1]

The newspaper account,[2] as quoted by Sitwell, continued:

"The spirit 'Marie' again appeared, and this time the
suspicion of Sir G. R. Sitwell and his friend being excited by
the sound of undressing behind the curtain where the medium
sat, the 'spirit' was seized by one of the visitors, while the
others, pulling aside the curtain, displayed the medium's
empty chair, with the discarded dress, stockings and boots.
The meeting then broke up in confusion and adjourned to a
room downstairs, where all present—excepting the officials,
one of whom took refuge in abuse—entirely agreed with
Sir G. Sitwell and his friends, as to the grossness of the
imposture, and thanked them for exposing it."

In another contemporary article[3] it was said:

"When one of the party had laid hold of the 'spirit'
another drew aside the curtains and discovered the medium's
chair empty, and with the knot of the rope slipped, while, to
make assurance doubly sure, the stockings, boots and other
discarded garments of the medium lay about in ungraceful
confusion. According to the report of Sir George Sitwell and
Herr Carl von Buch, the objects named were handed round
among the strangers and friends present to make certain of
their identity. It is almost needless to add that an official
connected with the show hastened to put the company in
total darkness, or that the persons belonging to the institution took refuge in recrimination and abuse. Sir George Sitwell, Herr von Buch and Mr. Fell put their case fairly and
temperately before the public when they say that, leaving
general conclusions on spiritualism to others, they claim to
have proved that in a society recommended to them as the

[1] *Left Hand: Right Hand!* (London, 1945), Vol. I, p. 27.
[2] The *Evening Standard*, 12 January, 1880.
[3] The *Daily Telegraph*, 13 January, 1880.

first of its kind in England the medium has been detected in the fraud of personation."

After the trouble caused by the seizure of Marie by Sir George Sitwell, Florence evidently decided to be even more careful than she had hitherto been. Although the case does not seem to have excited much comment in England the critics abroad treated it as a sensation and both Dutch and Norwegian newspapers featured it for some days. The Cook family too must have been much perturbed, especially as Mr. Henry Cook had died just previously on 10 December, 1879.

We do not know much about Florence's private life at this time, but there are indications that things were not going too well with her and Captain Corner. Her husband must have been aware that Crookes's effusive praise of her mediumship and his astonishing articles in *The Spiritualist* could not be explained merely by supposing that the scientist had been taken in by his wife, and he may have realized what had happened and consequently made trouble. Nevertheless, he had to keep silent in public since any statement by him as to the true character of Florence's mediumistic gifts would have been seen by Blackburn, or at any rate repeated to him, and such disclosures might dry up a golden stream in which Corner might well still think that he could share, even though it did not directly fall into his own family circle. Captain Corner was no fool: he was a man of the world, a bluff mariner who took a chance when he saw one and was never averse from getting hold of cash when he could. This might well explain the beginning of his interest in Kate.

In 1879 Kate Cook was still living with her parents and her sister Edith at 53 Eleanor Road, Hackney, where the family had moved from 6 Bruce Villas nearby in 1877. At this latter date Florence and her husband had set up an establishment of their own at 26 Malvern Road, Dalston, a few hundred yards from Eleanor Road. The family unity was, however, clearly still preserved. When Mr. Cook died[1] on 10 December, 1879, it was Captain

[1] In view of the comfortable financial arrangements which Captain Corner was subsequently able to make from the mediumship of his second wife Kate, a clause in Henry Cook's will is worth the notice of the reader. It was made on 1 November, 1879, and was an oddly elaborate document in the circumstances, appointing trustees to deal with his affairs, although his estate was under £450 and appears to have been confined to his house. The estate was left in trust to Mrs. Emma Cook and after her death was to

Corner, who had been present at the death, who reported it to the Registrar. The Cooks seem to have been a united family until Blackburn's death, and Florence and Kate in particular appear to have been on the best of terms until 1891. The only written message from Katie King at the last séance of 21 May, 1874, which has been preserved in the Britten Memorial Library reads, "To Kate Cook with Katie's love and best wishes for her future." When Blackburn wrote to Kate in 1879 with what seem to have been bitter criticisms of Florence, Kate replied on 8 April, "I do not understand what you mean about Florrie. Communications received through my mediumship always teach me to be sisterly and it pains me to hear people speak so unfeelingly of family ties." Florence's two daughters by Captain Corner, who were born in the 1880s, long after Kate's mediumship had commenced but before the death of Blackburn, were named after her sisters Kate and Edith.

The first letter from Kate Cook to Blackburn I have been able to trace during this later period was dated 18 April, 1880, and was from 53 Eleanor Road. This communication, which described a routine materialization by Lillie Gordon, was of additional interest in that it acknowledged receipt of a payment from Blackburn which differed very substantially in amount from the ten shillings mentioned in a letter three years previously. The payment acknowledged in 1880 had risen to seven pounds. 1880 was an interesting year in another respect. It seems clear from the payment by Blackburn in April that the suspicions he had entertained about Kate's mediumship in the early part of 1879 had been temporarily removed by the "test séance" in which Mr. and Mrs. Fletcher had assisted. These suspicions, however, returned in a milder form in the autumn of 1880, due, possibly, to Florence's disaster.

In September 1880 Blackburn was sufficiently doubtful regarding the nature of the phenomena arranged for his benefit to address a series of written questions to Kate upon some aspects of the

be divided equally between his four children. Mr. Cook said, somewhat significantly, that the shares of his estate bequeathed to his daughters "shall be for their sole and separate use and enjoyment free from the debts, control or engagements, of any husband and their receipts alone and no others shall be effectual discharges to my trustees". As neither Kate nor Edith was married this precaution seems to have been designed to protect Florence's inheritance from any undue cupidity on the part of Captain Corner.

séances which were causing him disquiet. These are sufficiently important and amusing to quote *verbatim*. The incident of the odd noises produced by the materialized figure's bowels has already been the subject of brief comment in an earlier chapter. Blackburn's questions were not dated, but Kate Cook's answers were made on 14 September, 1880, and the spirit letter from Lillie Gordon regarding the incident of the bowels was written on 28 September, 1880. Blackburn wrote:

"Lillie showed some white calico without any face or form in it next to you and acknowledged to me that I was right. Why do this to deceive me?"

Kate answered:

"I am sure you must be mistaken in saying that either Lillie showed calico without any form in it or acknowledged to you that she had done so. She has no object in deceiving you and has no wish to do so. I thought by this time you would have trusted us both better. Lillie denies saying such a thing to you."

Blackburn went on:

"When I had hold of you in the cabinet Lillie could not appear at the curtain. Why?"

Kate answered:

"If you touch a mesmerized sensitive even with the mesmerist's consent, if the sensitive were exceedingly delicate, it would instantly disturb the unconscious state. It is just so with me. Lillie is throwing all her influence on me so that she may keep solid, and when anyone touches me it causes confusion of influences and therefore she is unable to appear at the curtain while I am held."

Blackburn wrote:

"When Lillie stands beside me, I hear her bowels growling. Why, unless it be you transformed?"

Kate answered primly, "I think you had better ask Lillie herself when next you see her." Lillie's explanation probably approximated to the truth in some respects:

"It is quite possible that you have heard the sounds you mention to Katie. I have allowed many people to feel that I have a heart, then why should I not possess other organs? It happens only when I am perfectly formed and have been so some time. Of course Katie gets weak and the weakness communicates itself to my materialized form. I cannot write much. Why do you not ask me these things when you are with me? I talk easier than write. Sending you my best wishes and love, I am ever your friend in the spirit world, Lillie Gordon."

Blackburn evidently accepted the denials and explanations offered to him and this fact alone illustrates his credulity.

The doubts that Blackburn was showing do not seem to have prevented Kate from giving sittings to selected people. The Rev. Dr. Maurice Davies, who had already published such damaging statements directed against her sister and Crookes's behaviour at her séances, founded a small society called the Guild of the Holy Spirit which apparently provided its members with opportunities to attend séances. Before the sitting was held he conducted a short service for Holy Communion as he had the queer idea that through the religious atmosphere the little upper room in Great Russell Street might resemble the room on the Day of Pentecost. Mediums most favoured by Davies were trance mediums for clairvoyant description and visions like Miss Godfrey, but on 17 February, 1881, the medium was Kate Cook who had been specially invited. On the lights being put out and Kate's right hand being held by a lady sitter, raps were heard and then touches were experienced. One gentleman said a spirit hand undid his necktie and then the hands allowed themselves to be clasped by some of the sitters.

The sitting was so successful that she was again invited a few days later but evidently the results of the previous séance had been talked about and many strangers gained admittance which, it was thought, may have been the cause of the sitting being almost negative. Three months later, however, when the usual *habitués* were the sitters, the phenomena were excellent. Lillie Gordon came amongst the sitters showing her delicate little face by the aid of what she said was her spirit lamp. Finally she stood on the platform behind Davies and exhibited her arm as solid and moved it about in front of the luminous cross on the altar. It is not recorded that on this occasion Kate's hands were held in any way, and the sitting illustrates the mental condition of Dr. Davies and suggests that his derogatory remarks about the earlier Florence Cook sittings must have been aroused by conditions even more suspicious than were commented on at the time. It is clear that he must have had some belief in the reality of Lillie Gordon even though he had little in Katie King, in spite of her enthusiastic endorsement by William Crookes.

An event of first importance in the relationship between Kate and Blackburn occurred three years later. On 14 October, 1883, Lillie Gordon wrote a "spirit letter" to Blackburn from 53 Eleanor Road of which the following is an extract:

> "I hear you think of placing your daughter with Katie. If I may say so you could not do better. Katie will exercise a beneficial influence over her. I told Katie so some time ago. From what I have seen I cannot believe the case a hopeless one. It must grieve you to be away from her and I am sure if you could see her frequently she would get reconciled to you, therefore do not despair for a brighter time is coming for you and her. I am so glad you and Katie are such good friends. She is a good, intelligent girl and so deserves anyone's friendship."

At this time Eliza Blackburn was confined in Brook House Asylum, Upper Clapton, London, under the care of Dr. Josiah Oake Adams. She was probably suffering from some mild mental disorder and it was evidently necessary to keep her under institutional treatment. She was presumably sane in February 1879 when she took part in séances with her father and Kate at Didsbury,[1] but whether this involvement in spiritualism was a contributory factor in her ultimate breakdown is not known.

This letter, written by the materialized ghost to Blackburn through the mediumship of Florence's sister to whom he had now turned, is of great importance. The idea underlying it was brilliant. Blackburn's health was slowly failing and the cancer

[1] See p. 121, n. 1.

which finally destroyed him may have already begun to do its deadly work. Eliza was his pet lamb and he had nobody to whom he could entrust her after he had gone. Why not put her in the care of the Cooks? His dear Kate might look after her and he would see that she would not lose by it. It was an idea worth considering. For the Cooks such a plan was one to be furthered by all the means in their power. If they could work on Blackburn through Eliza then the golden stream might become a torrent. And what could be better than a recommendation to this effect through the hand of one who had already made her home in Summerland and who obviously knew more than the inhabitants of the earth how things should be done? Her medium, Lillie had said, was a good, intelligent girl who deserved anyone's friendship. Merely to be with Kate would do Eliza good.

Blackburn did not at first accept Lillie's recommendation and it became necessary to bring further pressure to bear three months later in a letter from Lillie Gordon to Blackburn dated 12 January, 1884. This letter is informative in that it was written on the engraved letterpaper of 105 Elgin Crescent, Blackburn's first London home, into which he moved either late in 1883 or early in 1884. The Cooks moved into the same house with him, and from that date until Blackburn's death in 1891 they had no home of their own and presumably lived entirely at his expense.[1] It would seem that by this time Blackburn was greatly under the influence of the Cooks for, as has been said, throughout the whole of his residence at Elgin Crescent Mrs. Emma Cook was listed as the official occupier. If she had been the architect of the plan to make sure of Blackburn it had succeeded beyond her wildest dreams. Having once got him they could make sure that he could never escape.

The letter of 12 January, 1884, said that Lillie Gordon had invisibly accompanied Kate Cook during a recent visit by her to Brook House where Eliza was confined. Kate had not been permitted to see her, but Lillie reported that she herself had been able to observe Blackburn's daughter in an excited and distressed condition, improperly dressed and under preventive restraint by two women attendants. Blackburn's response to this cruel

[1] After Blackburn and Kate had begun to live in the same house the communications from Lillie Gordon were evidently written on a blank sheet of paper placed in an unsealed envelope with a pencil by Blackburn, in completely uncontrolled conditions and usually after an interval of some days.

communication has not been preserved, but a reply from Lillie Gordon of 26 January, 1884, is sufficient to indicate its general substance. Lillie said that she would do all she could to satisfy Blackburn's natural anxiety about his daughter and that the following night she would write at greater length and advise him for the best. The nature of that counsel is not available for the promised letter has not been discovered, but its nature can reasonably be inferred from what followed.

On 22 December, 1884, Blackburn made his will which was a long and complicated document entrusting his affairs to several named trustees. Two items are important, and it may be suspected that the influence of Lillie Gordon had something to do with the first. Kate Selina Cook received a legacy of £750 free of estate duty, together with the whole of what must have been the very considerable contents of 105 Elgin Crescent. Blackburn added that it was his wish that Kate Cook would be a friend and companion to his daughter Eliza. The sum of £14,000 was to be set aside as a trust fund for the maintenance, support, benefit and comfort of Eliza, and it seems highly probable that it was upon what was in 1884 this very large sum of money that the covetous eyes of the Cooks now became directed. It is sufficiently obvious that even so substantial a sum in 1884 as £750 and a house full of furniture was unlikely to satisfy the cupidity of Kate and her mother when so much more was temptingly within their reach.

No letters between 22 December, 1884, the date of the main will, and 9 July, 1886, which was the date of the first codicil have been found. Obviously the opportunity for correspondence between Kate in her own name and Blackburn ceased when they began to occupy the same house in London although there were some spirit communications from Lillie Gordon after 1886 which have been preserved. The first codicil was short, and must have been regarded by the Cooks with at least qualified satisfaction. After a somewhat significant bracketed comment that Blackburn had already made a payment to Kate, presumably between 1884 and 1886, in lieu of the legacy of £750, the codicil said that Kate was to receive an additional legacy of £1,500 free of estate duty, with a further provision that should Kate Cook predecease Blackburn the legacy would be paid to Mrs. Emma Cook.

In 1887 Mrs. Cook was still listed as the occupier of 105 Elgin

IIIa. 105 Elgin Crescent, London W.11, where Blackburn and the Cooks lived from 1883 to 1887

IIIb. 34 Ladbroke Grove, London W.11 where Blackburn and the Cooks lived from 1888 until Blackburn's death in 1891

IV*a*. Oakfield, Llanbadoc, Usk, Monmouth, bought by Blackburn in 1889

IV*b*. Rear view of Oakfield. According to the present owner, who bought the house from Corner's trustees in 1930, the superstructure on the roof was added during the Cook/Blackburn occupancy. The reader may wonder why these rooms at the top of the house were necessary and who occupied them, and will notice that similar accommodation was provided when the Corners built Broad Oaks (Plate V*b*)

Crescent, but in 1888 Blackburn and Mrs. Cook became the joint occupiers of another large and fashionable house a short distance away, 34 Ladbroke Grove, Notting Hill, London, where Blackburn was to live until his death. This move was evidently made either in the latter part of 1887 or very early in 1888, for on 28 January, 1888, Blackburn wrote to the spirit Lillie Gordon on the notepaper of 34 Ladbroke Grove. This letter was sadly indicative of the extent to which the lonely and ageing Blackburn was now in the toils of Kate Cook. The former occasional suspicions had been replaced by a pathetic faith in Lillie Gordon, around whom the last years of Blackburn's life seem to have revolved. Blackburn recalled that at the last séance Lillie had told him that his daughter Ellen, who had died twenty-one years previously, had signed a card for him which had pleased him very much. He said that he wanted Ellen to write him a letter, adding that if Lillie could do this for him he would "for ever thank you both. Sincerely with love, Charles Blackburn".

The second codicil of Blackburn's will signed on 14 August, 1888, demonstrated the power which Lillie Gordon and the Cooks now exercised over him. He authorized his trustees to utilize the £14,000 which he had previously set on one side for his daughter's benefit and comfort to purchase a house for Kate Cook and her mother and to engage and pay companions, attendants and servants should Eliza Blackburn live with them. The same second codicil authorized the trustees to remove Eliza if her condition warranted it from the care of Dr. Adams at Brook House and place her under the sole and absolute control of the Cooks.

This instruction by Blackburn presumably referred to what was to happen after his death, but there seems to be no doubt that the Cooks knew of the bequest and set to work to prevail upon Blackburn to bring this plan, which would be highly beneficial to themselves, into operation in the immediate future. Correspondence in affectionate terms between Lillie Gordon and Blackburn continued during the autumn and winter of 1888. An amusing feature of an undated letter written by Lillie to Blackburn some time between August and October, 1888, was that the spirit asked that she be provided with a pencil with a sharper point for the occasion of her next communication!

The persuasions of Lillie Gordon were evidently effective, and in May 1889 Blackburn bought a house named Oakfield in Llan-badoc in pleasant surroundings near Usk in Monmouthshire. It is reasonable to assume from what followed in the fourth codicil[1] and the other attendant circumstances, that the whole plan envisaged in the second codicil was put into immediate effect. If the house cost something like £1,000, which would be a reasonable price in 1889, it means that the Cooks were provided with an income from the remaining £13,000 which would produce about £650 a year, to maintain the house and themselves, and to provide the necessary companions and servants for Eliza as Blackburn had instructed.

It was now a matter of striking while the iron was hot. The Cooks had Blackburn and his daughter virtually in their power and were in a position to demand further favours. These were secured by the fourth codicil which was signed by Blackburn shortly after-wards on 16 July, 1889. Blackburn bequeathed the house Oakfield upon trust for Eliza Blackburn during her life and after her death to Kate Selina Cook absolutely. A further legacy of £1,500, free of duty, was left to Kate Cook and a similar legacy to Edith Cook. Blackburn said that it was his wish that his daughter should be placed in the care of Kate Cook at Oakfield. This munificence was rounded off in the fifth codicil of 29 August, 1889, which be-queathed the contents of Oakfield upon trust to Eliza during her life, reverting after her death to Kate Cook absolutely. It was reasonable for Blackburn to anticipate that Eliza, who was forty-one years old at the time, would die before Kate who was only thirty.

It seems probable that these events influenced the resignation as a trustee of William Holliday Cornforth, a business friend of Blackburn, who had been named in the original will and was to re-ceive the considerable sum in those days of £1,000 for his services. Whether Cornforth could no longer conscientiously be a party to the making over of such substantial gifts of money and property to an adventuress like Kate Cook is not known. He did, however, ask to be released from his responsibility, and in the sixth codicil of 8 January, 1890, this was made effective and the legacy of £1,000 revoked. He was replaced by James W. Slater.

[1] The third codicil of 6 November, 1888, was very short and merely appointed Alfred Leaf, a solicitor, as a third executor.

The enjoyment by the Cooks of the substantial annual sum I have mentioned which in 1889 would be ample for the purpose for which it was provided, depended upon Eliza Blackburn being looked after at Oakfield. Surprisingly enough it seems that in 1890 and the early part of 1891 Kate's sister Florence lived at Oakfield and presumably undertook the care of Blackburn's daughter. This is shown by the fact that when Captain Corner witnessed the eighth codicil of Blackburn's will on 27 December, 1890, he gave his address as Oakfield, near Usk. A similar address was used by him when he reported the death of Charles Blackburn to the Registrar on 16 January, 1891. Mr. T. P. Holmes-Watkins, the Solicitor and Clerk to Pontypool Rural District Council, writing to the author in July 1960, said that he remembered Captain and Mrs. Corner with their two daughters living at Oakfield and afterwards moving to another house in Usk named Usk Vale "round about 1890".

As has been shown earlier, the Cooks were a united family at this time, sharing the bounty of their generous patron. Indeed, the only difference between this period and the early days of Florence's allowance, apart from the relative amounts of money involved, was that Kate had replaced Florence after the imbroglio with Crookes as a medium acceptable to Blackburn. No doubt Florence and Captain Corner were very willing to give up their house in Dalston and accept a free home in beautiful and healthful surroundings at Oakfield. It is possible that Florence was additionally remunerated for her attentions to Eliza out of the income provided, in some way which satisfied the requirements of the codicil. She may have been described as a "companion" to Eliza. As Captain Corner was a mariner it was clearly of no importance where he lived in England whilst not away at sea.

It may be urged that it is curious that Blackburn did not insist that Kate and Emma Cook themselves lived at Oakfield in strict conformity with the terms of the codicil to look after Eliza, particularly as after the end of 1874 he seems to have regarded Florence with dislike and suspicion. The truth of the matter may be that Blackburn was probably a very sick man indeed for a considerable period before his death from cancer in January 1891. In his last letter to Lillie Gordon of 4 January, 1891, he said that his condition had not been suitable for séances for many months. He may well have put his own comfort before that of his daughter when he became seriously ill. In any event, he was probably quite powerless to intervene in anything the Cooks chose to do; and it seems likely that he was entirely dependent upon them during his last helpless months at Ladbroke Grove. Kate and Emma Cook must have thoroughly enjoyed living in a large house in a fashionable district of London, for, as will be shown later, one of their first actions after Blackburn's will was proved was to purchase for themselves an equally pretentious house within a stone's throw of Ladbroke Grove.

It seems possible that the constantly increasing bequests to the Cook family resulted in disadvantages to others who had previously benefited under the terms of the original will. In the seventh codicil, which was signed by Blackburn on 17 September, 1890, a legacy of £1,000 to Catherine Messer and all previous trusts and dispositions in favour of Harriette Elizabeth Blackburn, the wife of Blackburn's son Henry, were revoked. Three months later, in the eighth codicil of 27 December, 1890, the trustees were additionally authorized at any time on the written direction of Kate Cook to provide a sum up to £2,000 or thereabouts for the purchase of a house in the south of England as a winter residence for Kate and Eliza Blackburn, where Eliza was to live entirely as directed by Kate Cook. The furniture for this house was to be provided from the estate. After the death of Eliza Blackburn the house and its contents were to become the property of Kate Cook absolutely. It is of great interest to notice that one of the witnesses to Blackburn's signature of this codicil in London was Captain Corner.

Charles Blackburn's life was now approaching its end and on 4 January, 1891, he wrote his last letter to Lillie Gordon:

> 34 Ladbroke Grove,
> Kensington Park Gardens,
> London W.

"My own dearest Spirit Lillie,
    You have written often to me for years and I want in my prostration a few lines of comfort from you, written with the enclosed lead pencil, *on the back of this letter*—and replace it where you take this from—*viz* my bed-room drawer.

From your side *can you see* if the doctors are working correctly for my restoration, and if *you don't know* can't you see Pierpoint or others to assist you in writing to me the best remedy—as I don't want to quit yet!

Of course we have had no séances of late and my condition not suitable for months. Still we know and feel you are about us and hope you will reply as usual and put it in small envelope which I enclose with pencil.

With my Love and Kisses, which I have so often received from you.

Sincerely,
Charles Blackburn."

Lillie Gordon's answer to this pathetic letter was not dated but was evidently written between 4 January and Blackburn's death in the small hours of 15 January, 1891. It was written in pencil on the verso of Blackburn's own letter and is reproduced below:

"My dearest friend,

Your letter gave me both pleasure and pain, *pleasure* in thinking writing interests you, pain to think that I cannot give you comfort by telling you that you will recover. All is being done for you that is possible both on your side and mine. Many are waiting to welcome you home and I shall be with you always.

You must think you have had a long and useful life and have been just to all connected with you.

Will you look forward to our meeting not as we have done but in perfect unity and friendship and together we will watch.

I must not close this without thanking you once more for your great kindness to Katie and those belonging to her and she will endeavour to repay you by attention to your daughter who will be happy with her.

Will you destroy this.[1] I have been long in answering it for so many influences are at work in your room, it is not want of desire to write.

---

[1] It is noteworthy that this letter is still in existence. It seems probable, on the assumption that Kate would have destroyed it herself if she could, after Blackburn's death, along with the rest of the Lillie Gordon correspondence, that Captain Corner possessed himself of all these letters for a purpose of his own. It seems highly significant that they were preserved for so many years.

Please believe me that I am *always* with you and am your faithful loving Lillie.

This is not goodbye."

The ninth and tenth codicils of Blackburn's will were hastily prepared and both were signed on 14 January, 1891. Blackburn was to die within a matter of hours and the documents bear an "X" in place of his normal signature. The Cooks must have been active during those last few days. The ninth codicil included two or three small bequests to Blackburn's doctor and his servants but the principal beneficiaries were, as always, the Cooks, *i.e.* Kate, Edith and Emma, who received between them 4,500 shares in the Lancashire and Yorkshire Railway, valued at that time at approximately £5,000. Captain E. Elgie Corner received the sum of £800. The final codicil underlined the intentions contained in the will and its codicils as a whole and seems to have been designed to secure the position of the Cooks.

Blackburn died at 2.35 a.m. on 15 January, 1891, at the age of seventy-nine. According to the particulars supplied to *The Medium and Daybreak*[1] by Edith Cook "he was conscious to the last and passed away most peacefully". In his obituary in *Light*[2] it was said that the Cook family formed part of his household and were to the last kind and attentive to him.

---

[1] 23 January, 1891, p. 53.
[2] 24 January, 1891, p. 43.

CHAPTER TEN

THE LAST YEARS OF FLORENCE AND KATE

W ITH the death of Blackburn the Cooks settled down to enjoy the results of their work. It could hardly be denied that they had been extremely successful. Before continuing the story of their subsequent adventures it may be of some interest to see exactly how they were living at the time of Blackburn's death. Kate Cook presumably was at Ladbroke Grove, on the evidence of Blackburn's final pathetic exchange of letters with Lillie Gordon between 4 January and his death, and it seems highly probable that Mrs. Emma Cook, the joint occupier of the house with Blackburn, was also in London. Edith Cook was there, for it was she who sent the brief details of his death to *The Medium and Daybreak*. We know that the ubiquitous Captain Corner had arranged to be in London at the right time, for he was a witness to the eighth codicil of Blackburn's will signed on 27 December, 1890, and he supplied the details to the Registrar of Blackburn's death, at which he was present, on 16 January, 1891. It is probable that since Blackburn died at 2.35 a.m. on 15 January, Corner was at 34 Ladbroke Grove on 14 January when he was named as a beneficiary in the final codicil of Blackburn's will made on that day.

The available evidence points to the fact that Florence was at Oakfield, Usk, at the time of Blackburn's death, deputizing for Kate and Emma Cook in the care of Eliza Blackburn so as to satisfy the conditions under which the Cooks were receiving their substantial income. On 11 February, 1891, probate of Blackburn's will and all its codicils was granted, and it is possible that Florence would then become aware for the first time of the full extent to which her sister Kate, and to a lesser degree Edith and Mrs. Emma Cook, had benefited from their association with Blackburn.

It will be recalled, against the background of the value of money in 1891, that on Blackburn's death Kate Cook inherited £1,500 free of duty under the terms of the first codicil, a further and similar duty-free legacy by the fourth codicil and one-third of

Blackburn's shares in the Lancashire and Yorkshire Railway stock amounting to £1,650 under the terms of the final codicil of 14 January, 1891, a total of £4,650. Under the main will of 22 December, 1884, she also inherited all the furniture, paintings, silver plate and other household effects contained in Blackburns' London home. She could look forward to inheriting the house at Usk with its entire contents after Eliza Blackburn's death, and under the terms of the eighth codicil of 27 December, 1890, she had the right to request Blackburn's trustees at any time to expend £2,000 on the purchase of a house in the south of England, which she would also inherit at the death of Eliza Blackburn.

Edith Cook inherited £1,500 free of duty under the fourth codicil and £1,650 from the Railway stock under the terms of the final codicil. Mrs. Emma Cook received £1,650 only, being a third share of the Railway stock bequeathed by Blackburn to the Cooks, whilst Captain Corner received £800 by the final codicil executed on the day immediately before Blackburn's death. As has been shown, it is extremely probable that Kate and Emma Cook also enjoyed an income of approximately £650 per annum for the maintenance of the house at Usk. Florence Corner alone received nothing whatsoever, and died thirteen years later in poverty.

It would be surprising if she was not distressed and resentful when the terms of the will were published, and it is extremely probable that it was this event which caused the breach between Florence and the remainder of the family.[1] It is also possible that Florence told Kate and her mother with indignation that they could arrange to look after Eliza Blackburn themselves in the future. However this may be, it is certain that by January 1893 when Anderson visited Florence at Usk she had moved from Oakfield to Usk Vale, and this is additionally demonstrated by a writer in 1894 who described a visit to Florence Corner's house in Wales.[2] A directory for 1895, the first published in the Usk district for some years, puts the matter beyond doubt, for Mrs. Cook was shown as the occupier of Oakfield, whilst Captain Corner was the occupier of another house called Usk Vale. These circumstances would seem to justify the bitter comment by Florence to

---

[1] As will be shown later Mrs. Emma Cook divided her estate between Kate and Edith Cook.
[2] L., 15 December, 1894.

Anderson in January 1893 that her sisters, Kate and Edith, living at a different house nearby in Usk, had persuaded a wealthy old man named Blackburn to bequeath considerable sums of money to them by means of fraudulent spiritualism, facts which Anderson could not possibly have known himself.

Where Captain Corner stood amidst this family division is a matter for speculation. He seems to have been a practical man of affairs in that he arranged to be in London at the right time in order to obtain some benefit from Blackburn's will even though his wife failed to do so. We have no means of knowing what his relations were with Kate Cook in 1891, and whether any regard he may have had for her was influenced by the fact that she was now in very comfortable financial circumstances by the standards of the late nineteenth century.

It would seem therefore that although he moved to Usk Vale with Florence he did not take any active part in the family quarrel. In any event, he was presumably away at sea a good deal and may not have spent much time with his wife. He was not there during Anderson's visit, and his name was not mentioned by the contributor to *Light* who visited Florence in Wales. Similarly although Captain Corner was later described in the records of the time as the occupier of 20 Battersea Rise, London, where Florence spent the last years of her life, he was evidently not with her when she died.

The directory issued by Kelly for 1891 is the last showing Mrs. Emma Cook and Charles Blackburn as the joint occupiers of 34 Ladbroke Grove. The issue of 1892 shows Mrs. Cook as the occupier of 7 Arundel Gardens, an occupation which continued until Mrs. Cook's death in 1901. This information is of twofold interest. No. 7 Arundel Gardens was, in 1891, a fine house in a first-class London residential district, substantially built of brick with a columned portico and stucco enrichments, and four storeys in height. Arundel Gardens itself is a short road joining Kensington Park Road and Ladbroke Grove parallel with Elgin Crescent, which itself extends on either side of Ladbroke Grove. Obviously Kate Cook and her mother had no intention of moving out of the select residential district to which they had become accustomed during the years that they had lived with Blackburn. It is equally obvious that Arundel Gardens was beyond their means, and it was quite possibly the purchase of this house and the cost of maintaining it which explains how much of the very considerable sum of money obtained from Blackburn was quickly dissipated in the following years. It is also noteworthy that Mrs. Cook kept her hand very firmly on the reins, in that she was listed as the official occupier of the house for the remainder of her life, despite the fact that it had obviously been purchased with Kate's money.

The decline in the fortunes of the family is first demonstrated by the history of Mrs. Emma Cook, who made her will on 23 March, 1898. This quite elaborate document, which appointed Mr. Edward W. Williams, solicitor, as her executor, divided her residual estate equally between her daughters Kate Selina and Edith Harriet Cook. This division was preceded by specific bequests of an immense mass of jewellery, principally to Kate and Edith. These items, which are listed in Mrs. Cook's will, must by themselves have been worth a considerable sum of money even in 1898, and presumably most of them were purchased out of the £1,650 which Mrs. Cook had inherited. But when Mrs. Cook died three years later at Arundel Gardens on 15 April, 1901, at the age of seventy-four, the gross value of her estate was proved at only £32 16s. 6d.

1901 was, it seems, the last year in which Mrs. Cook was listed as the occupier of Arundel Gardens. It was also the last year in which she was shown as the occupier of Oakfield, a position which she had assumed from the date that the house was bought by Blackburn in 1889. In the following years of 1901 to 1903 the "Misses Cook" were listed as the occupiers of 7 Arundel Gardens whilst Miss Kate Cook became the occupier of Oakfield. Oddly enough, despite the fact that at Christmas 1904 Kate and Edith Cook sent out a printed Christmas card jointly from 7 Arundel Gardens, in that year there was a change in occupation at the house from the "Misses Cook" to "Miss Cook". One wonders whether the necessity of maintaining Eliza Blackburn at Oakfield following the breach with Florence and the death of Emma Cook meant that Edith Cook was also called upon to do duty in Wales.

Although it is not certain how long Florence remained in Usk it seems that, towards the end of the century, she grew tired of an inactive life. Her husband presumably was often away on his maritime affairs; and at times Florence doubtless hankered after the old days and the financial rewards and excitement of being a famous figure surrounded by admiring sitters. Towards the end of the century these thoughts of the past seem to have prompted her to try once more to regain something of her lost position as England's greatest materializing medium. Sir William Crookes could, of course, no longer be relied upon to act as her manager and astute accomplice: she had to work alone and it merely remained to decide what form her mediumship should take to convince her dupes and above all to avoid a further exposure. It seems that probably after much cogitation she finally decided that the best plan was to insist on being tied to her chair within the cabinet as, knowing investigators from long experience, it was almost certain that she would be able so to manipulate her bonds that escape would not be too difficult. Once free she could then extract the various tools of her trade from where she had hidden them and use them to good advantage while posing between the cabinet curtains as a full-form materialization or producing little lights and other petty phenomena.

Acting upon this decision, she was bold enough in 1898 to accept an invitation from Lieut.-Col. G. L. Le Mesurier Taylor to visit him at his country house in Cheltenham and give some sittings to his own selected circle. Colonel Taylor had long been interested in psychical research. He had for some time been a prominent member of the London Spiritualist Alliance and of the English Society for Psychical Research and only a few years previously had been a tenant of the famous Ballechin haunted house in which he kept a journal of his experiences.[1] He was a careful and conscientious observer and recorder and his account of the sittings with Florence Cook is one of the best which have come down to us.[2]

The five sittings took place from Sunday, 21 August, 1898, and lasted until 25 August. A cabinet had been erected in a corner of the room, the sitters being ranged in a semicircle in front, the greatest distance being eight feet from the curtain. On a chair within the cabinet sat the medium who was tied in a variety of ways by cords, the ends of which were fastened to points outside

[1] Cf. *The Alleged Haunting of B— House*. Ed. by A. Goodrich-Freer and John, Marquess of Bute. (London, 1899.)
[2] First published in November 1921, in the *Journal* of the American Society for Psychical Research, XVI, pp. 499-519.

the cabinet. Unfortunately, no standardized method of this control was adopted and thus the amount of movement permitted to the medium varied from sitting to sitting. Generally speaking, nothing occurred of a spectacular nature; and although hands were seen and a vague figure in white now and then appeared between the opening of the curtains, there was little in Colonel Taylor's opinion that demonstrated the genuine nature of the phenomena beyond doubt. It is true that the figure shook hands with a member of the circle but at the time it was far from certain that the form was not that of the medium herself. Some of the phenomena were at times a little puzzling. For example, at the first sitting the curtain was apparently blown (*not* pulled) in towards the medium as if by a gust of wind, a curious and suggestive effect for which Colonel Taylor found no normal explanation. Since the medium was not searched on any occasion it was impossible to ascertain where, assuming fraud, came the white drapery with which the figure was veiled but, assuming that Florence was able to free herself from the ties, it would have been easy for her to extract these materials from where they were hidden.

The result of the sittings at Cheltenham may have suggested to Florence that perhaps her phenomena, if puzzling to Colonel Taylor, might be much more puzzling to investigators on the Continent. She had already connexions in Germany where she had stayed with Prince Sayn-Wittgenstein and it seems that towards the beginning of the year following the Cheltenham sittings arrangements were being made to undertake a trip to Germany and Poland. Thus early in 1899 she was invited by the Wissen-schaftliche Vereinigung "Sphinx" in Berlin, an organization of investigating spiritualists and others, to give a series of séances. In the Society's journal, *Die Übersinnliche Welt*, the first intimation of her visit was published in the January issue for 1899. Readers were here informed that Mrs. Corner was coming to Berlin at the end of the month and that members of the Society and other persons who wished to know something of her materialization phenomena and who approached the subject in a scientific spirit and free from prejudice would have the opportunity do so so. Members of the Society were informed that she was the medium whom William Crookes had investigated when she was fifteen and Mr. Volck-man's (so-called) exposure was lightly passed over by quoting the words of the famous Professor Zöllner who declared that it was "a flagrant violation of the privacy of a household". The editor of the paper, Mr. Max Rahn, went on to say that at the end of the official sittings given to the Society it was hoped that others might also have the opportunity to observe the phenomena.

In February 1899 Florence Cook arrived in Berlin and a note about some of her sittings was contributed by Mr. Rahn in the February issue. He declared that she was working under strict control conditions similar to those employed with the medium Emil Schraps and consisted of her being fastened to her chair with ties in which every knot was sealed in lead so that it was impossible to displace them. A number of sittings had already been held in subdued red light and under these conditions both large and small hands had been seen outside the cabinet quite different from the hands of the medium and veiled in a white silky material. Before every séance Mrs. Corner was searched by two ladies and in every case it was confirmed that she was clothed entirely in black and instead of underwear wore grey woollen Jaeger combinations. On several occasions she was stripped but it is stated that no white stuff was ever found on her which could give occasion for fraud. As in Cheltenham there sometimes clearly appeared standing for a moment in the space between the curtains a form fully clothed in white.

The sittings that Florence Cook held in Berlin from 29 January until 21 February must have been attended by a number of people.[1] From some of the notes published it would seem that a certain disappointment was experienced by the sitters as naturally they had hoped to see something more exciting than fleeting visions of white hands and filmy figures and were looking forward to seeing a phantom dancing in a circle in front of the cabinet. They expected also to see knots formed in endless pieces of rope, telekinesis and even clairvoyance. Nevertheless, nothing of the kind occurred. Moreover, somehow or other the rumour had got around that the medium had the white material for her hands and phantoms under her combinations, a story strongly rebutted by the editor who insisted that at every sitting two ladies, who were not always the same, were informed of this suspicion and every

[1] The material contributed by the Berlin Society on the Berlin sittings was published in *Die Übersinnliche Welt*, 1899, VII. Jahrg., pp. 32–3, 73, 105–11, 145–9, 185–91.

time were expressly reminded not to be content with any superficial examination but to convince themselves satisfactorily that
these suspicions were groundless. This examination was conscientiously performed and all the séances with the exception of
the first took place in the private house of Mr. E. Andreack, one
of the members of the Society.

In order to give some idea of what happened at the sittings it
may be of interest briefly to summarize the reports of two of the
sitters. The first is by Mr. M. Schnitzer, a reporter from the
Berliner Börsen-Courier, who was invited by the Society to be
present. Mr. Schnitzer appears to have been an ordinary German
newspaper man and he stated that the members of the Society
were neither dreamers nor fanatics. According to him they wished
simply to ascertain the facts and had no desire to be deceived by
simple trickery. When introduced to Mrs. Corner he found a lady
of about forty with clear-cut features from which shone a lively
intelligence. Her eyes were large and grey but their sparkle was
dulled as if a fine veil lay over them which gave them a somewhat
sleepy expression.

While the ladies were investigating Mrs. Corner's clothing
Mr. Schnitzer was invited to examine the cabinet, which consisted
of a firm oblong structure supported on stout iron posts. Curtains
surrounded it on all sides, while the back of the cabinet was the
wall of the room. Inside were various objects, such as a small table
on which lay a writing pad and a sharpened pencil whilst a tambourine lay in the corner. When the medium returned the two
ladies stated that under her black dress she was wearing that day
simple underclothing with black woollen knickers. The medium
then entered the cabinet and was secured to her chair. The fastenings were placed over the upper part of her body, her feet and her
hands and were twice knotted and secured with leaden seals. The
tying up was very thorough and the medium was in a position in
which she could hardly move at all. The light was turned down
and the room illuminated by a dull red glow. The first thing heard
was the clatter of the tambourine and then the cabinet curtains
billowed out and suddenly there appeared out of the opening
an object something like a hand which in the light of the lamp
appeared to be slightly luminous. After having opened and shut
the hand disappeared, only to show itself in another place and then

154

to disappear again. Meanwhile the sitters heard now and then the rattling of the tambourine and a whispered voice coming from the cabinet. Questions were asked and answers given. It was, for example, asked whether Mary, one of Miss Cook's phantoms, and Captain Williams ("Sweet Bill") would show themselves. Mary's voice, which spoke through the mouth of the entranced medium, promised this and almost immediately there fluttered out of the cabinet a veil-like formation, supposedly the materialized dress of Mary which looked like a sort of crape. At the next moment the material disappeared and Mary asked for the light to be extinguished and for those present to join hands. Scarcely had this been done when the luminous hand appeared again, holding the tambourine which the leader of the circle took at the request of the voice. Shortly afterwards the curtain of the cabinet was drawn aside and a white luminous form veiled in crape stood upright at the opening. While the voice was still speaking the form moved perceptibly, both to right and left and forwards and backwards. A crape veil was on its head and to Mr. Schnitzer it seemed that the features were those of the medium. Then suddenly the little table appeared in front of the cabinet and the form laid its head on it, a movement which was repeated.

Various questions were asked by the sitters, among them being whether Mary would write something today. Rustlings followed in the cabinet and then a paper on which something was written flew out of the cabinet, followed by a long piece of crape which whisked past a lady and swept the floor. One or two of the sitters touched the materialized substance. One of them thought that it felt like thin silk, while others had the impression of something rather thicker resembling cotton-wool. Then the tambourine again began to rattle and a deep voice, that of Captain Williams, was heard to make some discontented utterances. He declined to drink the whisky offered to him and explained in a somewhat cross manner that there was not enough strength today to be able to become independent of the medium.

The sitters were now able to free their hands and the phantom Mary, this time small, bent and shadowy, again showed itself, holding the tambourine in her hand. It was then announced that the power was exhausted and after a few raps had sounded within the cabinet all was still. After a short time the light was riased and

155

the leader of the circle carefully drew back the curtains of the cabinet and invited Mr. Schnitzer to enter. Florence was sitting in her chair, her head bent sideways and apparently in a deep sleep. The leader of the circle took her hands and called her several times by name. Opening her eyes wide and staring sleepily around her she asked to be untied. The fastenings and leaden seals were then examined and found to be undisturbed, deep creases being visible on the wrists of the medium on account of the pressure. The ties were then cut and the séance closed. Mr. Schnitzer was unable to give any explanation for what he had seen and in his report he adds that he has to say this because of his promise to be objective in his judgment.

A later report of a sitting by another observer, Mr. R, an official of some standing and a member of the Society, does not add very much to our knowledge of what occurred. He corrects various mistakes which he thinks were made by Mr. Schnitzer and his own account adds the detail that the medium's chair was fastened to the wall and that the freeing of the medium from her bonds could only have been occasioned by cutting. Again at this sitting no white material was found on the medium on investigation. The circle of some fourteen persons was harmonious and good results were to be expected. After a quarter of an hour little luminous floating lights were observed about two inches square with sharp edges and shining with a bluish glow, and after a short time some of the sitters said that a smell of phosphorus or something like garlic was perceptible. After the lights had been turned down sounds were heard in the cabinet like the clapping of hands, blows on the table and conversations between two or three persons. The materialized hands then showed themselves and a full-form clothed in white stuff became visible. The neat feet and lower part of one of the legs of the phantom could be seen by all the sitters. Mrs. X, a very sympathetic sitter, was invited to step forward to the cabinet and a quantity of fine white material was pressed into her hand which she felt along with the warm hand of the phantom. Mr. R was then himself invited up to the cabinet. His hand was seized by the left hand of the figure and he noticed that it had no rings, such as the medium wore on her hand. The necklace which was around the neck of the medium was then brought out of the cabinet and handed to one of the sitters. When

V*a*. 7 Arundel Gardens, London W.11, where the Cooks moved in 1891

V*b*. Broad Oaks, Benenden, Kent, built by the Corners in 1910

VI*a*. Florence Corner
(*circa* 1898)

VI*b*. 20 Battersea Rise, London
S.W.11, where Florence died in
1904

Mr. R was called for a second time to the cabinet the phantom allowed him to see her raised outstretched naked leg, which felt exactly like that of a living person. After some time Mary, speaking English, asked how Mr. R's name was written and a short time afterwards there was heard the sound of a pencil scratching in the cabinet. When the writing had finished a request was made to turn up the light and open the curtains, whereupon a sight of unbelievable confusion was made visible. Table, chair and everything was mixed up, while the medium was seated in a state of bodily and mental exhaustion. The knots were found intact and the medium was freed and awakened by magnetic passes. On the paper block had been written the words: "Dear Mr. R, I thank you, you speaking well about Florrie. We work with difficulties here, because I cannot talk. Your friend Mary."

Mr. R concludes his account by stating that all present were exceedingly well satisfied with the results of this séance.

At a later sitting which Mr. R attended a surprising phenomenon took place. Holding both Mary's hands in his own he suddenly saw appearing at the inner corner of the cabinet where the medium was seated fastened in her chair a long arm, the hand of which came quite close to his right hand. Unfortunately Mr. R did not try to take this hand, which, he stated, had obviously come so near to his for this very purpose. It could not have been an illusion or hallucination because it was seen by other sitters at the same time, among them being Mr. Rahn who sat immediately in front of the cabinet.

In his final discussion Mr. R maintained that the medium, being fastened in her chair which itself was attached to the wall, could not have moved, and he pointed out that after the sitting it was ascertained that everything was as it should have been. Luminous phenomena had occurred without the medium being in possession of any lights, phosphorus or other luminous materials: the phantom showed intelligence and in the darkness was able to write a clearly legible letter: a third hand was materialized although the medium had only two such parts at her disposal.

The Berlin sittings with Florence Cook were clearly of the same type as those which she had been developing in her later years. On the one occasion when the features of the figure were visible the resemblance to the medium's own face was noted and it is obvious that to produce the phenomena exhibited, some release from her fastenings was imperative. Without the necessary details of how these ties were applied it is impossible to discuss them profitably, but it may be pointed out that it seems very probable that the leaden seals mentioned by the sitters were like those commonly used in other European séances. These are without any value for the purposes of security and although their inadequacy ought to have been apparent when they were first used, they were still being employed at the *Institut Métapsychique* in 1925 with a physical medium whose speciality was to show materialized hands when she herself was encased in a sack. The success of her performance was entirely due to her having discovered how to manipulate these leaden seals.

The appearance of the third hand was certainly a somewhat striking phenomenon and from the account given it is not easy to suggest the method by which it was accomplished.

From a consideration of the Cheltenham and Berlin series it is fairly clear that Florence Cook was still able to puzzle investigators who did their best to avoid deception. But, relying as they did on a control by ties instead of holding the hands of the medium, they invited failure from their point of view and the medium obviously took full advantage of it. It was possibly due to these successes that Florence accepted the invitation to Warsaw where she gave half a dozen or so sittings in 1899. Dr. Watraszewski, the medical officer of the St. Lazarus Hospital in the city was in charge and in his report he describes what occurred.[1] The phenomena appear to have been of the same type as those that occurred at Cheltenham and Berlin, but the conditions were much stricter. Although the leaden seals were used evidence was obtained that slipping had taken place and other more secure methods were resented by Mrs. Corner who insisted on being secured in the way she herself desired. Moreover, the fact that she had left her chair was ascertained by an electrical device, presumably without her knowledge. When searched in order to discover any white material for use during the séances the medium was found to be wearing "for medical reasons" a kind of bandage which itself excited some suspicion.

The Warsaw Committee was bitterly disappointed. They could not believe that the Florence Cook investigated by Sir

[1] Cf. *Psychische Studien*, 1899, XXVI, pp. 546–51, 604–9.

William Crookes could be the same person as the Mrs. Corner of Warsaw. Upon consideration of all that they had seen they came to the conclusion that the phenomena could be reduced to nothing but "miserable, badly conducted comedy" and had nothing in common with mediumship. Mrs. Corner, they comforted themselves by thinking, must have lost her power. It naturally never occurred to them that she never had any and that her great British protector and friend was her accomplice.

With the Warsaw sittings this period of Florence's mediumistic activity seems to have ended. She must have at last realized that even a moderate knowledge of how things should be done would effectually prevent her from bringing her new performance the success she had hoped for. Her active mediumistic career before a European public was at an end.

With the exception of a strange episode in 1901 we have no further detailed accounts of Florence's séances. But at Christmas time of that year she is said to have given a sitting at a country house-party in Gloucestershire at which one of the guests was Captain (later Sir) Ernest Bennett,[1] a member of the Council of the Society for Psychical Research. Captain Bennett said of the appearance and disappearance of the figure of Marie that the mystery, so far as he was concerned, was unsolved and unsolvable, and that the séance was one of the strangest experiences of his life.

It is true that Captain Bennett's account was not published until nineteen years after the events it purported to describe,[2] and that so far as I have been able to ascertain it lacked corroboration of any kind. Apart from the single piece of information that the house was in Gloucestershire its location was not disclosed. Not one of the persons present at the house-party was named other than the medium and her daughter. If notes were taken by Captain Bennett in 1901 no mention of them is made in the account of 1920. It is odd that Captain Bennett contributed no account of his extraordinary experience to any of the publications of the Society. Moreover, he was a member of the Committee for Experiments, yet it seems he made no attempt to arrange a series of sittings

[1] Sir Ernest Bennett was M.P. for Central Cardiff and Assistant Postmaster-General (1932–5).
[2] "What was the Figure? A Real Christmas Ghost Story." *The Wide World Magazine* December 1920, pp. 193–6. The article was reprinted in *Psychic Science* July 1927, pp. 113–17.

under the auspices of the Society in order to confirm or otherwise the extraordinary phenomena he stated he had witnessed. Florence had been tied up with yards of material bound round and round her, yet during the séance Marie, the full-form materialization, had come out of the cabinet and walked around. In view of what we know of her sittings at this period the account by Captain Bennett is frankly incredible. Either the whole account was pure fiction written as a Christmas ghost story or Captain Bennett's memory had completely betrayed him. It is another instance of the extreme caution that should always be observed in lending credence to the tales of their experiences told by parapsychologists.

By 1901 Florence had finally left Usk and had returned to London, living at 20 Battersea Rise. Up to 7 April, 1903, Florence was still giving sittings but these, unlike her previous séances, seem to have been very private affairs. One of her most faithful friends and sitters was Miss Mack Wall and from November 1902 to within a few weeks of her death she sat at her home circle in Battersea. Racked by a cough which shook her body she is said to have remained cheerful and resigned to her lot. As Miss Wall said: "She had had a difficult life and done much service, *how* difficult perhaps none of us fully realize". It was at Battersea Rise that Florence Corner died of pneumonia on 22 April, 1904, her death being reported by her daughter, Kate Corner, of 3 Ilminster Gardens, Battersea. There is nothing to show why Florence's unmarried daughter was living at a different address from her mother. Florence apparently left no will and no Letters of Administration were taken out by her husband, who was not present at her death. The famous medium died without possessions, in striking contrast with the circumstances of her sisters.

After the death of Florence Corner we do not know what pursuits her husband was engaged in. But it seems that his thoughts were still directed towards sharing in the family fortunes and the long association of his family with the Cooks made any complete breakaway difficult. We have, of course, no information as to when the idea came to him to marry his sister-in-law Kate. It was legally impossible immediately after Florence's death in 1904, but on 28 August, 1907, the Royal Assent was given to the Deceased Wife's Sister Act, and on 11 October of the same year Edward Elgie Corner married Kate Selina Cook at Wandsworth Register

Office. Corner, who gave his address as 38 Nightingale Square, Balham, was aged sixty-two and described himself as a marine surveyor. Kate gave her age as forty-eight and her condition that of a spinster, her address being 7 Arundel Gardens, Kensington Park, London, W. It is of some interest to recall that Kate described her deceased father, Henry Cook, as a "publisher's agent". Kate had been the informant of her mother's death in 1901 and at that time she had described him as a "mercantile clerk".

Whether Corner was in fact a marine surveyor at this time I do not know. On the face of it it seems unusual for a captain in the merchant service to become a competent valuer of ships, and it is curious that when Kate died in Kent in 1923, to be survived by Corner for five years, she was described on her death certificate as the wife of "Edward Elgie Corner. Army Captain, Retired". The reader will notice other indications here and there in the story that after Kate had obtained Blackburn's money her Hackney background began to recede behind a façade of large houses, expensive calling cards and crested notepaper and a deceased father with an occupation somewhat removed from that of the humble compositor of Eleanor Road. It seems possible that Corner, who also came from Hackney, shared these social aspirations, for on the marriage certificate his deceased father was described as being of independent means.

We have no information as to how long this somewhat autumnal romance had been in existence. The speed with which the marriage followed the introduction of the legislation which made the union permissible would indicate an established attachment. Corner's desire to marry Kate probably arose from material considerations, and may have dated back to the death of Florence. He may indeed, have become interested in Kate at the time when it first became apparent that she was going to replace the discredited Florence and benefit substantially from Blackburn's wealth. Why Kate should have been willing to marry him is a matter for speculation. It is possible, of course, that she had regarded Corner romantically from the early days at Hackney when he was the accepted lover of Florence. On the other hand, as will be suggested later, Corner may have been in a position to persuade her to become his wife.

If there were a liaison between Corner and Kate of some years standing this might provide an explanation of the mystery of why

Corner was a beneficiary under Blackburn's will when his wife was excluded. Corner may have suggested to Kate that Lillie Gordon should recommend a legacy for him be included in the final codicil. It is noteworthy in this connexion that Corner was one of the two witnesses to the penultimate codicil, from which Kate was the only beneficiary, and which ultimately provided the means for the building of the house in Kent where he and Kate were to live during the last phase of their lives.

For some years after their marriage in 1907 Captain Corner and his new wife lived at 7 Arundel Gardens and until 1910 directories continued to name Mrs. Corner as the official occupier of Oakfield. It was, it seems, at about this time that increasing financial difficulties could no longer be ignored. We have seen that by her death in 1901 Mrs. Emma Cook had spent the whole of the money which she had received in Blackburn's will. It is reasonable to suppose that serious inroads had been made into Kate's ill-gotten capital, whilst the income provided for the upkeep of Oakfield and Eliza was becoming less profitable with the decline in its purchasing power as the years went on. Unfortunately Oakfield did not belong to Kate until Eliza's death; and therefore the position had to be at least superficially maintained in order to satisfy the terms of the will. It is of some interest to discover from directories, which were published only infrequently in the Usk district, that in 1911 and 1914 Oakfield appears to have been untenanted. Eliza was evidently no longer living there after 1910.

There was, however, one thing which could be done in 1910 in order to improve the diminishing fortunes of Captain and Mrs. Corner whilst still complying with the provisions of the will. It will be recalled that under the terms of the eighth codicil of 27 December, 1890, the trustees were empowered at any time at the request in writing of Kate Cook to purchase at a price not exceeding £2,000 a house in the south of England as a residence for herself and Eliza Blackburn, to be held on trust during Eliza's lifetime and after her death to revert to Kate Cook absolutely. No advantage had been taken of this codicil until 1910 for the probable reason that even the improvident Kate realized the impossibility of keeping up three houses. It was at this time that the decision may have been taken to build a house in Kate's native county of Kent under the terms of the codicil to which Eliza could be moved and Oakfield abandoned. In 1911 E. Elgie Corner is listed as the occupier of Broad Oaks, near Benenden, Kent, a remotely situated house approached by a narrow and unfrequented lane.

I have visited the house, and informants in Benenden and the nearby village of Biddenden remember the house being built by Captain Corner, so that its lonely position was evidently purposefully chosen. One of the inner doors of the house is still decorated by a glass panel made up of faded transparent photographs depicting Corner, a large bearded man, and a small attractive woman strongly resembling Florence Cook whom I assume to be Kate, together with a number of other persons who cannot now be easily identified.

Corner is remembered in the district as a picturesque and forceful character. He was a man of considerable physical strength with a booming voice and an impressive vocabulary of oaths. A valued patron of the village inn, he followed no occupation, and according to his own account his income was derived from the ownership of property. His wife seems to have made little or no impact upon the people of the Kent countryside. She is remembered, by those who remember her at all, as being a quiet woman who made no friends in the district. Eliza Blackburn, the third occupant of Broad Oaks, was seldom seen and was said to suffer from "a deficiency".

Kate was evidently reluctant to relinquish the fashionable house in Arundel Gardens as long as it was possible to maintain it, and among the Britten Memorial Library manuscripts is an engraved visiting card reading "Mrs. E. Elgie Corner, 7 Arundel Gardens, Kensington Park, W. and Broad Oaks, Benenden, Kent". This situation continued until 1914 which was the last year in which a London directory showed Mrs. Corner as the occupier of 7 Arundel Gardens. It seems possible that by that date the maintenance of the house had gone quite beyond the means of the Corners. On the other hand, the outbreak of the First World War may have been the cause of their deciding finally to abandon London. From that date forward, at any rate, Captain and Mrs. Corner lived solely at Broad Oaks and it is certain that Eliza lived with them, for only in these circumstances could they continue to draw the annuity of about £650 which probably formed a substantial part of their income.

On 25 October, 1914, Kate Corner, giving her sole address as Broad Oaks, Benenden, made her will, the terms of which go far to confirm some of the assumptions I have made. The whole of her estate was left on trust to her husband who was one of the two trustees, the other being a solictior. The trustees were entitled to manage the real estate, and the rents and profits accruing were to be paid to Edward Elgie Corner who with his co-trustee had the right to accept surrenders of leases, arrange tenancies and so on. This provision clearly referred to Oakfield. It was shown as untenanted in the 1914 directory, but by the date of the next issue in 1923 it was listed as being occupied by Mr. John H. Houghton who was still the tenant in 1926. The rent of Oakfield was therefore added to the income of the Corners.

At what date it became impossible to continue having Eliza Blackburn living at Broad Oaks is not known. We have no details of the conditions of the household, except that Broad Oaks was remote from other dwellings and difficult to approach, making the advent of visitors unlikely. Whether the situation of the house was deliberately chosen by Kate, or more probably Corner, for some reason connected with the accommodation of Eliza we do not know. Her mental health was not likely to improve as she became an elderly woman. She was ultimately removed to the Lascelles Nursing Home run by Mrs. Simmonds at 15 Lascelles Terrace, Eastbourne, which was probably the nearest town to Benenden where a suitable home could be found. She died there at the age of seventy-three on 18 April, 1921. At this date, if the conclusions so far advanced be correct, the income from the trustees for the upkeep of Eliza would cease, whilst Kate Corner would become the owner of both Oakfield and Broad Oaks.

Kate Corner died at Broad Oaks on 17 October, 1923. She was sixty-four years old and the cause of death was apoplexy. The details of the probate of her will show that the gross value of her estate was £2,742, the net personalty being the trifling sum of £119. It seems clear that the balance of £2,600 represented the value at that time of Oakfield, which was now let to a tenant, and Broad Oaks itself. It may have been that Kate was persuaded by Corner to make over to him the money received from the sale of 7 Arundel Gardens. It will be remembered that Henry Cook in his will thought it desirable to take special precautions to prevent

Florence's small inheritance falling into the hands of her husband; and it is noteworthy that Corner was possessed of a considerable sum of money, in addition to property, when he died.

In this connexion it is difficult not to speculate on the reason for the incriminating correspondence between Lillie Gordon and Charles Blackburn having been preserved by the Corners for a period of nearly forty years after Blackburn's death. We know that these documents were in the hands of Corner at the end of his life. Is it possible that he had possessed himself of them at a much earlier date? Did he use them to influence Kate in money matters, or even perhaps to persuade her to marry him in 1907? We shall never know the answers to these questions. All we know about these papers is that the collection was sent to the Britten Memorial Library in 1946 by Captain Corner's niece, Miss L. Dixon, who presumably came into possession of them in 1928 when Corner died. How they came into her keeping is not recorded as far as we know. She was not an executor of Corner's will and in that document there is no mention of any private papers. So little attention was paid to them when received at the Library that they were not even acknowledged, and a second letter had to be written to inquire if they had been received. It is quite possible that Captain Corner possessed himself of this correspondence when Charles Blackburn died on 15 January, 1891. He was, as we know, in Blackburn's London house at that date. Lillie Gordon (or Kate Cook) specifically asked Blackburn to destroy her last letter, which was nevertheless preserved and has been already quoted. It is reasonable to suppose that had Kate been able to destroy the letter after Blackburn's death, together with the rest of her somewhat incriminating correspondence, she would have done so.

Much of this private material is fragmentary and a good deal is missing. Miss Dixon made it clear in her letter to the Library that certain of the letters which had been in her possession were of a private and personal nature, and it is reasonable to suppose that these would be amongst the correspondence that was destroyed.

In this connexion it is of interest that Crookes's biographer remarked that some of the scientist's correspondence was not available to him. He wrote:[1]

---

[1] E. E. Fournier d'Albe, op. cit., p. 176.

"But much has been lost or destroyed. This is notably the case with Crookes's numerous letters to Florence Cook as well as to W. H. Harrison, editor of *The Spiritualist*, and to and from a number of other spiritualists. These, if ever recovered, would bring us much additional light."

Copies of seventy-three letters written by Crookes between November 1873 and December 1874, including thirteen to Florence Cook, thirteen to Charles Blackburn and seven to W. H. Harrison were destroyed, presumably with the replies to them of which there was no trace. D'Albe wrote (p. 180):

"The originals were copied into a letter-book and indexed. The copies were subsequently removed, but the index was left intact, and the above numbers are extracted from the index. I have been unable to ascertain why and by whom these copies were removed."

The reader will observe that the period during which deliberate destruction of this correspondence occurred, November 1873 to December 1874, corresponds roughly with the period of Crookes's association with Florence Cook, and may therefore not be without significance.

It should be explained that not all the correspondence in the Britten Memorial Library is dated. Florence and Kate Cook in particular sometimes merely indicated the day of the week on which a letter was written. Fortunately, however, Charles Blackburn in many cases recorded upon such letters the date upon which they were received. Moreover, known changes of address, the dates of which have been established from public records, changes in letter-paper (both Florence and Kate Cook were much given to frequent experiments with crests and monograms) and references to events and persons mentioned in the contemporary spiritualist journals have enabled approximate dates to be established for virtually all the correspondence quoted.

Despite his advanced age, Captain Corner continued to live at Broad Oaks after his wife's death until 1927. By the date of his death on 5 November, 1928, however, he had moved to Poplar Farm at Wittersham, near Tenterden, another Kentish village not far from Benenden. He was eighty-three, and it is interesting to reflect that with the possible exception of Edith, whose later history I have not tried to ascertain, he outlived all the other actors in the drama. His estate totalled the not inconsiderable sum in those days of £4,838, exceeding by £2,000 the amount left by Kate. Thus Captain Corner ultimately benefited financially from spiritualism to a greater extent than either of the two mediums he married.

What were his thoughts as he walked in that lonely garden at Broad Oaks in the years that remained to him after the death of Kate? Would his principal memories be of the warm, irresistible Florence, whom as a young man in 1874 he had so desperately desired that he had agreed to a marriage that was to be kept secret from Crookes and Blackburn until it was expedient to announce it? Or would he think of the pretty scheming Kate who, according to Lillie Gordon, seemed outwardly cold despite her "sincerely affectionate nature", and whose extraction of money and property from Blackburn had enhanced her attractions for a middle-aged man?

Whatever the answers to these questions may be, it will be pleasing to some to be able to record that Florence was not entirely forgotten. Corner had no children by Kate but there were two daughters of his marriage to Florence, both of whom were married and were living in South America. By the terms of Corner's will his estate was divided equally between them.

CHAPTER ELEVEN

CONCLUSION

THE story of the Cook family is now told. Those who have followed the details can now decide for themselves whether Florence and Kate Cook were genuine mediums exhibiting the most extraordinary phenomena and whether Sir William Crookes was right in his judgment regarding Katie King. The story is a remarkable one, whatever interpretation be placed upon the complex events with which it is concerned. One useful way to consider the evidence is firstly to try to decide, in isolation from her association with Crookes and her story to Anderson, whether Florence Cook was a genuine medium or not.

In this connexion the many recorded instances throughout her career of her exposure in flagrant trickery can hardly be regarded as other than extremely damaging. Moreover, the detection by Edward Cox of Florence's friend, Mary Showers, in the act of glaring and fraudulent imposture, wearing the "ghost head-dress" but still in her own frock, is of great significance, when it is recalled that Florence and Mary Showers gave a joint séance at Mornington Road and their respective materializations marched around Crookes's laboratory with their arms entwined. The conclusion here seems inescapable that both were genuine or that both were fraudulent.

As to Kate, her correspondence with Blackburn, the evidence at the Fletcher trial and the other surrounding circumstances demonstrate beyond much doubt that Kate was a calculating adventuress and that her alleged mediumship, in which she was at first encouraged and assisted by her mother, was wholly fraudulent. The pair seem to have devoted themselves from 1875 onwards to the unscrupulous extraction of large sums of money and property from Charles Blackburn, and they pursued their object with cruel and insatiable persistence until literally the day of his death. The fact that Florence was a member of such a family, and remained on affectionate terms with Kate and Emma Cook whilst this swindle was going on, seems to offer a distinct clue as to Florence's own character.

It is also of interest to remember that Kate was able to start her career as a fraudulent medium by stepping into the breach immediately Florence had lost the confidence and favour of Blackburn. The alleged phenomena Kate produced by trickery precisely duplicated the supposed manifestations which had occurred during the mediumship of her sister, even following the same cautious development by stages over the years from "spirit faces" to a full-form materialization. Kate's ability to do this can only be understood if Florence's mediumship had been dependent upon the same tricks. Living in the same house, Kate would be familiar with every detail of the various deceptions. All she needed was the guidance of Emma Cook, which was readily available, and the acquisition of the necessary skill and confidence which came with practice. She started, as Florence had done, by learning the simple trick of freeing herself from restraint (or even allowing the "spirits" to tie a suitable slipknot as Florence did in her earliest days) and then standing on her chair in the Punch and Judy cabinet and producing "spirit faces" at the aperture for the delighted spiritualists.

As for Florence's mediumship, the most damaging inference which can be drawn from the information we possess about Kate is the fact that both girls started their careers under the wing of their mother, who was constantly in attendance at their early séances which she organized and controlled. Is it possible to believe that Emma Cook could have been both the reverent impresario in regard to genuine and incredible paranormal phenomena produced by Florence and at the same time the accomplice and mentor of the fraudulent Kate?

It was possibly in the early days of her membership of the Dalston Association of Inquirers into Spiritualism that Emma Cook decided that it was likely that appreciably more money could be made from fraudulent mediumship than was being provided by her husband, who seems by turns to have been a printer, a traveller and a clerk. Whether she was encouraged and assisted in her purpose by people like Thomas Blyton and William H. Harrison, who also profited substantially from the mediumship of Florence Cook, is a matter for surmise; but the circumstantial evidence seems to suggest that this probably was the case. However this may be, Emma Cook's assessment of the financial prospects offered by spiritualism proved to be right, as she must have realized complacently in 1891 when she compared No. 7 Arundel Gardens, in the fashionable district of Kensington Park, with her old home in Eleanor Road, Hackney.

It is unlikely that as early as 1871 the complete future operation of the swindling of Blackburn, including the moving in to his household of the Cook family and the persuasion and pressure successfully brought to bear to extract money and property from him on an ambitious scale, was planned in detail in advance; but as soon as Blackburn showed his willingness to pay a regular income to the Cooks in return for the thrills of Florence's mediumship, then the possible shape of things to come began to be discernible. The exposure of Florence by Volckman was an unfortunate accident which had to be overcome by whatever measures were necessary, and led directly to the snare set for Crookes and his planned involvement with Florence. If all had gone well, and the chain of events set off by the Volckman incident had not occurred, Kate would probably have not featured in the story at all. But as we have seen, emotional entanglements and pressures led Florence into deceptions and indiscretions which ended in disaster so far as her relations with Blackburn were concerned, and Kate took her place.

Edward Elgie Corner is another significant link between the two mediums. A study of his life with Kate Cook and his behaviour towards Charles Blackburn shows that he was a man who was quite willing to profit financially from fraudulent spiritualism. If this be accepted, then much light is thrown on the chain of events which culminated in his secret marriage to Florence. The inference is that Corner knew that Florence was a fraud and was willing to play his part in securing the allowance from Blackburn, and his reason for attacking Volckman at the sitting of 9 December, 1873, becomes clear.

The weight of evidence appears to show that Florence Cook's mediumship was as shamelessly fraudulent as that of her sister. Once this is accepted, then the conclusion that William Crookes became her accomplice seems inescapable. His position as controller of the séances, his freedom to enter the cabinet and his own accounts of the conditions of the sittings make it clear beyond doubt that he was the one person who could not possibly have been deceived.

The disappearance of Crookes's correspondence with Florence removed any *direct* evidence which may have existed regarding a sexual liaison between the scientist and the medium. It can hardly be doubted from Crookes's own writings and the published comments during his lifetime by Maskelyne, Davies, and others that he was at the very least infatuated with Florence Cook. It may also be significant that a man so intolerant of criticism as Crookes should have refrained from defending himself against the published suggestions that he was "peculiarly susceptible to feminine influences", or that he was "much too far gone for 'investigation' ". This restraint, however, does not prove beyond doubt that Florence Cook was actually his mistress. That can only be a matter of surmise against the background of the story as a whole.

It is in this connexion that I have examined with some interest the romantic lines of poetry which Crookes included in his final letter published in *The Spiritualist* of 5 June, 1874.[1] They were clearly included purposefully by Crookes in his eulogy of the beauty of Katie King and therefore, presumably, of Florence Cook, and throw some light on the problem as to whether Florence Cook was Crookes's mistress and not merely a young girl with whom he had fallen in love. In the absence of the private correspondence, which might have told us so much had it not so mysteriously disappeared, these lines are probably the only direct clue remaining to us, appearing as they do in a letter written by Crookes.

The six lines of verse, so far as I am aware, have never been the subject of any comment in the literature of psychical research apart from their quotation by J. N. Maskelyne to which reference has been made in an earlier chapter, and a remark about them quite recently by Dr. A. da Silva Mello.[2] Maskelyne, not unreasonably, merely quoted the poetry as part and parcel of the "gush upon her loveliness" which, in his view, indicated that Crookes was "too far gone" to be able impartially to pronounce upon the genuineness or otherwise of the phenomena. He was evidently not sufficiently curious to wonder whether Crookes composed the

[1] *See* p. 63.
[2] Op. cit., p. 394.

verse himself or if it was an unacknowledged quotation from the work of another writer. Silva Mello said that Crookes "wrote verses throbbing with the love which had been inspired by the young girl whose beauty he considered to be indescribable", and evidently concluded without investigation that Crookes was responsible for the lines himself.

It may be significant that Crookes did not give the provenance of the verse in this instance, for on page 8 of his book he quoted fourteen lines from Thomas L. Harris's *Lyric of a Golden Age* with acknowledgement to the author. It is germane to what is to follow to remark that these fourteen lines were quoted accurately, showing that Crookes copied them out and did not rely upon memory alone.

Here are the unacknowledged lines:

> "Round her she made an atmosphere of life,
> The very air seemed lighter from her eyes,
> They were so soft and beautiful, and rife
> With all we can imagine of the skies;
> Her overpowering presence made you feel
> It would not be idolatry to kneel."

The precise ten-syllable lines and unusual rhyming suggested that the verse was an example of the quite rare variation, introduced by John Hookham Frere in 1817, of the *ottava rima* stanza, mutilated by the omission of two lines, and it was soon identified as the seventy-fourth stanza of the third canto of Byron's *Don Juan* (1818–21) which reads as follows, the lines *omitted* by Crookes being in italics:

> "Round her she made an atmosphere of life,
> The very air seemed lighter from her eyes,
> They were so soft and beautiful, and rife
> With all we can imagine of the skies,
> *And pure as Psyche ere she grew a wife—*
> *Too pure even for the purest human ties*;
> Her overpowering presence made you feel
> It would not be idolatry to kneel."

A number of inferences can be drawn from this discovery. First, the accurate quotation of the six lines, even to punctuation except in one instance, means that Crookes was not relying upon memory. He had copied the stanza and the omission of the fifth and sixth lines was therefore deliberate. Secondly, an attempt to conceal the omission was made by transferring Byron's semi-colon from the end of the sixth line after "ties", to follow "skies" at the end of what became the fourth line in the mutilated version. The reason for this is fairly obvious; the last two lines were a new and separate thought and had to be preceded by at least a semi-colon. Unless this change had been made the omission might have been apparent. The lines were clearly directed by the infatuated Crookes to Florence as an expression of his passionate love for her, and their ostensible reference to Katie King was merely a fiction, which indeed failed to deceive even critics of the time. Unable to compose verse himself, Crookes secretly used Byron's description of the beautiful Haidee, hoping no doubt that Florence would be flattered and impressed. It will be recalled that at this time her secret marriage to Corner had not been revealed.

Haidee was young, beautiful, desirable and pure. Crookes considered that the lines of Byron's stanza were appropriate in all other respects to his passionate eulogy of Florence so long as the two lines relating to Haidee's innocence were omitted. The conclusion that Crookes and Florence shared the knowledge that she was not innocent seems difficult to avoid.

The disclosures made by Florence Cook to Francis Anderson and Jules Bois can now be viewed in the light of what we know. She said, it will be remembered, that her mediumship, and that of Kate Cook, was fraudulent. She described the details of her sister's trickery, which she said enabled Kate to extract large sums of money from Charles Blackburn, a fact which Anderson could not possibly have known. She said that William Crookes had been her lover, and that their affair had been in progress during the famous séances at which he had ostensibly played the part of a scientific investigator but had in fact secretly been her accomplice in fraudulent deception.

If this confession be true, and it is certain that the greater part of it was true, then the story of Florence Cook, William Crookes and Charles Blackburn is one of the most extraordinary in the whole sordid story of modern spiritualism. Crookes received not only a knighthood and the Order of Merit, but the Presidency of the Royal Society. These honours were, of course, conferred on him because of his important and original scientific work, and it is more relevant here to note that he was also created not only President of the Society for Psychical Research but remained a Vice-President to the day of his death. This Society was founded in 1882 with the expressed aim of approaching the problems of psychical research "without prejudice or prepossession of any kind, and in the same spirit of exact and unimpassioned inquiry which has enabled Science to solve so many problems". The Society's first President, Mr. Henry Sidgwick, in his inaugural address, said that the Society hoped to obtain sufficient evidence for paranormal phenomena to convince the scientific world, and that "however good some of the evidence may be in quality, we require a great deal more of it". It is of some interest to note that he stated, "I do not presume to suppose that I could produce evidence better in quality than much that has been laid before the world by writers of indubitable scientific repute—men like Mr. William Crookes, Mr. Wallace,[1] and the late Professor de Morgan". Such a statement, made only eight years after the Katie King séances,[2] when the exposures and criticisms of Florence Cook must have been still fresh in the President's mind, seems somewhat disingenuous.

Despite the protestations of scientific impartiality, it is quite clear that the President himself regarded it as of prime importance to convince the "advocates of obstinate incredulity", and for this purpose thought that "every additional witness who, as A. de Morgan said, has a fair stock of credit to draw upon, is an important gain". Crookes, in other fields, certainly had a very good stock of credit and so perhaps the means seemed to justify the end. We now know of Crookes that not only did he support and encourage a person whose mediumship, one might have thought, could have deceived no one of sane mind, but he encouraged her to swindle an innocent and credulous old man on the basis of his recommendation. Never in the long history of parapsychology has a better example been found of the mistake, still so often made, of

[1] Alfred Russel Wallace, whose defence of the "remarkable mediumship" of Florence Cook was published the year before Sidgwick's address. Mr. Wallace claimed to have seen even more marvellous phenomena than those produced by Florence, but his testimony is almost entirely worthless.

[2] The statement was made, moreover, only two years after the public exposure of Florence Cook by Sir George Sitwell in 1880. (*See* pp. 132-4.)

trusting to the *bona fides* of the investigators themselves, however distinguished they may be. In this instance at least, one of the aims of the first President of the Society for Psychical Research has been achieved. Almost the closing words of his address were: "We must drive the objector into the position of being forced either to admit the phenomena as inexplicable, at least by him, or to accuse the investigators either of lying or cheating or of a blindness or forgetfulness incompatible with any intellectual condition except absolute idiocy." The doubts so often expressed by orthodox scientific men are founded upon very real and solid facts.

APPENDIX

THE story of the Cook family and their circle has been written in chronological order, so that the general reader with no special interest in psychical research will encounter as few difficulties as possible in following a narrative which is necessarily based upon a mass of somewhat complex material. I have added this note of the circumstances and order of the inquiry itself for the convenience of those readers who may like to know why and how the investigation was undertaken.

It seems clear from the writings of Maskelyne and Davies and some others that suspicions were openly entertained as long ago as the 1870s that William Crookes was probably infatuated with Florence Cook. However, the books in which these opinions were printed, like the old volumes of *The Spiritualist* containing contemporary comments upon the dubious quality of Florence's early mediumship, have long been collectors' items and difficult to obtain. The significance of these accounts of nearly a century ago, moreover, has been overlaid in the literature of spiritualism by the illogical emphasis placed by modern writers upon Crookes's scientific achievements in the years subsequent to his involvement with Florence Cook, and an insistence that the "Katie King" materialization must therefore of necessity have been genuine. The testimony of Anderson, given to the S.P.R. in 1922 and 1949, remained a secret buried in the archives of the Society, the Presidential Chair of which had been occupied by Crookes for one of its longest periods, although rumours about it have been current for many years.

In September 1959 Dr. Eric J. Dingwall addressed a meeting of the Churches' Fellowship for Psychical Study at the Froebel Institute at Putney on "The Evidence for Materialization". He said:

> "It would take me all night to deal with the story of Florence Cook. She was a fascinating and irresistible young woman. I have no doubt that she fascinated Sir William. It was a case of two hearts beating as one."

Dr. Dingwall added that the S.P.R. possessed important evidence in its files regarding the case, but that he had been unable to obtain permission to disclose the details to the Churches' Fellowship that afternoon as many of the members of the S.P.R. Council were on holiday. He and the S.P.R. were violently challenged in the columns of the spiritualist newspaper *Two Worlds* to produce the evidence, if it existed.[1]

On 26 January, 1960, Mr. George Zorab, the Dutch parapsychologist, delivered an uncritical lecture on the Katie King séances at the College of

---

[1] "Astounding Allegations about Katie King Séances," *Two Worlds*, 19 September, 1959.

Psychic Science in London. He was asked about Dr. Dingwall's revelation but he said that he was unable to comment upon it. Mrs. K. M. Goldney, formerly Organizing Secretary of the S.P.R., who was present, however, said that she was able to do so. She told the audience that she had known the author of the evidential document very well and that she did not regard her conversations with him as being in any way confidential.

Mrs. Goldney gave the meeting an epitome of the Anderson deposition, which was reported on the front page of *Two Worlds*:[1]

> "He said that when he was a student he had occasion to call on Florence Cook. She was then in her thirties, married, and her husband was away at sea. They had a liaison, in the course of which she stated that she had also had an affair with Crookes. Their séances were merely a cover-up for the liaison. Sir William had concocted his findings for a similar reason."

The editor of *Two Worlds* expressed the indignation of the spiritualists, pointing out that at the time the deposition was made both William Crookes and Florence Cook were dead:

> "So, when all is said and done, the allegations against Crookes rest on uncorroborated statements, made at a time when none of the other parties could be questioned. Obviously he [Anderson] could not produce any evidence that Florence Cook said what he said she did. Even if she did say it, what evidence is there that she was speaking the truth?"

The editor added, in support of his violent contention that nothing could shake Crookes's evidence, that the materialization of Katie King had been seen in electric light by Crookes and eight other witnesses at Mornington Road, and that Crookes had ridiculed the idea that an innocent schoolgirl of fifteen could successfully maintain so gigantic an imposture for three years.

The matter rested there until May 1960 when Mrs. Eileen J. Garrett, the President of the Parapsychology Foundation of New York, wrote to invite me to undertake an investigation of the whole case in the interests of psychical research and to publish the result, whatever it might be. As it seemed that nothing but benefit could result from an impartial inquiry into the affair I gladly consented to do the work which would be necessary.

Through the efforts of Mrs. Goldney, who reassured me that the Anderson story was given to her and was not confidential, I was able to pay for a copy being made for me of the deposition in the S.P.R. files. When this was available, I read with great interest for the first time Florence Cook's secondary narrative about her sister Kate and the swindling of Charles Blackburn, a story which seemed to me to be of great importance. The literature was entirely silent about it, which seemed an additional reason for investigating it. I was already reading the volumes

---

[1] "Sex (in Psychics) Rears its Ugly Head. Light on a Mystery Document that attacks World-Famous Séances." *Two Worlds*, 26 March, 1960.

of spiritualist journals of the time and had discovered that Blackburn had died in 1891, so that the task of obtaining his death certificate and copy of his surprising will and its codicils was a simple matter.

As Blackburn was a Manchester man it seemed possible that information about his activities as a spiritualist might be available in the Britten Memorial Library, which forms part of the headquarters of the Spiritualists' National Union at Britten House in Tib Lane, Manchester. It was there, in the summer of 1960, that I found the box of unsorted correspondence which had been sent to Mr. E. W. Oaten, a former President, by Miss L. Dixon in 1946. As the reader knows, this mass of material contained much more information than I had expected to find.

The building up of the eventful lives of the characters in the story was a matter of routine work at Somerset House and the Probate Registry, the examination of directories of the period, visits to the scenes of the events and the reading of the periodical spiritualist literature of the times and the unpublished correspondence. The reader will scarcely be interested in the prosaic details of how the pieces of the jigsaw were found and ultimately fitted together, after the mistakes and frustrations which distinguish real life investigation from its fictional counterpart.

This book is a study of the fraudulent practices of a group of spiritualists in the nineteenth century. An interesting point about it is that by far the greater part of its documentation has come from the writings and the publications of the spiritualists themselves.

INDEX

Adams, J. O., 138

American mediums, pioneers of alleged materialization phenomena, xii; performances in England, xii, 19n, 126–30

American Society for Psychical Research, *Journal* of, 151n.

Amsterdam, 10n

Anderson, F. G. H., liaison with Florence Cook, 99ff; Florence's confidant, 99ff, 115n, 148–9, 173; his evidence recorded by S.P.R., 100ff; attainments, 100; seduced by Florence, 101

——, Mrs. (*sen.*), 100–1

Andreack, E., 154

Annales des Sciences Psychiques, 67, 107n

Antwerp, 112n

Arundel Gardens, purchased by Cooks, 144; description of, 149; expense of, 149–50; vacated, 163

Athenaeum, 66

Attwood, Miss, xiiin

Balfour, Earl of, 97

Ballechin House, 151

Balliol College, 100

Battersea Rise, death of Florence at, 149, 160

Beckwith, F., ix

Belsey, Miss, 56

Benenden, 163–7

Bennett, Sir E., 159–60

Berlin, Florence's séances at, 153ff.

Berliner Börsen-Courier, 154

Berry, S. B. C., 16–17

——, *Experiences in Spiritualism*, 16n

Biddenden, 163

Bielfield, H., 61

Binney, F. A., *Where are the Dead? Or, Spiritualism Explained*, 14n, 19n

Bird, E., 56

——, Mrs. E., 56

Blackburn, C., association with Crookes and Cooks, xviii–xix; payments to W. H. Harrison and *The Spiritualist*, 8, 8n; payments to Florence, 9ff.; payments to F. Herne, 12, 17n, 21, 23; delight at Florence's mediumship, 25; present at Volckman exposure, 31; letters in Britten Memorial Library, 31, 120, 125n, 135–7, 141, 144–5; took Florence to Paris, 39; deceived

by secret marriage, 39n; his occasional suspicions, 46; suggested electrical test, 47n; convinced by Hackney séance, 55–6; and by Crookes's letter, 59; received lock of hair, 69; persuaded to continue Florence's allowance, 73; swindled by Kate Cook, 102–3, 106, 117; told of end of "Katie King", 109; subsequent payments to Florence, 111, 113, 114–16; told of "psychic arm", 112; hostility to Florence and Crookes, 113, 113n; relations with E. E. Corner, 113n; payments to Kate, 117ff.; suspicions of Kate, 118, 124–6, 135–7; and Emma Cook, 118n; and "Lillie Gordon", 118ff.; and Kate, 119–20; E. H. Britten on, 120; his children, 121; letters to "Lillie Gordon", 125n, 144–5; threat to stop payments, 125, 130; criticism of Florence, 135; suffered from cancer, 138–9, 143; moved to 105 Elgin Crescent, 139; bequests to Cooks in will and codicils, 140ff.; moved to 34 Ladbroke Grove, 141; placed Eliza Blackburn under control of Cooks, 142; purchased Oakfield, 142; final letter to "Lillie Gordon", 144–5; death, 146; bequest to E. E. Corner, 146

——, Ellen, 121, 141

——, Eliza, and Florence, 113n; in Brook House Asylum, 121, 121n, 138, 139, 141; mental condition, 121, 138, 139–140, 141, 163; at Didsbury séances, 121n, 138; Cooks' plan regarding, 138–9; provision of £14,000 for her maintenance, 140; lived at Oakfield, 142, 143, 147; looked after by Florence, 143, 147; left Oakfield, 162; at Broad Oaks, 163; at Lascelles Nursing Home, 164; death, 164

——, Harriette E. (Mrs. Henry Blackburn), 144

——, Henry, 121, 144

——, W., 121

Blanc, L., xi

Bloomsbury Place, séances at, 126–30

Blyton, T., secretary of Dalston Association of Inquirers into Spiritualism, 4; friend of Florence, 4ff., 8n; attended and publicized Florence's early

181

Eleanor Road, Cooks lived in, 1ff.; Florence's early séances in, 4ff.; "spirit-faces" in, 7ff., 111–12; F. Herne in, 11; Volckman exposure in, 27–32; materializations in, 25ff.; final "Katie King" séances in, 39, 54ff.; Kate's early séances in, 119ff.; death of H. Cook in, 134; vacated by Cooks, 139
Electrical experiment, devised by C. F. Varley, 47; applied to Florence by Crookes, 47–53; Varley's account of, 48–50; W. H. Harrison on, 48, 50; Crookes on, 50; E. W. Cox on, 53
Elgin Crescent, Blackburn and Cooks in, 118n, 139; contents bequeathed to Kate Cook, 140
Ellidge, R., ix
English Mechanic, 93
Evening Standard, 133n

Falmouth, 74
Fell, J. C., 133
Flammarion, C., and D. D. Home on Florence's trickery, 84
—, *Mysterious Psychic Forces* 84n
Fletcher, J. W., fraudulent séances of, 126–30; and Kate, 126, 129–30
—, S. W., fraudulent séances of, 126–30; trial, 126–30; in prison, 127n
Fodor, N., *Encyclopaedia of Psychic Science*, 40n
Fournier d'Albe, E. E., Crookes's biographer, xvii, 47, 88–9, 90, 91–4, 97, 115, 165–6
—, *The Life of Sir William Crookes*, xviin, 47n, 88n, 90n, 91n, 92n, 93n, 97n, 165n
—, *New Light on Immortality*, 25n, 40n
Fox, K., *see* Jencken, K.
Fraser, G., 14
Frere, J. H., 172
Froebel Institute, 177

Galaxy, 19n
Garrett, E. J., President of Parapsychology Foundation, x; confidante of H. A. J. Bois, 107; invited author to make investigation, 178
Gay, S. E., *John William Fletcher: Clairvoyant*, 126n
Gay Young Widow of Balham (The), 41n
Ghost Club, 97n
Gloucester Square, séance at, 48
Goldney, K. M., 99–103, 178
Goodrich-Freer, A., and Bute, Marquess of, *The Alleged Haunting of B—— House*, 151n
Goodwin, E., 115

"Gordon, Lillie", *see* Cook, Kate
Great Russell Street, séances at, 137–8
Guild of the Holy Spirit, 137
Gulat-Wellenburg, W. von, Klinckowstroem, Graf von and Rosenbusch, H., *Der Physikalische Mediumismus*, 50n
Gully, J. M., Crookes's colleague, 40; and "Katie King" photographs, 40; President of British National Association of Spiritualists, 40; his disgrace, 41n
Guppy, A., xviii, 16

Hackney and Kingsland Gazette, 6n
Haigh, K. M., x
Hall, K. E., x
Hall, S. C., 60
Harper, E. K., 43n
Harrison, W. H., editor of *The Spiritualist*, xv and *passim*; Florence's early supporter and publicist, 1ff., 7ff.; financially supported by Blackburn, 8, 8n; suppressed Florence's critics, 8, 18, 25; and F. Herne, 12, 12n; and Dr. J. E. Purdon, 18; and H. Cholmondeley-Pennell, 21; and Lord Arthur Russell, 22–3; and W. Volckman, 27–30; and electrical experiments, 48, 50; and Hackney séances, 56ff.; and Mary Showers, 76–8; and Florence's Paris holiday, 113; lecture to Dalston Association, 118; probably encouraged Florence in fraud, 169
—, *Spirit People*, 119n
Hart-Davis, J. A. T. H., 127
Harwich, 112
Havana, 93
Hayes, F. W., 41
Hayes, G., 41
Herne, F., séances of, xiv, 10n; Florence's mentor, 11; early séances with Florence, 11–12; financially supported by Blackburn, 12; exposures of, 12, 12n, 18n; and "spirit faces", 14, 16; and Mrs. Berry, 17; and "direct voice", 37
Hipp, W., exposure of Florence, 18, 18n
Hofmann, A. W. von, 89
Holborn Viaduct Hotel, 124
Holmes, N., séance with Florence, 19, 19n, 20
— (Mrs.), 19, 19n, 20
Holmes-Watkins, T. P., 143
Home, D. D., investigated by Crookes, 33, 75n, 93–4, 96n; and E. W. Cox, 75; letter from E. W. Cox, 80–4
—, *Lights and Shadows of Spiritualism*, 80n